MW01285849

Champions of Oneness

Louis Gregory and His
Shining Circle

Champions of Oneness

Louis Gregory and His Shining Circle

Janet Ruhe-Schoen

Bahá'í
PUBLISHING

Wilmette, Illinois

Bahá'í Publishing
401 Greenleaf Avenue, Wilmette, Illinois 60091-2844
Copyright © 2015 by the National Spiritual Assembly
of the Bahá'ís of the United States

All rights reserved. Published 2015
Printed in the United States of American on acid-free paper ∞

181716154321

Library of Congress Cataloging-in-Publication Data

Ruhe-Schoen, Janet.
  Champions of oneness : Louis Gregory and his shining circle / by Janet Ruhe-Schoen.
    pages cm
  Includes bibliographical references.
  ISBN 978-1-61851-081-5
  1. Bahais—United States--Biography. 2. Bahai Faith—United States—History—20th century. 3. Gregory, Louis G. I. Title.
  BP390.R836 2015
  297.9'3092273—dc23
  [B]
                                              2015000342

Cover design by Misha Maynerick Blaise
Book design by Patrick Falso

In memory of my sister artist Barbara Stephens,
who carried oneness in her heart;
and dedicated as ever to my family,
particularly my incomparable Christopher.

When shall a few of us go to seek our kindred,
Riding intrepidly over the white crested waves
With our garlands of greeting?
—Doris McKay

Contents

Acknowledgments

Thank you to Cap Cornwell and Fares Behmardi at Palabra Publications for suggesting this project and patiently awaiting its completion; to the U.S. Bahá'í Publishing Trust for taking it on subsequently; to Lewis Walker at the National Bahá'í Archives of the United States and Baher Seioshansian at the Bahá'í Archives of Washington, DC for their thorough efficiency and goodwill; to the wonderfully supportive, open-hearted Bahá'ís of Charlottetown, Prince Edward Island; and especially to Louise Mould, Pat and Vivian O'Neill, Bob and Shirley Donnelly, Paul Vreeland, Anne Boyles, and Louis Pollard. Thank you also to Patti Tomarelli, Judy Hannen Moe, Anneke Schouten-Buys, Anthony Lee, Claire Vreeland, and Gwendolyn Etter-Lewis for unstintingly sharing information, unpublished manuscripts, and taped interviews even though much couldn't be incorporated in the final manuscript. And thank you to diverse groups at Green Acre Bahá'í School, Desert Rose Bahá'í Institute, the Maritimes Bahá'í Summer School, the New York City Bahá'í Center, and my home region in New York State for listening to readings from the manuscript-in-progress with such love, empathy, and enthusiasm, and for providing invaluable encouragement.

Champions of Oneness

Louis Gregory and His
Shining Circle

1

Heritage: The Concept of Oneness

. . . The concept of oneness, a concept to be loved as a reality,
for itself . . .

—*Doris McKay*

My friends and I sit or sprawl on the living room floor and on
assorted pieces of furniture in the home of two aged ladies in Brat-
tleboro, Vermont. The ladies are our teachers, for we're new members of the Bahá'í Faith (and interested pals), and they are veteran
Bahá'ís. The ladies aren't so very old, perhaps. But it's 1968, we're
flower children, and they're definitely a long way over thirty. Being
young at heart and thrilled to have guests, they're gracious, non-
demanding teachers who don't seem at all worried about their spin-
dly-legged, splay-footed furniture or hand-tatted doilies. We play
our guitars, recorders, kazoos, flutes, harmonicas, spoons, drums;
we sing, laugh, sip tea, munch Lorna Doones and Fig Newtons,
debate world peace, race relations, the existence (or not) of God,
and whether (or not) religion is good for anything. Our hostesses
bring on the chocolate-covered graham crackers and keep us talking.

But eventually I separate myself out and sit on the rug by the
bookshelves, paging through volumes of a certain encyclopedia—
The Bahá'í World—doting on the "In Memoriams." The obituaries.
Reading up on the dead. That's not as lugubrious as it sounds. These
particular dead led venturesome lives of travel in places I've never
heard of and had lives full of the kinds of heroic quests, sacrifices,
services, epiphanies, and personal miracles I've always longed for.

From a vantage point of color TV, psychedelia, *Sergeant Pepper's
Lonely Hearts Club Band* and *His Satanic Majesty's Request*, my new-

found heroes from the first half of the twentieth century mostly look plain, dowdy, and doddering in their grainy black-and-white "In Memoriam" photos. But to me, despite my Twiggy eyeliner and my Janis Joplin boas, beads, and plumed hats, they're the princesses and princes of fairy tales. They risked all, wandered their dark nights of the soul in realms of mystery and monsters, to find their destined light and live by it forever.

The ones that fascinate me most actually met Abbas Effendi, called *the Master* by His Father. However, Abbas Effendi preferred the title 'Abdu'l-Bahá, which means *Servant of Glory*. While His Father was alive, He was prince regent serving Bahá'u'lláh, whose name means *the Glory of God*.

Bahá'u'lláh was the Prophet-Founder of the Bahá'í Faith. After He died in 1892, His followers learned from His Will and Testament that they were to turn to the Master as their authority, the only interpreter and elucidator of Bahá'u'lláh's teachings. Obeying this ordinance, the Bahá'ís stayed united. Through harsh battles pitting spirit against the ogres and dragons of ego, they avoided the fate of preceding religions—that is, becoming divided into splinter groups and sects. For my heroes, 'Abdu'l-Bahá was the king enthroned at the heart of the mystery, the warmth in the ice cave, the blue light of love within the flame.

"So He is for me," I decide. Servant of Glory. Servant-as-king. I've read and reread those popular books of quest, *The Journey to the East* and *The Prophet*, seeking someone like the Master, but I was always disappointed in the end. Ordinary writers, trying to explicate mystery, seem to only diminish and annihilate it. But from what I know of 'Abdu'l-Bahá, nothing diminished Him in life, and now His memory and heritage keep growing stronger. No wonder another of His titles is *the Mystery of God*.

If only I'd lived while He was alive. In 1912, He was actually in the United States, spent nine months traveling from coast to coast, with words and example inspiring people to envision universal oneness and live/act in its spirit. What if I'd been on the dock in New

York City, watching His ship come in? What if I'd followed Him to Washington, DC and Boston? Or what if I'd been unaware of Him until I suddenly saw him on a street in Chicago, or in a train chugging over the mountains to California, or at a whistle-stop somewhere in Colorado?

What if I'd gone to meet Him in the Holy Land? If only I'd been among the first group of pilgrims from the Western world to climb the flight of worn stone steps to Him in His house in 'Akká where He, having lived most of His life exiled, a prisoner in a walled city, manifested incontrovertible freedom.

I'm comforted by the fact that He wrote a special prayer and said that to recite it was like meeting him face-to-face. It begins: "O God, my God! Lowly and tearful, I raise my suppliant hands to Thee and cover my face in the dust of that Threshold of Thine, exalted above the knowledge of the learned, and the praise of all that glorify Thee . . . Lord! He is a poor and lowly servant of Thine, enthralled and imploring Thee, captive in Thy hand, praying fervently to Thee, trusting in Thee, in tears before Thy face, calling to Thee and beseeching Thee, saying: O Lord, my God! Give me Thy grace to serve Thy loved ones . . ."[1]

Alone in my college dorm room, I recite this prayer and weep as I say it, as if to convince God of my sincerity. I haven't yet learned to trust God. After enduring intense loneliness and trauma during childhood and youth, I conceive of God almost as an enemy or antagonist, an extremely critical male superspy. I certainly have trouble praying. I have to give up on the prayer. I'm too paranoid and self-conscious to feel the unconditional love and acceptance that people said emanated from the Master. How I want it! Instead of praying, I hungrily read descriptions of Him: He had hazel eyes that most often appeared blue, silvery hair and beard, and gestures and a smile that seemed to summon his listeners to come up, come up, be gathered in. He walked like a shepherd but also like a king.

If only I'd heard His ringing laugh and resonant voice, seen Him placing coins in the hands of the homeless or sitting next to the bedsides of the sick; if only I'd touched the edge of His hand or the hem of His garment; if only I'd been one of the few who heard Him praying and sobbing in the night—then I would have felt the love I'm longing for, would have recorded Him in my mind, engraved Him on my heart, spent the rest of my life breathing His love into the world.

Such is not my destiny. But I can read about those whose destiny it was, people such as May Maxwell, Howard Colby Ives, Loulie Matthews, Lady Blomfield. He lives in their books—*An Early Pilgrimage, Portals to Freedom, Not Every Sea Hath Pearls, The Chosen Highway*—and in the many memories briefly (too briefly) noted in the volumes of *The Bahá'í World.* My heroes pioneered in His name, leaving their homes and families, traveling into storm and war, chaos, poverty and revolution, braving all varieties of culture shock, to establish Bahá'í communities all over the world. They found their light of love, carried it with them—this romance in their hearts, forever—and lived happily ever after. Happy, yes. Free of pain and suffering, no.

What wonderful pain! How I want a bitter taste of it, to prove my mettle. Let's look ahead a bit. I'm in my early twenties, and I transplant myself to the Mescalero Apache Reservation in the arid, southwestern United States to help form a Bahá'í community there. To me it's a gritty, lonely, and alien place, a rude awakening. I live at Mescalero for a couple of years and then return to my green East Coast, realizing that my rude awakening has been to my own shortcomings, not to Mescalero. Someday I'll be a better person; someday I'll try again.

A few years later, I'm working in the Public Information Office at the U.S. Bahá'í National Center, writing copy for the newspaper and magazine, reporting on community activities. But I want to write an historical feature for the magazine. Perhaps I can express my love for 'Abdu'l-Bahá and His adorers via research and composition since I'm having trouble expressing it through extroverted action. I put together an article based on a telegram sent from the Bahá'í

World Center in Haifa when Marian Jack, perhaps one of the greatest Canadian Bahá'ís, died in Bulgaria shortly after World War II.

The telegram was written by the Master's grandson, Shoghi Effendi, the Guardian of the Bahá'í Faith. He said Marian Jack had joined "her distinguished band (of) co-workers" in the Abhá Kingdom, and he named them: Lua Getsinger, May Maxwell, Martha Root, Keith Ransom-Kehler, Hyde Dunn, Susan Moody, Dorothy Baker and Ella Bailey. I immerse myself in research for a few weeks, then write short profiles of each of them. I title the piece "A Love Which Does Not Wait," from a statement in Martha Root's obituary that she "became the embodiment of a love which does not passively wait, but which goes forth, with a wholehearted reckless spending of personality, of time, of strength."[2]

After the article is published, I receive compliments, feel happy with what I've done, and that's that—or so I imagine. Several years later, living in upstate New York, I hear that the article has been translated into Spanish and published as a booklet in South America. I want a copy, but there's no way to find one until 1980.

At that point, I'm testing my mettle again, living in the desierto lunar—the moonscape desert, as they call the Sechura in Peru—trying to be of service in the small city of Piura. And finally I'm able to get my hands on my article as a little Spanish booklet with a yellow cover that reads "Un amor que no espera."

A decade later, I'm living in Chile (still testing that old mettle, which is getting pretty worn in spots) and I drop in on an international Bahá'í youth conference in Santiago. On the wall facing the entrance I see a little paper sign lettered in magic marker: "Un amor que no espera," with an arrow pointing down the hall. I learn that a Persian scholar from Brazil is basing classes on the little booklet. Soon, I meet him; he's elderly, spry, bald, tearful with his admiration of those who rushed forth "with a love that does not wait."

There are certainly more of those than the nine in my article. He's one of them himself. He pioneered in Brazil for forty years and is considered the spiritual father of the Brazilian Bahá'ís. (Flash forward to 2010, and the book *A Love Which Does Not Wait* is translated into Portuguese and published in Brazil; *Um amor que no espera* is dedicated to him, Habib Taherzadeh.)

But at that youth conference, I'm not aware of his stature. However, because of him, it occurs to me: "Why not make the article into a full-length book? Expand each profile into a chapter?"

Long story. To make it much shorter: in 1998, I'm living in upstate New York again, and Palabra Publications releases the book *A Love Which Does Not Wait*. Over the years, the book gains friends, so that, when I visit in Haifa in 2009 as a pilgrim to Bahá'í holy places, the first thing a new friend says to me is, "Oh, you wrote *A Love Which Does Not Wait!* Thank you!"

As I pray in the shrines, I think, "Perhaps I should write a companion volume to *A Love* . . .?" But back home on my desk is a mass of documents, notes, books, and different versions of a manuscript: I'm finishing a biography of the martyr Ṭáhirih, now published as *Rejoice in My Gladness: The Life of Ṭáhirih.* Do I really want to follow it immediately with another research and writing project? No. Work on the book, which is at the time titled *Rent Asunder,* is taking me upwards of a decade and is rending *me* asunder. I don't think I want to write more biographies; maybe I don't want to write anything more, at all. However, after returning home, I get a call from Palabra.

"We're bringing out *A Love Which Does Not Wait* in paperback. Do you want to add anything to it?"

"No."

"Do you want to write a companion volume?"

———

Well.

I begin poring over old volumes of *The Bahá'í World* even as I hammer away at the last chapters of *Rejoice in My Gladness.* Who should I include in a companion volume? Palabra told me they wanted the new book to complement a study circle course on oneness. So I'll focus on Bahá'ís who specifically championed oneness, who bravely—sometimes at the risk of their lives—bridged ethnic and cultural divides.

A Love Which Does Not Wait has a natural flow, being focused on the people mentioned in Shoghi Effendi's telegram, and while writing it, I had the deep and satisfying adventure of discovering that every one of them had personally met the Master and been transformed by the contact. That gave the book a wonderful coherence. In fact, to me, the book is as much about 'Abdu'l-Bahá as it is about its various biographees. Others often refer to it as "that book about the women," although there is a male in it, Hyde Dunn. A sweet and mild Englishman, he seems to get lost among the eight females. Nothing I can do about it: that's who's mentioned in the cable.

I want the new book to be about Bahá'í heroes of various ethnicities, men as well as women. I want them to be people whose halcyon years were in the early twentieth century, the same time period when the people of *A Love Which Does Not Wait* were living in their prime. I want them all to have met the Master. Unfortunately, there's no other telegram memorializing a crew of people who meet my criteria! Where's my natural link? Who will make the companion volume a true child of the first?

I begin reading *To Move the World*, Gayle Morrison's biography of Louis Gregory. He was among the first African-American Bahá'ís, a man of tremendous spiritual stature, a true trailblazer of interracial amity. I already know I want to write about him, for he met the Master and lived by His wisdom, radiating His presence as an ambassador of the new/ancient one-world.

But *To Move the World* is a challenging read, so, for a change, I pluck the book *Fires in Many Hearts*, by Doris McKay, from my bookshelf. She wrote the quote that gave me the title for *A Love Which Does Not Wait*. I've had her book for years but haven't read it. Now I'm drawn to it. Thinking it's probably extraneous to my search, since Doris became a Bahá'í after 'Abdu'l-Bahá died, but always being one for detours, I open it.

A few days later, I write in my journal, "This is amazing. What a link I've found! Doris McKay's first action, the night she became a Bahá'í in 1925, was to pray to be freed from prejudice. She understood that oneness is the heart of Bahá'í belief and that if she, a racist, didn't overcome her prejudice against African Americans, she could never really enter that heart. She awoke in the morning feeling free, and within months she was acting upon that freedom. With her husband, Willard, she hosted racially integrated Cherry Blossom Picnics on their farm (which was in Klu Klux Klan territory even though it was in the northeast) and convened race amity conferences. Willard traveled and taught with Louis Gregory across a southern U.S. ruled by segregation—the two were like early Freedom Riders. In the 1940s, Doris went to Memphis, Tennessee to fight an uphill battle to persuade white Bahá'ís to stop demanding segregated meetings and join their black brethren to build a true Baha'í commun . . ."

Doris was a great believer in love. She'd been a confidante of Martha Root's. She recalled that, when asked to write Martha's "In Memoriam," she "sat down and said, 'Martha, I know you will want to go on teaching through this article, so what do you want me to say for you?' Her spirit, so newly arrived in the next world seemed for a moment to fuse into mine leaving me physically shaken up. The answer I sensed was 'love' and that she was telling me to project that atmosphere of Love-only that she had made her habitual state. She had experienced the power of love and found that nothing (more) was needed in the way of brilliant exposition or show . . ."[3]

Then there was the link with the Master. Doris wrote, at the end of her memoir, "My early days in the Faith had begun four short years after the passing of 'Abdu'l-Bahá—early days which had a story-book quality. There were few Bahá'ís in 1925 and our first teachers were like apostles . . . For years their radiance was like stardust that brushed off on our young souls . . ."[4]

And it wasn't just their radiance. It was their understanding of the source of that radiance, of how to keep it shining. After one meeting with Mabel and Howard Ives, Doris was imbued with "the concept of oneness . . . a concept to be loved as a reality, for itself."[5] Why else would she have prayed immediately to be free of the race prejudice that was a heritage of her childhood? Instead she adopted another heritage: Love. And she spent her life putting roots down into its rich soil.

"So much is said about Love in the Teachings," she wrote, "not only because it is kind! It is a great and vital Power, a worker of miracles because it is the key to the heart of the True One. It is, to quote from the short daily prayer, the reason why we were created. Bahá'í love is a heritage passed on to the young Bahá'ís, the first link in the love-chain that was made by 'Abdu'l-Baha . . ."[6]

At the end of her life, to share the heritage, she began to record the stories of her intimate friends Dorothy Baker, Martha Root, May Maxwell, Grace and Harlan Ober, Howard and Mabel Ives, Louis Gregory, and others. "At that time," she said, "biographies of these people had not been written and the young Bahá'ís were so eager for 'real-life' stories about the heroes and heroines I had known. It seemed as if, at the mention of their names, these angelic beings came and joined us. I remember telling the stories in one place where the people stayed up all night and we continued at breakfast the next morning . . ."[7]

Doris McKay. Her instant prayer for freedom from prejudice; her instant actions that proved her sincerity; her belief in love; her deep, personal connection to people featured in *A Love Which Does Not Wait*; her desire that their stories and those of other apostles be told; her own greatness and her utter willingness to share her story. While in her nineties, she wrote in her memoir, ". . . the secrets of the hearts of the Bahá'ís are events in the history of the faith. I am moved to turn myself inside out to share with you the true record of those days in which we were revealed to ourselves."[8]

So, Doris' honest purity, courage, and love help me focus and choose people to write about. Slowly. Very slowly. Years later, after much research and several long, experimental manuscripts, I see that my way to a unified book is by centering it on the towering figure of Louis Gregory and his fellow workers for race amity. I arrive at *My Book of Oneness: Louis Gregory and His Shining Circle*, which is then transformed into *Champions of Oneness: Louis Gregory and His Shining Circle*. This phrase is how Louis Gregory often signed his letters to fellow race amity workers: "Love to you and all your shining circle."

With his life as the anchor, I'm able to delve into the lives of his fellow champions of oneness—his wife Louisa Mathew Gregory; Pauline and Joseph Hannen; Robert Turner; Roy Williams; Mírzá Abu'l-Faḍl; Zia Bagdadi, and more. All of them personally met and were transfigured by the Master. Others, who came into the Faith after the passing of 'Abdu'l-Bahá have to be eliminated, not only for the sake of coherence, but to keep the book down to an accessible length.

Does that mean eliminating Doris and Willard McKay?! How can I do that?

I can't. Doris learned of the Faith in 1924 from Howard and Mabel Ives. Because they radiated the incandescence of 'Abdu'l-Bahá no matter how tired they were or how inept they felt, the Ives almost instantaneously, in one meeting, communicated to Doris the reality and importance of oneness. The last chapter of this book, "Heritage: Doris and Willard McKay" includes the story of that happening and other relevant doings of Doris and Willard, for they were definitely of Louis Gregory's shining circle, which went on shining long after 1921. And three of the stars of *A Love Which Does Not Wait*—Dorothy Baker, May Maxwell, Martha Root—come out and shine for us a little more in this final chapter.

But the focus of the book is, loosely, the period from 1898, when Robert Turner became the first African American Bahá'í, to 1921, when the Bahá'ís of the United States convened the first Race Amity

Convention. Following 'Abdu'l-Bahá's example and instructions, they'd struggled for years to be an integrated group in a segregated society torn by race warfare, and the convention was a giant step for them, a victory along an arduous road. They were helping to deepen and firmly establish the other American tradition—other than racism—that has persisted from 1776 onward: race amity, the coming together in friendship of people of every ethnicity to fulfill the dream of all of us living in oneness, in peace.

Shortly after the first Race Amity Convention, 'Abdu'l-Bahá died peacefully at the age of seventy-seven, in Haifa. That the Bahá'í world has continued following in His footsteps, creating an ever-increasingly diverse and integrated community, is evident in current Bahá'í events, but *Champions of Oneness* takes place during our spiritual spring, a season of beginnings in the sun of His presence.

And in fact it was spring, 1911, when Louis Gregory, a pilgrim, met 'Abdu'l-Bahá. As 'Abdu'l-Bahá Himself wrote, referring to the beginnings of Bahá'u'lláh's Revelation, "How wondrous was that springtide and how heavenly was that gift!"[9]

2

In Egypt

He came, a dark youth, singing in the dawn
of a new freedom . . .
—*James D. Corrothers*

April 10, 1911. Louis Gregory, very tall, reed-thin, well-dressed
in a three-piece suit, a handsome young African American with the
presence and bearing of an actor or dancer, follows an Iranian friend
down a street of gracious villas and gardens by the sea in Ramleh,
Egypt. If they should try to make conversation, their words would
be nearly swallowed by whooshing surf and wind. But it's likely that
Louis is quiet, for suspense and excitement belying his outer poise
sweep his inmost being.

I imagine his suit is light-colored for the Mediterranean weather,
and soon he'll be sipping tea on the Hotel Victoria's wide veranda,
beneath the famous, outsized clock. But now his friend opens the
gate of a modest, comfortable villa and leads him through the front
garden, where he leaves him for a moment at a side door to enter
the house and run upstairs. He quickly returns and guides Louis to
a second-story reception room where people sit conversing. Among
them is the Master, 'Abdu'l-Bahá.

At the sight of Him, Louis feels (he will later write) "a natural
impulse" to kneel. So he does, with his singular grace, at the threshold of the room. The Master rises and goes to him, bends over him
and kisses his bowed head.

Louis is the second African-American Bahá'í pilgrim ever to visit
'Abdu'l-Bahá. Robert Turner, in 1898, was the first; he came with
the first group of pilgrims from the western world to the Master's
side. Now, fourteen years later, Louis cannot know how deeply

happy he makes 'Abdu'l-Bahá, although, during the years of their association, the Master will intimate it, always. Two years ago, Louis requested permission to come on pilgrimage, but the Master told him to postpone the trip. Now he's here by the Master's express invitation. The Master seats him with the other guests in the reception room, which is, as far as Louis is concerned, heaven.

The guests include all sorts of visitors, but there are a few fellow pilgrims, among them Louisa A. M. Matthew, a dainty, petite, dark-haired Englishwoman with big brown eyes and an earnest, forthright gaze. She's an empathetic person with great concern for social justice, so, knowing the inequities of life for people of color, she likely feels happy and affirmed in her faith as she watches Louis interact with the Master. But she never imagines that within a year she'll be Louis' wife.

When the Master seats Louis and asks him how he is, Louis feels it's no routine "how are you?" 'Abdu'l-Bahá senses not only Louis' voyage over several seas to His side but his voyage over life's ocean, along with the very tide and surge of the blood in his heart, the pulse of his soul. And Louis realizes that "the weariness of the long journey, the suspense and excitement of landing for the first time at an Oriental port," have vanished. He feels "more peaceful and composed" than ever before.[1]

This unusual psychic balance, this gift of quiet joy, comes naturally to Louis, but he hasn't always felt it. However, from that moment in Ramleh until the end of his life, it's one of his most distinguishing characteristics, one of his graces.

Shortly after welcoming Louis, the Master has a question for him: "What of the conflict between the white and colored races?" Louis smiles, feeling that, although 'Abdu'l-Bahá hasn't been in the United States, He knows more of conditions there than he, Louis, can comprehend. Louis answers that there's much friction between the races. Bahá'ís hope for "an amicable settlement of racial differences," but others are "despondent." Even among the Bahá'ís, some are earnestly eager "for a closer unity" and hope for guidance from 'Abdu'l-

Bahá, but some want to arrange meetings so a "central" one is "open to all races, while group meetings might be organized along racial lines." In other words, the Bahá'ís are struggling against their own prejudices to practice Bahá'u'lláh's central principle of oneness. The Master replies, "There must be no distinctions in Bahá'í meetings. All are equal."[2]

As the visit draws to a close, the Master shakes hands with Louis and arranges for him to sup that evening with an Iranian friend, a former minister of state who's now a Bahá'í, making it clear, as He'll continue to do throughout Louis' pilgrimage, that Louis is not to be shy but to go everywhere among all people. Although in Louis' country, a system of stern segregation—a racial apartheid enacted under laws known as "Jim Crow laws"—is growing like a malignant tumor, he can be secure in his stature as a world citizen.

'Abdu'l-Bahá sees himself and everyone as world citizens. Some 160 hard-pressed Bahá'ís in the remote Iranian village of Kishih recently received a Tablet from Him in which He mentioned each by name and told them to look beyond local troubles and see "the implications of unity on a global scale." They're cut off from the world's social, technological, and intellectual developments, living under an authoritarian patriarchy that terrorizes and persecutes them mercilessly, yet He summons forth the right of each of their souls to independently investigate truth, and He guides them in how to function via consultative democracy in "this . . . the century of light."[3]

No wonder that Louis always feels at home with the Master. During the ensuing days, he's in a state of happy, alert absorption as he revels in his new surroundings and observes 'Abdu'l-Bahá conversing in a group or one-on-one, or walking about Ramleh with his mutable entourage. In *A Heavenly Vista*, his memoir of his pilgrimage, Louis will vividly describe Him: medium height, very erect, strongly built; symmetrical features and a "slightly aquiline" nose; parchment-toned skin; "deeply furrowed face;" light blue, penetrating eyes; "silver hair . . . long enough to touch the shoulders," a white beard, and hands and nails that are "shapely and pure," a voice that's powerful yet "capable of infinite pathos, tenderness and sympathy;" simple, neat, light-colored robes and turban. His brow has a kingly grandeur, also "the meekness of the servant." The summary: "Majesty and beauty are His adornments."[4]

The feeling of happiness is mutual. The morning after their initial greeting, Louis is writing in his diary in one of the ample lounges of the Hotel Victoria, awaiting the arrival of two fellow travelers, when he looks out the window and sees "coming up the steps leading to the broad veranda—'Abdu'l-Bahá." Louis goes "joyfully to meet Him." "I came specially to see you," 'Abdu'l-Bahá says, taking Louis' hand.[5]

Louis had been expecting a British pilgrim, Neville Meakin, and one of the Master's translators. Neville is a spiritualist; like Wesley Tudor-Pole, Alice Buckton, and some other British leaders of occult movements, he's entranced with 'Abdu'l-Bahá. He has a society called "The Order of the Table Round," a mystic circle bound up in Arthurian mysteries and the Chalice Well at Glastonbury. He's also one of the many invalids of that era afflicted with tuberculosis; no doubt he and his doctors hope the famously salubrious air at Ramleh will be good for him.

'Abdu'l-Bahá, too, is in Ramleh for His health. After forty years as an exile and prisoner, He's finally free. He was en route to Europe and North America to visit and strengthen the new Bahá'í communities there, but He fell ill in Port Said and ended up convalescing in Egypt for almost a year.

'Abdu'l-Bahá's style of convalescing is, as we see, highly active. The public knows him by his given name, Abbas Effendi. Louis will report that "Abbas Effendi might at times be seen walking about the streets. Ofttimes he would ride upon the electric tramway, making change and paying his fare in the most democratic fashion. His reception room was open to believers and non-believers alike. Upon a visit to some unfortunates one day, I asked if they knew Him. 'O yes,' they responded, 'He has been in this house.'" Louis adds that many who visit the Master's reception room aren't Bahá'ís, and, in general, "thousands of persons" have the "opportunity to see Abbas Effendi."[6] He wonders how many among them perceive 'Abdu'l-Bahá, the Servant of Glory?

Certainly the Master never seems to anyone like a sick man as he attends to His missions of charity, mercy, and elucidation of theology and philosophy. He feels his illness and long stay in Egypt have a purpose. He's already sent his dear friend, the scholar Mírzá Abu'l-Faḍl to Egypt for the same purpose, and now he himself assists in fulfilling it. Egypt is an intellectual and cultural hub, a meeting place between the ancient Islamic East and the galumphing, colonizing Christian West. Leaders of thought from both horizons—including various journalists with a great deal of outreach—find their way to 'Abdu'l-Bahá's door, hungry for His philosophy, and He initiates and mediates dialogue between them.

But what exactly is His illness? He has lingering effects of the tuberculosis He suffered at age seven and which caused doctors to despair of His life; and He has lingering effects of chains, dungeons, malnutrition, extreme cold, and extreme heat. He has intermittent fevers—called nerve fevers at the time—probably linked to prison episodes of typhus and malaria as well as to ongoing exhaustion and insomnia. He has stress galore, for He carries the weight of the Bahá'í world and, implicitly, of the whole world, on His shoulders.

In *A Heavenly Vista*, Louis describes the effects of this load: the exhaustion, agitation, and sadness that overwhelm 'Abdu'l-Bahá while He and Louis discuss a sad situation in the Washington community arising from racial prejudice. "Although the expressive and beautiful face of 'Abdu'l-Bahá was nearly always joyful during my stay at Ramleh, here was a glimpse of Him who carries the burden of the world. Like One of old, how truly must such an [sic] one be 'a Man of sorrows and acquainted with grief.'"[7] The quote is Isaiah 53:3 from the King James Bible, a famous passage Louis knows from his Christian upbringing as "The Suffering Servant."

So Louis sees that 'Abdu'l-Bahá is excruciatingly sensitive to disunity. That's how it must be. For 'Abdu'l-Bahá is a unique creation, the center of unity for the Bahá'í world, the Center of the Bahá'í Covenant, which is "the axis of the oneness of the world of humanity . . ."[8]

That's why 'Abdu'l-Bahá, born to foment and maintain love and unity, feels the wrenching-apart that comes from hate and disunity as a personal loss, an agony, and He mourns. He also mourns because tragedy stalks the Bahá'ís of Iran. He's the first to receive news of the persecution that haunts them and of their heartbreakingly heroic martyrdoms. He's sixty-eight when Louis meets him. Some of the lines that Louis sees in His "deeply furrowed" face score His cheeks like the tracks of tears, so deep, so staining, He might have wept tears of blood. Yet, He revels in life, radiates vitality.

After Louis greets the Master on that sunny morning at the Hotel Victoria, he hears Him "going along the corridor and saying in a strong voice, 'Good Morning!'" 'Abdu'l-Bahá is on His way to visit a sick friend. But soon he sends for Louis, who finds him "seated in the bay window of a room on the third floor." He dictates Tablets to two secretaries. Louis presents messages and presents sent by American Bahá'ís, and feels glad because the "simple and inexpensive" gifts represent "much love on the part of the friends." When 'Abdu'l-Bahá opens the last gift, a bottle of perfume, He rubs some on His beard and then on His secretaries' hands, increasing Louis' happiness.[9]

Fellow pilgrims and local Bahá'ís also make Louis happy. One evening, he joins Neville Meakin and several Iranian Bahá'í men for a "late Oriental dinner" and a visit to an invalid brother of one of the men. After some hours spent in "the best of humor," Louis "could not forebear to express" to these friends his "admiration for their noble qualities." Yet he admits that he has a strange feeling, as if he's with them under false pretenses, as some sort of imposter. Their courtesies to him are "out of proportion" to his "station," he tells them. He is only of "humble rank among Americans."

They kindly accept his compliment to themselves, but when the translator begins telling them about Louis' "humble rank" they won't let him keep speaking, refuse to hear it. The translator explains to Louis that they value him with no regard as to whether or not he has "worldly power." [10]

——◆——

Louis is a son of the Deep South, that region of the United States built and fueled from the 1600s into the 1860s by slave labor. His grandmother was stolen from Africa and brought to America. She was one who survived the inhuman torture of the slave ship—"Voyage through death," the poet Robert Hayden has described it, "voyage whose chartings are unlove." [11] Louis' mother and father were both born into slavery. Louis, born after the Emancipation Proclamation, in the first decade after slavery, has always been free, but that doesn't mean he hasn't felt the oppression of bondage. He's only one generation removed from it, his life intimately linked with his grandmother's and, of course, his parents'.

There are fascinating parallels between Louis Gregory's early life, the history and philosophy of his grandmother and parents, and the lives of Bahá'u'lláh and 'Abdu'l-Bahá. Just as we can see how Christ took up the cross for us, suffered the ills and pains of the world for us, so we can see how Baha'u'llah's bondage and chains, exile from His homeland, and His imprisonment during the nineteenth century paralleled the sufferings of Louis' grandmother and other African slaves. 'Abdu'l-Bahá, from the age of nine, was also an exile; He bore the weight of chains; He was a prisoner for over fifty years. He and his father endured stoning, vile insults, and beatings. The same abuse and bullying that dogged African Americans also dogged Them. They were wrenched away from their loved ones in heartbreaking circumstances and watched them get killed or succumb to illness.

Yet Bahá'u'lláh and 'Abdu'l-Bahá appeared to live by the same philosophy that Louis imbibed from his grandmother: "It's better to be light-hearted than broken hearted."[12] He remembered his grandmother telling humorous tales of life on the plantation until he practically fell off his chair, crippled with laughter. When Bahá'u'lláh was imprisoned in the barracks in 'Akká, every evening, at his behest, the Bahá'ís imprisoned with Him took turns telling the most comical things that had happened to them that day; despite the nightmare surroundings, they often laughed till they cried.

No wonder that when 'Abdu'l-Bahá looks into Louis' eyes in Egypt, He recognizes and welcomes a kindred, deep, abiding soul. And among the pilgrims and others that Louis meets, he finds other kindred souls, chief among them Louisa Mathew. Being with 'Abdu'l-Bahá, she and Louis share an atmosphere that another who met Him described as "'alchemizing'" to "'incidents forgotten and hidden in the recesses of one's being'" so that "'veils that inhibit necessary spiritual development'" are removed.[13]

But it's more than atmosphere; His teachings revolutionize the spirit. Louis and Louisa hear Him more than once praise the efficacy of interracial marriage for integrating a community. For instance, He teaches, "'Intermarriage is a good way to efface racial differences. It produces strong, beautiful offspring, clever and resourceful.'"[14]

Right now, over a century later, given current social, cultural and demographic trends—our progress toward becoming the rainbow race—some people take umbrage at rhetoric about beautiful and talented offspring of interracial unions. They assume that stereotypical qualities of whites and blacks are being singled out and praised: "good hair" from the "white side," "rhythm" from the "black side," and such. In truth, these stereotypical assumptions are often the norm, and African Americans feel it's patronizing on the part of whites and reveals a lack of self-acceptance in themselves that they need to overcome. However, perceptions are changing rapidly even as I write this, so that people are not limiting themselves to one standard of beauty for the entire world. Perceptions can't change fast enough for me!

Meanwhile, we know from other things that the Master said and by His actions that His support of intermarriage and its offspring had less to do with looks than with forging unbreakable family, human bonds transcending skin color. That's what He wanted.

In His day, while there was some public rhetoric about the beauty and intelligence of racial "mixtures," the prevailing sentiment was that "mixed race" people (and we're just about all mixed race, actually, but I use the term in its limited sense here) were scorned as worse than people of "pure" racial stock. "Mulattoes" had a "touch of the tarbrush"; "half-blood Indians" had a "taint." People with a partially Jewish heritage could be rejected for jobs, education, marriage, etc., if they were "found out." People with oriental background experienced some of the worst rejection of all. Racists didn't want such folks infiltrating "pure white" strongholds, potentially "tainting" others.

For, what could they be but children of sin? At the time, miscegenation (a word that even sounds like a sin), was viewed by many as depraved, even if sanctioned by marriage. And interracial marriage was excoriated or illegal, or both, almost everywhere in the United States. It was so controversial that, when Louis published *A Heavenly Vista* in around 1914, he only had five hundred copies printed. 'Abdu'l-Bahá saw Louis keeping his diary at Ramleh and urged him to write as freely as he wished, but when it came time to publish the journal, advised him to produce a limited edition because of the statements on interracial marriage.

Knowing 'Abdu'l-Bahá's encouragement of variegated families and his intuitive trust in Louis and Louisa, of which we'll see ample proof, it's interesting to consider whether or not He engineered their meeting. In afterthought, they believed He did. Louisa, like Louis, had to put off her pilgrimage until it just happened to coincide with Louis'. Did the Master foresee this? Did he foresee, even there in Ramleh, that Louis Gregory and Louisa Mathew would form a union of equals in which each nurtured the other's soul while braving a prejudiced society that could have destroyed them? Did he foresee how they would each follow, while maintaining their unity, an individual path of service with such passion and purity that Louis would posthumously be named a Hand of the Cause of God, and Louisa hailed as a "'faithful, consecrated handmaid of 'Abdu'l-Bahá?'"[15]

3

An American Childhood and
Young Manhood

Let me not hate, although the bruising world decries my peace,
Gives me no quarter, hounds me while I sleep,
Would snuff the candles of my soul . . .

—*Georgia Douglas Johnson*

Louis and Louisa became good friends while on pilgrimage, and they promised to write to each other, but that was the extent of it. Louisa was the daughter of an affluent merchant family in a prosperous English town. She was born one year after Louis' mother and grandmother left the plantation to taste the first fruits of freedom — some of which were bitter, indeed.

Louis was born in 1874 in Charleston, South Carolina. Although they were poor, both his parents were literate. His father, Ebenezer George, was a blacksmith. His mother, Mary Elizabeth George, called Elizabeth, was a tailor. Elizabeth's mother, Mariah, was known as Mary Bacot.

Mother and daughter had been slaves on a plantation called Elysian Fields in Darlington, South Carolina, the famously verdant low country, home to the richest plantations and the largest slave population in the United States. Louis was the son and grandson of slaves, but he was also the grandson of George Washington Dargan, descendant of Irish immigrants. He was a lawyer, judge, and state senator, and he owned Elysian Fields. "My grandmother, wholly of African blood, was without ceremony his (Dargan's) slave-wife," Louis wrote. Senator Dargan was Elizabeth's father.[1]

The senator owned 119 slaves. He died several years before the Emancipation Proclamation ended slavery in most of the United States in 1863. Louis' grandmother told him that a female relative of Senator Dargan's taught her and Elizabeth the Christianity of salvation, forgiveness, and gratitude. Mother and daughter were true to their religion, although life gave them reasons not to be, among them the lynching of Mary Bacot's real husband.

After leaving Elysian Fields (and perhaps we'll never know if that name was meant to be ironic or not) Mary "lived with her husband in a small city in the south," Louis wrote in his unpublished manuscript, *Racial Amity*. He continued:

He was a blacksmith and a right good one, regular in habits, thrifty in living and pious in life. He saved enough from his earnings to purchase first a mule and later a horse, a considerable investment of capital in those days for a former slave. These two animals he used to drive out together for recreation after the Sunday worship, which followed the week of toil. Such a display of luxury by one of lowly estate quickly aroused the resentment of the Klan. Would it not spoil all the other darkies and make them ambitious and proud? Late one night, he and his wife were rudely awakened by stern voices. He was ordered out of his modest abode and instantly killed. Someone in the ranks of the Klansmen cried, "Shoot into the house and kill that woman, too!" Another declared that action unnecessary. This thought prevailed and so, narrow was the escape of Grandmother after being in earshot of her husband's sudden and violent taking off. This tragic story she told simply and sadly, but entirely without abuse of the wrong doers. Early in life, under the driving force of pain, she had found peace of heart divinely given.[2]

Lynching—the murder, often by hanging, by a large or small mob, of a frequently wrongly accused victim—was common in the South and also occurred in other parts of the United States. Most of the victims were black. The murderous posse was often rallied by the white supremacist hate group, the Klu Klux Klan.

Charleston, South Carolina, where Louis grew up, was the city where three-quarters of all U.S. slaves had first set foot in the country. For almost two hundred years its streets saw scenes like this: "They would bring people off the boat. They would parade them up the street in chains. White plantation owners and local slave traders would get on the sidewalks. They'd watch them as they went up the street. They would follow behind . . . have their slave auctions. Anybody they didn't sell that day they would keep in . . . slave depots."[3] Slaves were chained in coffles of 100 or more adults and children. The traders herded them along using whips and guns. African men and women fell to their hands and knees, pleading with slavers not to separate them from spouses and children, but families were wrenched apart, wailing with terror and grief. Louis Gregory's grandmother had been sold to Senator Dargan under such conditions. She was part of the Maafa (Swahili word for holocaust) that cast over ten million Africans into bondage during the four centuries of the Atlantic Slave Trade.

The attitude that typified Louis, that his grandmother and other millions of the Maafa passed on to their descendants, is well-described by Cain Hope Felder: "Slavery and oppression provide a wilderness experience where people raise ultimate questions and they are on the breaking point. They are on the brink. And at that special place between sanity and insanity, breaking or not, is where I think God encounters us best. And I think at that point either you break or you get the sense that there's no need to break. And I think a lot of black people got the sense that there was no need to break."[4]

Mary Bacot and her ilk endured slavery stoically; then, with emancipation, their hopes and expectations rose, and, after the Civil War, it did indeed seem that the balance of power might shift in the South. During Reconstruction, in places like South Carolina, where the majority of people were black, African Americans successfully entered politics. In the year of Louis' birth, a freeborn black man was state senator; he'd also served as secretary of state. Six black men represented South Carolina in the U.S. Congress. The next year, the federal government passed the Civil Rights Act, mandating integration. However, it didn't grant African Americans land or any other form of compensation for their slave labor.

In 1883, when Louis was nine, the Supreme Court threw out the Civil Rights Act, allowing the southern states to legislate segregation. They did it with zeal. Sixty-five years later, the hysterically rigid segregation known as apartheid would become the law of the land in South Africa. That tragedy directly followed Nazi oppression in Germany, and elsewhere in Europe, of people viewed as "other," a reign of terror that caused the institutionalized murder of millions deemed not Aryan enough to live. But segregation law, or reign of terror, in the Deep South wasn't called apartheid or Nazism. It was named Jim Crow, a derogatory term for African Americans, which came from a popular minstrel show character. Jim Crow was a white man in black-face who capered grotesquely and lewdly, singing, "I jump just so / And every time I turn about, I jump Jim Crow."[5]

Apartheid-like practices became unspoken custom in most of the United States. Federal law gave black men the right to vote; now states invented and implemented ways to disenfranchise them, such as poll taxes, impossible identification requirements, and more. Daily humiliations piled up in the lives of people of color: they couldn't walk on the same staircase with white people, they couldn't use the same bathrooms as whites, they had to ride the "Jim Crow cars" of trains, they had to walk into the train station beneath a door marked Negroes, they couldn't sit at the same restaurant counter as whites, they had to step off the sidewalk to allow a white person to pass. When driving a vehicle—horse and buggy, or automobile—a black driver had to move out of the way of a white one and stay out of the way until the white driver passed by. And more. Every African American child, born carefree, as is human birthright, had his or her moment of pain and shame when the truth struck and wounded him or her. "You do not belong. You are not good. You are other." The wounding and re-wounding went on for life. Countee Cullen summed it up in a famous poem:

> Once riding in old Baltimore,
> > Heart-filled, head-filled with glee,
> I saw a Baltimorean
> > Keep looking straight at me.
>
> Now I was eight and very small,
> > And he was not much bigger,
> And so I smiled, but he poked out
> > His tongue and called me "Nigger."
>
> I saw the whole of Baltimore
> > From May until December;
> Of all the things that happened there
> > That's all that I remember.[6]

Louis' grandmother, Mary Bacot, could have lamented when she looked around at how the South had so quickly fallen from the hope of Reconstruction into the lewd lap of Jim Crow, especially in light of her own tragedies, but her sense of humor and self-worth overcame her woes. Also, she had a lot to do. She could barely read but had been a nurse on the plantation, and she was a healer: all her life, people consulted her for her deep knowledge of practical medicine. Perhaps her most practical medicine was storytelling and the resulting, liberating laughter.

Louis' mother, Elizabeth, was a lovely woman with refined sensibilities despite her hard lot. After Ebenezer died, she worked as a tailor, struggling to support Louis, his older brother Theodore, and her mother in a crowded tenement called Blackbird Alley at 3 Burns Lane, in the poorest quarter of Charleston.

Louis was four when his father died. He wrote that Ebenezer succumbed to tuberculosis and he himself had tubercular tendencies — not uncommon in those days, when TB was practically endemic. Like polio, Lyme disease, and other ailments, once contracted, it afflicted its survivors for life with relapses and recurring symptoms. But according to one of Louis' closest friends, Roy Williams, Louis saw Ebenezer get beaten in the street and lynched. Roy said that was the formative event of Louis' childhood. Did Roy, in his eighties when he told the tale, mix-up what he'd heard about Mary Bacot's husband getting lynched right before *her* eyes? Or is it possible that Louis was at his grandmother's house when his step-grandfather was killed, and that he did not disclose this when he wrote about it?

According to Louis' biographer Gayle Morrison, author of the masterful *To Move the World*, Louis didn't have any memory of his father. His father was mortally ill with TB, but perhaps a beating hastened his death? Roy said the killing happened right outside the Gregory family's door. "The little four year old child stood and looked. And so he made up his mind he wanted to do something, get ahold of something, so that he could fight back and the way he could do that was to get an education. He wanted to destroy all phases of lynching and hate, therefore he lived a life of peace and he would not say anything about certain things of the past. Louis Gregory was a man of peace."[7] Whatever the full details, we get the reality of the violence that roiled around Louis and his noble-hearted reaction to oppression.

When Louis was seven, his existence got easier because his mother married George Gregory, a leading black citizen of Charleston, who became a real father to her boys. Louis happily took his last name. George Gregory was freeborn and had never been a slave. He was influential in an interracial carpenter's union, and his family had owned property in town since pre-Civil War days. Although some freeborn African Americans owned slaves, George Gregory hated the practice. A Union Army veteran, he vehemently advocated freedom. He didn't follow Louis into the Bahá'í Faith, but he often distributed Bahá'í literature, and when he died at a ripe old age, one thousand people, black and white, attended his funeral. He had a comfortable house at 2 Desportes Court in Charleston (now the Louis George Gregory Museum) where Louis benefited from the benign, encouraging atmosphere and his parents' support of his fierce ambition to be well-educated.

Louis' schoolteachers were almost always white. When he got to the higher grades, he went to missionary schools and colleges where the teachers felt called to serve Christ by educating African American children. Many of them had been abolitionists, champions of African Americans before the Civil War, and now that it was over, they continued their mission. His high school, Avery Institute (now the Avery Institute of Afro-American History and Culture), sent most of its graduates to college, and many of them became leaders in education and civil rights.

The South was dense with missionary activity, and Louis later recalled sitting in a mission center on a special day of prayer for students. His classmates were singing a song he'd suggested, with the lyrics, "O the future lies before me and I know not where I'll be." Louis, however, wasn't singing. He'd fallen silent, for, as they sang, he "saw himself, running to and fro, delivering a message like unto heavenly music." He shook himself out of his reverie, ignoring it "as a creation of fancy."[8]

It may have seemed particularly fanciful because in 1890, during Louis' senior year at Avery, his older brother died of pneumonia, and the next year, when he graduated, his mother died of spinal meningitis. This cruel mixing of the bitter with the sweet would have been enough to sour any character, especially when combined with the poverty and loss of Louis' earliest days and the depredations that Jim Crow laws steadily made on any sense of liberty that Louis might have happened to develop. By the time Louis reached young manhood, he'd lost interest in the old-time religion of his mother and grandmother. He was agnostic and enraged at the spiritual, political, and financial bondage of African Americans. He felt that only radical action could break the chains.

However, Louis' stepfather never failed him, and he gained a loving stepmother when George married Lauretta Noisette, a member of one of Charleston's most prominent black families. He also gained a good brother in her son, Harrison.

Louis graduated from Fisk University, in Nashville, Tennessee, in 1896. George Gregory had apprenticed him to be a tailor, and after George paid for his freshman year, Louis worked his way through college by tailoring—mending, cleaning and pressing clothes for fellow students—and waiting on tables. Like Avery, Fisk had opened as a missionary school right after the Civil War. The white teachers lived in the dorms, ate with the students, went to student parties. They were highly qualified, and they "sacrificed income and position," Louis wrote, "to devote their lives to the children of former slaves."[9]

The professors and administrators at Fisk, Avery, and other schools, along with the founders of the schools, exemplified the American tradition of race amity—whites reaching out to people of color to help and assuage—that had always run counter to slaveholding and segregationist policies in the United States.

Louis taught for a time at Avery, then studied law at Howard University in Washington, DC. In 1902, he gave the commencement oration at his Howard graduation, speaking on the development of international peace laws and emphasizing disarmament. He opened a law office in Washington with a friend who later became the first black judge in the Capital District.

Washington, DC, was "the start of the North," Isabel Wilkerson writes in *The Warmth of Other Suns*, "filled as it was with grand squares and circles named after northern heroes of the civil War—Ulysses S. Grant, William Tecumseh Sherman, George Henry Thomas, David G. Faragut—names, to this day, reviled in the South."[10] Louis Gregory was part of the Great Migration of African Americans northward, away from Jim Crow. Though they faced grim prejudice and danger in the north, they were better off working in a factory for wages than breaking their backs sharecropping for a landowner who could whip them if they didn't work fast enough to suit him, pay nothing to them at the end of the growing season if he "broke even," or pay them nothing and tell them they owed him money for buying things on credit at his store. An African American who had a university degree had some chance at white-collar work in the north, or at least work besides picking oranges or cotton. It was an American dream, a risk worth taking.

> Many thousands rise and go
> many thousands crossing over
> > O mythic North
> > O star-shaped yonder Bible city . . .[11]

"Yonder Bible city" was the African-American part of town, like Harlem in Manhattan or the South Side in Chicago, and a major part of it was paved, having indoor plumbing and streetlights in ever-growing quantity, and beckoning with opportunity. Washington, DC, as a whole had its Southern characteristics, its great drawbacks of institutionalized prejudice, but Louis could function as a professional there, and he functioned very well. The broad green campus of his alma mater, Howard, was at the heart of African-American Washington, the so-called Secret City, with its Black Broadway full of favorite restaurants and clubs. Washington's black elite was made up mostly of educators and other professionals, as well as people who worked in civil service jobs, and there was a burgeoning arts community, soon to be tapped by famed philosopher and litterateur Alain Locke when he began publishing and publicizing African American artists during what would become known as the Harlem Renaissance. A good portion of this movement came from Washington, not to mention Chicago.

Louis was regarded as one of black society's most eligible bachelors, his doings reported in *The Washington Bee*, the capital's most important African American newspaper. The paper also reported his activities as a leader of the black intelligentsia and published his opinion pieces.

Louis ardently supported W. E. B. DuBois and the Niagara Movement. Until the advent of DuBois, progressive African Americans mostly followed Booker T. Washington, founder of Tuskegee Institute and author of *Up from Slavery*. Washington's philosophy was called accommodationist. Though he himself was a high achiever (putting it mildly), Washington felt African Americans should settle for being separate but equal. Let young African Americans develop vocational skills and aim for stable, well-fed existences. Don't strive in ways that make whites feel threatened, don't push for voting rights. Washington theorized that steadily increasing black prosperity and property ownership would eventually result in social equality.

DuBois, a Harvard graduate and literary genius, understandably considered the accommodationist stance counterproductive and self-defeating. No matter how low a profile African Americans tried to keep, bullying them—terrorizing and intimidating them, vandalizing and stealing their property—was a commonplace sport for many whites, and it easily exploded into lynching, arson, riots. Louis Gregory knew about that, first-hand. All the accommodating in the world couldn't stop it.

DuBois wanted real freedom, real equality, and full political enfranchisement for African Americans. He felt that had to come before they achieved the economic stability Washington envisioned. He upheld the reality of "the New Negro," first described in an 1895 *Cleveland Gazette* editorial as the new class of prosperous, educated African Americans "that had arisen since the Civil War."[12] The term certainly described Louis.

DuBois published his landmark book *The Souls of Black Folk* in 1902. A collection of fourteen essays, with various poems adding to its eloquence, and one fiction piece, it was as much a portrait of its author as of a people, and Louis loved it. Years later, he called

Dubois a "Cavalier of the Quill," and described *The Souls of Black Folk* as the "jeremiad of a poet-evangelist," but sadly saw that though it "stirred his vast congregation to remorse and even tears" it did not move them to "repentance."[13]

Describing the inner state of the African American in a world that demanded his invisibility, Dubois famously observed, "it is a peculiar sensation, this double-consciousness, this sense of always looking at one's self through the eyes of others, of measuring one's soul by the tape of a world that looks on in amused contempt and pity. One ever feels his twoness—an American, a Negro; two souls, two thoughts, two unreconciled strivings; two warring ideals in one dark body, whose dogged strength alone keeps it from being torn asunder."[14]

It's hard enough for a person to integrate her physical, emotional, intellectual and spiritual selves—hard enough to feel inner oneness. In his foreword to *To Move the World*, Glenford Mitchell points out, "This psychological dichotomy, it could be reasoned" is "an acute example of Bahá'u'lláh's meaning when He lamented that 'No two men can be found who may be said to be outwardly and inwardly united.'"[15]

Add to that the pressure of having roots in a homeland that rejects one's very humanity because of skin color, that sees her as other or alien so she feels she must abase herself, excuse herself, and disappear—while, within, her basic life force commands: appear! Most African Americans have a mixed heritage that makes this "double condition" even more wrenching—a white, slaveholder forebear like Senator Dargan, or a Native-American mother. The black poet Langston Hughes wrote of his ancestors, ". . . a Jewish slave trader in Kentucky . . . a distiller of Scotch descent . . . French . . . Indian . . . an ancestor related to "the great statesman Henry Clay," another to a "famous Jacobean poet." The great bandleader W. C. Handy described walking down Beale Street in Memphis, Tennessee, shaking hands with his black brethren—"ebony hands, brown hands, yellow hands, ivory hands."[16]

When DuBois identified what he called the color line as the major problem of the twentieth century, he was talking of prejudice and Jim Crow, but his impassioned writings disclosed a much deeper line—or lines—drawn within himself and his brother and sister African Americans, rifts and wounds that perhaps only the grace of God can heal. If that grace doesn't flow from human being to another, through human love, it can't be felt. When it does flow, it creates not only unity but amity, deep friendship.

In 1905, DuBois, with the black leaders Mary Burnett Talbert and the more militant William Monroe Trotter, started the Niagara Movement—so called because the first meeting convened at Niagara Falls—to demand full civil rights for African Americans. During the same year, artist/professor John Henry Adams Jr. wrote about the New Negro and made prototypes of his ideals in photos. He called attention to "what it actually *costs* in human effort to be a man and at the same time a Negro."[17] Photography in the hands of black artists had the same effect as literature by black writers: it revealed people of color as multidimensional human beings to the whites who viewed them as "others." Viewers of Professor Adams' pictures saw people, not caricatures. (Perhaps the worst caricature ever was the grotesque Jim Crow himself.)

At the second meeting of the Niagara Movement, in Harpers Ferry, West Virginia, DuBois delivered a speech "to the nation" condemning the rise of Jim Crow law. He demanded voter protection, i.e., full enfranchisement for black men (as yet, no women had the right to vote), and an end to segregation. He said:

In the past year the work of the Negro-hater has flourished in the land. Step by step the defenders of the rights of American citizens have retreated. The work of stealing the black man's ballot has progressed and the fifty and more representatives of stolen votes still sit in the nation's capital.

Discrimination in travel and public accommodation has so spread that some of our weaker brethren are actually afraid to thunder against color discrimination as such and are simply whispering for ordinary decencies. Against this the Niagara Movement eternally protests. We will not be satisfied to take one jot or tittle less than our full manhood rights. We claim for ourselves every single right that belongs to a freeborn American, political, civil and social; and until we get these rights we will never cease to protest and assail the ears of America.

The battle we wage is not for ourselves alone but for all true Americans. It is a fight for ideals, lest this, our common fatherland, false to its founding, become in truth the land of the thief and the home of the slave, a byword and a hissing among the nations for its sounding pretensions and pitiful accomplishment."[18]

He delineated Jim Crow / Apartheid in no uncertain terms: "Never before in the modern age has a great and civilized folk threatened to adopt so cowardly a creed in the treatment of its fellow citizens born and bred on its soil. Stripped of verbiage and subterfuge and in its naked nastiness, the new American creed says: Fear to let the black men even try to rise lest they become the equals of the white. And this is the land that professes to follow Jesus Christ. The blasphemy of such a course is only matched by its cowardice."[19]

That same year, the James Weldon Johnson poem that's now the African American National Anthem was set to music, and five hundred black children sang it in Jacksonville, Florida, at a Lincoln's Birthday celebration—

> Lift every voice and sing, till earth and Heaven ring,
> Ring with the harmonies of liberty; Let our rejoicing rise,
> High as the listening skies, let it resound loud as the rolling sea.
> Sing a song full of the faith that the dark past has taught us,
> Sing a song full of the hope that the present has brought us;
> Facing the rising sun of our new day begun,
> Let us march on till victory is won . . .[20]

Against the beautiful eloquence, bravery, and passionate purpose expressed by leaders like DuBois and Johnson, race war loomed in ugly, sporadic, but constant outbreaks. An epidemic of race riots and lynching bloodied the United States from the 1800s long into the twentieth century. In 1900, there were two major race riots, one in New York City and one in New Orleans, and riots in smaller places in the Deep South. Over one hundred black people were lynched. In New York City, police joined a mob of some ten thousand white men attacking every black man they could see. In 1906, Atlanta, Georgia, exploded in one of the South's worse riots, a four-day pogrom against the black population.

What could ignite such violence? There were various triggers, but one efficient way to incite a race riot and/or lynching was to accuse a black man of raping, or merely making advances to, or even looking at, a white woman. When newspapers and politicians went to work on such stories, the irrational fear of black men's sexuality that afflicted many white men and women ensured that hysteria, violence, and death would ensue. Ironically, it was white men like Senator Dargan—slaveowners, and, later, others in positions of power, such as farmers lording it over sharecroppers—who were guilty of raping black women. These men projected their crime onto their victims: the fathers, husbands, lovers, and brothers of the women they preyed upon and violated. Their unacknowledged sense of guilt because of their own sin fueled their fury.

Black people spent their lifetimes with their backs to the wall, up against this and other monumental lies. W. E. B. Dubois expressed the anguish in his Litany of Atlanta, written after the 1906 riot:

> "Bewildered are we and passion tost, mad with the madness of a mobbed and mocked and murdered people; straining at the armposts of Thy throne, we raise our shackled hands and charge Thee, God, by the bones of our stolen fathers, by the tears of our dead mothers, by the very blood of our crucified Christ: What meaneth this? Tell us the plan; give us the sign;

whisper—speak—call, great God, for Thy silence is white terror to our hearts! The way, O God, show us the way and point us the Path!"[21]

The genius and passion of DuBois were never more apparent than in that prayer. The very term "white terror" with its connotations of hooded and white-sheeted Klu Klux Klan posses and other hate-driven white supremacists, and its purposeful straying from the usual, clichéd image of dark terror, is just one example of his brilliance.

It described the feelings of many, among them Louis Gregory. As he entered his thirties he did indeed feel traumatized by "white terror," felt "bewildered . . . and passion toss'd" but, he didn't feel like calling upon God. He later said that he had been seeking truth, but not finding it, "had given up." He felt that nothing less than "fiery agitation" could win justice for African Americans.[22]

Louis was suffering the worst oppression there is. Bahá'u'lláh defines oppression as "the want of capacity to acquire spiritual knowledge and apprehend the word of God." This was an oppression Louis' grandmother had not experienced, for faith never left her heart. Bahá'u'lláh asked, "What oppression is more grievous than that a soul seeking the truth, and wishing to attain unto the knowledge of God, should not know where to go for it and from whom to seek it?"[23] In a photo of Louis taken at that time, his gaze is defiant, his posture rigid. There was truth in what DuBois said, and truth in Louis' rage, but his spirit demanded a different kind of truth if he were to survive.

4

Amity: Meeting the Other American Tradition

with Pauline Hannen, Mírzá Abu'l-Faḍl, Ali Kuli Khan

As my anger ebbs,
The spring stars grow bright again
And the wind returns.

—Richard Wright

At the time of his greatest despair and anger, Louis began working in the U.S. Treasury Department. We don't know why he went to work as a clerk instead of staying in his law practice; possibly he did both. But the government work turned out to be a blessing because he sat at a desk between two fellow clerks, who unexpectedly became his saviors. In his recollections, he credits them with giving him real friendship—amity—that grace that alone can solace an alienated heart.

Certainly, on his first day in the office, meeting the good gentlemen, Louis couldn't have suspected that he'd eventually view them with such gratitude. They were both advanced in years. One was from the South, the other from the North. Both were white. One had fought for the Union in the Civil War; the other had sided with the Confederacy. They absolutely hated each other. However, with Louis, they both carried out that other American tradition of amity. Louis had benefited from this other tradition in many ways, notably at the various schools he attended. But it was constantly counteracted by toweringly negative experiences and observations that stemmed from the racism inherent in American culture.

Outwardly, Louis didn't give away his inner alienation. Talking with him, his two office mates found him articulate and eloquent, with a soft, mellow voice and a slight Southern accent. He was obviously bright, carrying out all his duties with confidence and dispatch, moving quickly and deftly. Despite his inner anger, once he decided he liked somebody, he was engaging, kinetic, charismatic, and affable.

The two old soldiers loved to talk, and they soon found that Louis always had something to say. Louis also discovered, to his delight, that they "could be thrown into controversy at any moment by a question about the Civil War," about which they, of course, disagreed mightily. Louis had a keen sense of mischief and, in that winter of his discontent, reveled in argument. As he put it, back then he was "quite disputatious" and his workdays simply sped by when he could "stir up the animals"—get the two oldsters into a rousing quarrel.

Besides enjoying their fury at each other, Louis vented his anger to them, expounding his radical ideas. He gave them articles he was writing, and he shared writing by other authors. They listened patiently to Louis and read everything he gave them. The only thing on earth they agreed about, it seemed, was that Louis' opinions were not good for Louis and would only turn people against him. Louis' bellicose stance remained "unyielding" but "their friendship, even affection" for him grew. He often arrived at work with "ruffled" feelings, and they took care to soothe him. Their kindness and interest "made an indelible impression" on him. They lent him books, which he read.[1]

Then the Southerner heard about the Bahá'í Faith. He attended a meeting or two. He thought it would be good for Louis, though he wasn't interested in it for himself. He made Louis promise to go to a meeting.

Louis didn't want to go, and he procrastinated as long as he could, but, having promised, he finally went to the Corcoran Building (now demolished) across the street from the Treasury on a winter night in

1907. The weather was most inclement, so the story of Louis' Bahá'í life begins as many stories do: It was a dark and stormy night.

Louis made his way in out of the cold and found the designated meeting room. Pauline Hannen, a tiny, very young-looking white woman, was the only person there. Louis looked down into her earnest eyes as she turned her piquant face up to greet him, telling him he was about to hear "something very wonderful, though difficult" that would give him the same kind of opportunity he would have had if he'd lived on earth at the time of Christ. She urged him to try to get a full understanding of the message, "that through it a work would be possible that would bless humanity."[2]

Louis did want to do a work that would bless humanity; it had been his earliest dream. He'd been disappointed in the possibility of being able to fulfill it, but it still lived in his heart. As Roy Williams explained, Louis "was dedicated to one object in his life. Remembering the horrible picture from his early childhood of lynching in the South, he'd made up his mind as a boy to dedicate his life and education to trying to stop this venomous hatred, terror and malice of racial injustice in his lifetime."[3] So Louis took Pauline seriously, and his trust wasn't misplaced.

Despite her girlish appearance, Pauline was married and had two sons; she'd been a Bahá'í for five years when she met Louis. She was among the first Bahá'ís in Washington, DC, and had been the first in her Lutheran family to accept the Faith. She had immediately, without hesitation, transformed herself to put into action the principle of oneness, fearlessly espousing interracial amity. She was a true original and a leader.

In 1902, when she started out, Bahá'ís in the United States were almost all white, middle- or upper-class Americans. Occasional Iranian visitors added some diversity. The Washington Bahá'í community at the time had two Iranian guests who had been sent to the United States by 'Abdu'l-Bahá. One was a wraith-like, elderly philosopher in turban and robes; he was the teacher. The other, a young man in Western attire and fluent in English, was his interpreter.

Pauline was twenty-eight years old when she began going to their classes in a house on Massachusetts Avenue. She used to leave her infant son in his carriage at the front door of the house (yes, that's how the story is told—times were different!) and climb the stairs to the second floor to listen to the philosopher explain Messianic prophecies and give logical explanations of the Bible. Although one of his books was called *Metaphors and Miracles*, he didn't rely on miracle stories. He spoke in Persian, sometimes in Arabic, stopping from time to time so the young man could translate.

The venerable scholar loved his tea, brewed in a samovar, highly sweetened. After his talk, he'd make the tea and serve it in little glasses. Pauline would drink it, bid the two gentlemen adieu, go downstairs and take her baby home. She was one of a group of young parents who came to learn about the Bahá'í Faith. But she was so petite and quiet, she seemed like a solemn child.

"Does this little girl understand what we're talking about?" the younger man finally questioned his mentor. "Is she really interested?"

They agreed that she must be, or she wouldn't keep coming back. But the young interpreter decided to make sure. The next time she came, he asked if she was satisfied with the explanations or if she had questions. She smiled brightly and said, "How could there be anything more wonderful than this great Faith? After you have received this, what else in the world would you wish to possess?"[4]

Bahá'í literature in English was sparse at the time, but Pauline did have the small book of succinct counsels, *The Hidden Words of Bahá'u'lláh*, and she came upon this passage: "O children of men! Know ye not why We created you all from the same dust? That no one should exalt himself over the other . . . Since we have created you all from one same substance it is incumbent on you to be even as one soul, to walk with the same feet, eat with the same mouth and dwell in the same land, that from your inmost being, by your deeds and actions, the signs of oneness and the essence of detachment may be made manifest."[5]

Pauline's family had come to America from Germany but she, the youngest of three sisters, was born in the United States. She grew up in the Deep South—in Wilmington, North Carolina. From childhood she'd feared black people and she'd never questioned their subjugation. She later wrote, "I had known of the frightful retribution visited by whites on negroes for offenses of which I assumed they must be guilty." Perhaps she, like Louis, had witnessed a lynching, but from the other side. Lynching sometimes took place in public; spectators even brought picnics.

What she read in *The Hidden Words* made her think anew, act anew, disenthrall herself—(to paraphrase Abraham Lincoln). It was Thanksgiving time when she became a Bahá'í. She was walking down the street in a November snowfall when she saw a black woman coming toward her, arms laden with parcels and bundles, untied shoelaces dragging in the snow. Pauline knelt before her—thus stopping her in her tracks—and tied her shoes.

"She was astonished," Pauline recalled, "and those who saw it appeared to think I was crazy."[6] But Pauline made up her mind to teach the Bahá'í Faith to African Americans, to serve them, to share with them her vibrant conviction that humanity must be "as one soul . . . walk with the same feet . . . eat with the same mouth . . . dwell in the same land . . ."

Pauline's heart was pure, receptive and generous, her mind questing and open. She was also completely transformed by the logos of Bahá'u'lláh. It not only jolted her out of her prejudice, it freed her from fear.

And there was another influence at work: her teacher, the wraith-like Iranian scholar. 'Abdu'l-Bahá called him "a standard-bearer of the oneness of the world of humanity."[7] In many ways, the unity of the U.S. Bahá'í community, which gave it the ability to welcome 'Abdu'l-Bahá to North America in 1912 with some understanding of His mission and presence, was due largely to Mírzá Abu'l-Faḍl. For the sake of ease, and because his friends in the United States often referred to him simply as Mírzá, the title of respect given him because of his princely qualities, we'll refer to him by this name, too, and take a deeper look at him in the coming chapter.

5

Persian Prince of Amity: Mírzá Abu'l-Faḍl

I have seen a vision of the marriage of East and West . . .
a love-union of the two hemispheres;
a mystic ring on the finger of the world . . .
—Bernard Leach

Bahá'u'lláh was still alive when Mírzá Abu'l-Faḍl became one of His followers in 1883, and He wrote a Tablet to Mírzá a few years later telling him to travel and teach the Bahá'í Faith. In his obedience to this injunction, Mírzá, originally from a small inland Iranian town, would gaze upon seascapes, mountains, city skylines—far horizons he never would have imagined in his boyhood. Born in 1844 into a family of distinguished religious scholars, he was almost the exact same age as the Master and of his new religion.*

When he was a boy, townspeople thought Mírzá had supernatural powers because of his amazing memory and intelligence. In his youth he studied Arabic, the Qur'án, Islamic jurisprudence, and all

---

* On the night of May 23, 1844, in an upstairs room of a house in the city of Shiraz, in southern Iran, young Siyyid 'Alí-Muḥammad proclaimed Himself the Herald of the New Age. That night is celebrated by Bahá'ís around the world as the birthdate of their Faith. The young man seated in front of Him became the first to publicly believe in Him; His wife and an Ethiopian servant also believed. He took the title *the Báb*, which means *the Gate* or *Portal*. He explained that after Him, Bahá'u'lláh would make Himself known. He, the Báb, was preparing the way. His religion, the Bábí Faith, was destined to live only a few years, and so was He. His was "the first act of a sublime drama" and He was "its Master Hero," as Shoghi Effendi wrote one hundred years later in *God Passes By* (p. 4).

the other subjects included in the education of one destined to be not a mere mullah—though we will call him that to simplify our vocabulary—but a mujtahid, able to render judgment in cases tried by Islamic law. But he didn't stop there. He never stopped learning. He studied religious history with two Buddhists resident in Tehran, and learned about European science from Western instructors at the technical college there.

Before he was thirty, Mírzá was established in a hallowed madrassa (religious college) in Tehran both as teacher and superintendent. His given name was Muḥammad, but he took the name Abu'l-Faḍl for himself. It means "the father of knowledge." Later, the Master addressed him as the father of knowledge, and its mother and brother.[1] It also means *Father of Virtue*, and the Master used to make that plural: *Father of Virtues*.

A spare, ascetic man with especially black, deep-set, penetrating eyes, Mírzá was among Iran's most revered authorities on Shi'ite Islam, the Arabic language, the Qur'án, philosophy, history, and other branches of study. He regarded Bahá'ís as ridiculous upstarts and was surprised and annoyed when he found out that a farrier whose wisdom he admired despite the man's illiteracy was a Bahá'í. When he was about thirty-two, he began going to Bahá'í meetings to expose the folly of the faith. But he couldn't do it. Learned Bahá'ís disarmed his pointed attacks, but worse, relatively unschooled Bahá'ís—tradesmen and craftsmen—employed logic to defeat his most erudite arguments.

Trying to best them all, he read every bit of Bahá'í scripture he could find. When he read *The Book of Certitude*, lauded as Bahá'u'lláh's masterpiece, he remarked that if it was "a proof of Bahá'u'lláh's claims, he himself could certainly write a better book." The next day a woman came to his university looking for a scribe. Could a student write a letter for her? She was prestigious and the task was important, so the students sent her to Mírzá. When Mírzá picked up his pen and poised it above a piece of paper that he balanced on his knee in the usual Persian way, he couldn't even compose an opening sentence. He made small doodles in the corner of the paper. He drew little lines on his fingernail. The woman finally snapped, "If you have forgotten how to write a simple letter why don't you say so?"[2]

She swept out of the room, and he was utterly mortified. Then he recalled what he'd said the night before about *The Book of Certitude*. Had he been arrogant? Was this his punishment? With this thought, it seemed a glimmer of light came to him from his farthest horizon.

Yet it took him quite awhile to capitulate. He came to believe with his intellect but not his heart. He finally said that he'd only become a Bahá'í if Bahá'u'lláh's prediction of the downfall of the Turkish sultan* came true. Since he thought that would never happen, he regarded himself as saved from Bahá'í contamination. Now perhaps he could save *them* and bring them back to the truth. But the more he tried, the more his efforts were in vain, and he began to shun the Bahá'ís.

One day in 1876, when he saw two Bahá'ís talking together on the street, he pulled his *aba* (cloak) over his head and crossed to the other side. But they recognized him and called out the news that the sultan had been dethroned. He yelled, "It is no concern of mine . . . I am not a relative of his." They said, "Didn't you make your acceptance of the truth of this Faith dependent upon this event?"[3]

Completely enraged, Mírzá hurried back to his house. Weeping, he begged God to assist him so he wouldn't be misguided. When Bahá'ís came to see him at the front door, he snuck out the back and didn't return till nightfall. They came again. And again. After several days, he finally spoke to them, only to remind them that Bahá'u'lláh had also predicted the sultan's assassination. A few more days passed. News came that the sultan was dead. Suicide, the palace mutineers contended. But people knew he'd been murdered.

---

* 'Abdu'l-Azíz (1861–1876), thirty-second Sultan of the Ottoman Empire.

"I went out of my mind," Mírzá later recalled, "and was utterly perplexed. I was so agitated that I even aimed blows at myself. At one time I would fight with God, at another I would turn unbeliever, then I would repent and beseech God to assist, guide and protect me . . . I could neither eat nor sleep . . . I only drank tea and smoked and wept."

One night he had to settle down and face facts: for over a year Bahá'ís had been besting him in argument. And he was "the father of knowledge." Was the insightful logic of the Bahá'ís born of the divine spark? He had to admit that he admired their virtuousness. Perhaps he should not consider their words the breathings of Satan? Perhaps he should peruse Bahá'í writings "with the eye of justice and fairness?"

He took one of Bahá'u'lláh's tablets, which he'd kept for a long time without opening, and began to read. Then he felt as if a divine voice summoned him: "Am I not your Lord?" And in his heart he answered, "Thou art, thou art!"[4]

And Mírzá discovered in his innermost being the true meaning of Islam, which is, we are taught, submission. He had been a mystic huntsman, going after the Bahá'ís with his nets of traditional rhetoric and knowledge, but another mystic hunter, his own fate, had been after him and had now snared him in the web of oneness, a knowledge much deeper than tradition.

Being extremely straightforward, Mírzá immediately told his students at the madrassa about his new beliefs. He was arrested, chained, and imprisoned for five months. He lost his job. His brothers dispossessed him of all the family property, and he was penniless. He took a job teaching at a Zoroastrian school; he acted in a play, commissioned by the Parsi from India who ran the school, about the beginnings of the Bahá'í Faith.

In the early 1880s, he was imprisoned for two years in Tehran, in fetters and chains, sometimes in an underground dungeon. He was frequently interrogated and always expected imminent execution. Shortly after a brief period of freedom, he was again arrested and imprisoned for six months.

Upon his release, he received word from Bahá'u'lláh telling him to travel as a Bahá'í teacher. He began to earn his living as a scribe, writing letters for people or copying scripture. With this income, he could sometimes support the cost of a donkey for luxurious transportation as he covered great distances over desert and mountain and down into the humid regions by the Caspian Sea. Often he had nothing to eat but a staple of the poor, a delicacy called "crisp bread and water."[5] He thanked wealthy Bahá'ís who offered support, but accepted nothing.

Bahá'u'lláh instructed Mírzá to tell people of the "Most Great Announcement," to show them the "Most Exalted Horizon." Mírzá had thought he shouldn't presume to put pen to paper while Bahá'u'lláh Himself was alive and writing. Then he met a man who had heard Bahá'u'lláh say that "the believers should each one write books" in support of the Faith. When asked if Mírzá Abu'l-Faḍl should be employed in such service, the answer was yes.[6]

Mírzá became an ambassador of oneness. He wrote a book of proofs for the Jews of Hamadan, which was translated into Hebrew and circulated widely despite the fact that Islamic clerics imprisoned him for five days in Hamadan and then kicked him out of the city. He wrote to Zoroastrians in their own dialect of ancient Persian. His research and subsequent treatise on Bahá'u'lláh's genealogy, naming Yazdigird III, the last Zoroastrian king of Iran, as one of His forebears, had great influence on Zoroastrians.

Bringing the Faith even further afield—to new horizons—he went to Central Asia in 1889 and lived in the city of Ashgabat (then called Ishqabad), Turkmenistan, which was Russian territory. Shortly after his arrival, a Bahá'í friend of his was brutally martyred—hacked to pieces—in broad daylight in the marketplace. When the Russian overlords couldn't stop the wave of persecution that arose against the Bahá'ís, Mírzá represented the Bahá'ís in court and also before the governor-general. He established that the Bahá'í Faith was independent of Islam and therefore was not a heresy. The murderers were condemned to death; then, with other Bahá'ís, Mirzá won clemency for them.

In His Tablet of the World, revealed in 1891, Bahá'u'lláh celebrated the magnanimity of heart as well as the dedication to justice evinced by Mírzá and his companions. He thanked God that the influence of His teachings on the "characters and conduct" of His followers had been affirmed by "an event which hath truly cheered the eye of the world, and is none other than the intercession of the friends with the highest authorities in favor of their enemies."[7]

The atmosphere of animosity toward the Bahá'ís in Ashgabat changed to one of amity, or at least grudging respect. Was it a coincidence that in 1902 the first Bahá'í House of Worship* in the world was erected in Ashgabat? For a time, Ashgabat had a flourishing Bahá'í community with two schools near the House of Worship and a Pilgrim House.

Mírzá wanted to bring word of Bahá'u'lláh to more remote regions. Samarqand beckoned, then Bukhara. Mírzá had evolved far, far from his roots as a traditional mullah, sharing meals and conversing with non-Muslims, people he would once have avoided as ritually unclean. Within his transformed heart, he could see how their languages, cultures, and histories synthesized into a narrative of the oneness of humanity, and he imparted that narrative with the invaluable soupçon of unconditional love and acceptance.

But when he learned of Bahá'u'lláh's death in 1892, Mírzá went into a depression and decline. 'Abdu'l-Bahá summoned him to 'Akká, where he spent ten months recovering, under Abdu'l-Bahá's care. Then the Master suggested that he move to Egypt, and they consulted about a strategy for teaching the new faith as effectively as possible there.

Mírzá went to Cairo in 1894 but didn't contact the Bahá'ís. He started spending time at "the University of al-Azhar, the foremost institution of learning in the Muslim world . . . (where) his pro-

---

* Unfortunately it is no longer standing. During the 1930s, it was appropriated by the Soviet government and used as a museum. In 1948, an earthquake damaged it severely, and subsequently, it was demolished.

found learning caused a group of the students of the University to gather around him. From these he picked a few who were more open-minded and began to speak to them about the Bahá'í Faith. Eventually some thirty of these students became Bahá'ís . . ." They were Egyptians, and that was important because, up until then, all the Bahá'ís in Egypt were Iranians.

A mystique grew up around Mírzá. With his brilliant interpretations of scripture and mystic truths, he became "a point of adoration for scholars and a centre of pilgrimage for those who yearn after knowledge and understanding." Some people assumed that he was a chosen one of God, with special powers, "exalted above other men."

A particularly enthusiastic student said to him, ". . . Why do you hide from me? If you are a chosen one of God . . . please tell me and I will accept and follow you." Mírzá laughed and said the student would find an answer to his question later. After a time, the student had to go to the Haifa area, and Mírzá told him to meet 'Abdu'l-Bahá while there. After that, when the student saw Mírzá again, he reported, ". . . When I attained the holy presence of the Master, I realized that you are no more than a drop in relation to that billowing ocean." Mírzá, ecstatic, threw his arms around the student. "Now I know that you have recognized the truth," he cried.[8]

Mírzá also befriended journalists, and the intelligentsia published articles about him in reform-minded magazines and newspapers; they called him Shaykh Faḍlu'lláh Irani, which roughly translates as *the virtuous, wise elder from Iran.*

But in 1896, Mírzá rushed to the defense of the Bahá'ís when a powerful man at the Iranian Embassy accused them of complicity in the assassination of the shah. In so doing, Mírzá revealed that he himself was a Bahá'í. Shortly afterwards, two of his books were published: *The Peerless Gems*, defending Bahá'u'lláh's *Book of Certitude*, the very book he'd vehemently denigrated at first reading; and *The Shining Pearls*, or *Miracles and Metaphors*, essays on the history of religion. Fellow professors at the al-Azhar brought manuscripts to him for comments before publishing them. But, although respect for him continued and grew, Egyptian Sunnite mullahs officially declared him an infidel.

In 1900, the Master requested his help in the United States. Laura Dreyfus-Barney, a North American who was one of the foremost early Bahá'ís of Paris and Washington DC, had asked 'Abdu'l-Bahá's permission to bring him there. The community, pressured by enemies-from-within, was in danger of splintering and needed a wise guide who could impart and instill Bahá'í teachings on unity.

It was Mírzá's deepest prayer to be able to feel and understand universal oneness. He had a "devotion to the Faith of God within every great religion" that was "matched only by his selflessness and his (not typical of scholars) humility."[9] He believed that before the intuitive knowledge possessed by a Messenger of God, all of his insights were nothing.

In a missive written in the last year of Bahá'u'lláh's life, Bahá'u'lláh had sent him a prayer: "O my God! I beg of Thee by the King of Names and Maker of Heaven and earth; by the rustling of the Leaves of the Tree of life; and by Thy Utterance through which the realities of things are drawn unto us, to grant me . . ." (Here, Mírzá could name his supplications). In one typed copy of the prayer, there's a supplication appended: "To grant that each time we read these Divine Words we may realize Thy Oneness and Thy Singleness; there is no God but Thee, the Powerful, the Mighty, the Everlasting."[10] Unity was Mírzá's longing, the deep desire of his heart.

That prayer was to be said at midnight and followed by ninety-five repetitions of the Greatest Name, "Allah'u'Abhá!"—"God is Most Glorious!" We can imagine Mírzá with his bright black eyes closed, prayer beads clicking through his fingers, chanting the prayer Bahá'u'lláh had given him, then stating his heart's desire, and then repeating the mantra, the Greatest Name.

Ali-Kuli Khan, who accompanied Mírzá in the United States as his interpreter and aide, said that he "was almost continually in a state of prayer." He would lock himself in his room and apply himself to his devotions with "such fervor, and such weeping" because of "his concept of the greatness of God and his own nothingness . . ." Khan would admonish him, "You, a holy being, weeping like this. If *you* are a sinner, then what hope is there for the rest of us?" And he would reply that someday Khan would understand "the degree of devotion worthy to serve as a language by which we can praise Bahá'u'lláh."[11]

Mírzá was rigorous in his recitations of the obligatory prayers and reminded an inquirer of the secrets of spiritual success as given in the Qur'án: "The most exalted titles belong to God, so call on Him through them."[12] He must have sought help frequently by chanting the Greatest Name.

Before reaching the United States, Mírzá spent some months in Paris, teaching the small group of Bahá'ís there, and they experienced such uplift in Mírzá's company that they could hardly bear it when the time came for him to continue his journey. Lua Getsinger, another of 'Abdu'l-Bahá's great favorites, named by Him to herald the Covenant, who would be the first Bahá'í speaker that Louis Gregory would hear, was in Paris at the time. She said 'Abdu'l-Bahá had told her to love Mírzá "as my own Father and I have always done so—but I did not realize how great and deep that love is—until I went to say 'good by' to him—yesterday—and then when I saw him again this morning—my heart broke! . . ."[13] In fact, she's buried in Cairo, in the same tomb as Mírzá Abu'l-Faḍl. They were knit together in the web of oneness, more than either of them knew . . .

Mírzá spoke no English, so Khan interpreted everything. However, Khan noticed that Mírzá could tell whether or not the translations rendered the essence of his words by looking at the faces of the listeners. When he gave a public talk, he didn't use notes; but he referred to notes when he gave classes, or as he answered questions sent in the mail or asked in person.

Khan was a poet with the pen-name Ishta'il (Aflame). He had exquisite literary sensibilities in Persian and any other language to which he was exposed. During his youth in Iran, he'd felt a great hunger for knowledge of English, so he'd pursued it, not knowing why. As an ardent new Bahá'í, he went on an odyssey across deserts and seas to reach 'Abdu'l-Bahá in 'Akká, where he worked closely with him as a secretary and translator. He was one of the few Persians of his generation able to be deeply proficient and eloquent in English, and he would go on to fulfill (through great storm and strife) ambassadorial posts for the Iranian government.

After his months in Paris, Mírzá arrived in New York in August, 1901, and soon went on to Chicago where Khan awaited him. Mírzá was still spare and ascetic, and now growing old; sometimes on the city streets he looked like a leaf blown by the wind in his oriental garb and white beard. Khan, more substantial looking but with a rather poignant smile, was clean-shaven except for his well-groomed black mustache, and he generally wore a smart, three-piece suit and derby hat; women thought he was very romantic looking. The press in Chicago gave Mírzá lots of attention, stressing his leadership of the Egyptian intelligensia.

There was another Iranian in Chicago who had arrived sometime earlier to teach the Bahá'ís, but he had allowed his supposed greatness to go to his head and was imparting fanciful philosophy while spending a good amount of time interpreting dreams for people, particularly ladies, who would then tell Mírzá that they "were personally led by the spirit, or had had a vision warning them against a fellow-believer," or some such thing. Mírzá called them *djinn-gir*— "spook chasers." They decided their preferred teacher was "spiritual" and that Mírzá was "intellectual." Khan was disturbed by this but Mírzá, hearing that he was regarded as "a brain divorced from the spirit . . . was much amused."[14]

His solution was to tell a person who felt specially guided by the spirit to compare that guidance with the counsels found in Bahá'u'lláh's writings. If the inspiration accorded with the Teachings, well and good; if not, the person was being guided by his or her own imagination.

Unfortunately the soothsayer's audience grew, and since he aggrandized himself and inflated people's egos, he fomented disunity. His goal was to build the Bahá'í Faith around himself. He was, in short, breaking the Bahá'í Covenant, which had the Master, and no one else, as its center. Mírzá didn't want to write to the Master about the situation and add to His burdens. But Khan wrote, and the Master summoned the soothsayer back to Haifa.

In December, 1901, Mírzá and Khan left Chicago for Washington, DC. Mírzá liked Washington, where springtime came early. The cherry blossoms and magnolias in the green squares and along the wide avenues and boulevards, and the pink petals drifting on gentle breezes, suited him much better than the Hawk, that bitter gale that blew in Chicago, the Windy City.

They stayed in a boarding house, in rooms on the top floor where Mírzá would hopefully not be bothered by traffic noises, babies crying, and cats yowling. Although he loved babies and was fond of cats, he required quiet. Mírzá also didn't like the food at the boardinghouse—and fact, he couldn't stand American food—and he subsisted on tea imported from Egypt, an occasional delicate cookie or two, and thin, black, Egyptian cigarettes.

After criticism from the Americans, Mírzá stopped smoking. He refused to quit gradually. He went from inveterate chain-smoking to zero in a minute, and felt awful. The ever-loyal Khan also quit smoking; he'd been smoking since the age of fourteen, so he didn't feel very good himself. But he cut back gradually on tobacco, and he ate normally. He was very worried about Mírzá, who had even ceased to order food from the boarding-house kitchen. But he'd promised Mírzá, at the beginning of their venture, that he would not interfere in his personal affairs. However, one day he found Mírzá unconscious on the floor of his room—he'd fainted from lack of food.

Khan went to Laura Dreyfus-Barney and told her and her mother, the renowned artist Alice Pike Barney, the situation. Alice asked her chef to cook a chicken for Mírzá. She brought it to the boardinghouse and presented it to Mírzá, saying, "I heard downstairs that you, dear Mírzá, are not ordering any meals, and so I have had a nice chicken cooked for you in my own kitchen." Mírzá admired Alice greatly and he was also very courteous, so he thanked her politely—but he cast a condemnatory gaze on Khan, as if to say, "So this is how you keep your promise not to interfere in my personal life?"[15] Khan, however, had no complaints as he watched Mírzá eating roasted chicken.

In North America, Mírzá had a special assignment from 'Abdu'l-Bahá to write a book, *Bahá'í Proofs*. Khan was in charge of making sure it got done, translated, and published. This was a difficult task because of Mírzá's temperament and the constant interruptions, the calls upon both his and Khan's time. But they did manage to finish and publish the book in 1902.

Mírzá had no trouble with writer's block. Khan said that "he was a careful, painstaking stylist" (writing in his inimitably fluid Arabic) "and yet he wrote very rapidly, with no corrections, no crossing out."[16] He used a reed pen, the kind that's characterized by Persian poets as having a shrill voice because of the way it seems to shriek and sing while crossing the paper. 'Abdu'l-Bahá was very pleased with *Bahá'í Proofs*. It was directed to Christians who were looking into the Bahá'í Faith, and it proved extremely useful.

Typescripts of Mírzá's talks also circulated among the Bahá'ís, and for many years they served as important references. And Mírzá maintained a huge volume of correspondence; 'Abdu'l-Bahá often referred inquirers to him. Some of his books and pamphlets resulted from questions sent by scholars such as the British orientalist, E. G. Browne. Some were defenses against attacks by clerics of various faiths—one of the most famous of those was *The Brilliant Proof*, written to refute anti-Bahá'í statements by Peter Z. Easton, a Christian clergyman. But Mírzá knew his true audience wasn't limited to scholars.

Khan later wrote, "In Washington a small group of men and women were drawn to our gatherings and meetings which were held for the public, besides the afternoon classes which Mírzá Abu'l-Faḍl conducted in our own living quarters. I remember many a young mother and father with one or more infants, some in baby carriages and others holding the parent's hand. I cannot forget how those young mothers and fathers came to us as seekers, and when I would translate Mírzá's words concerning the new Revelation, in some instances I would be surprised that my words met with, what I then thought, was seeming indifference. But, as facts proved later on, those young people had, in their own words, been awe-struck by the overpowering announcement of the new Revelation . . ."[17]

According to Moojan Momen, Mírzá's teachings were particularly relevant because of his "keen understanding of contemporary currents of thought . . ." His expansive expositions on Bahá'í principles withstand the test of time. Momen writes, "One of his concepts, for example—that even religions that appear to consist of idol-worship and are condemned as heathen were in fact originally true religions from God, the original pure teachings of which have been lost over the ages mainly through the action of religious leaders—has clear implications for the encounter of the Bahá'í Faith with ethnic religions in Africa and other parts of the world."[18]

In the summer of 1903, Mírzá went to Green Acre in Eliot, Maine, where he taught Bahá'ís and people of various philosophies. Green Acre at that time was a nondenominational retreat, a capital of late transcendentalist thought. There, Mírzá, cultured and polite to the nth degree, kindly, yet so pure and austere, was a star among the Ivy League professors, prominent artists, political activists, and other influential folks. Someone once announced that they saw a halo glowing around his head while he was giving a talk.

A little over a year later, in November, 1904, he left the United States. Despite occasional jarring events such as schoolboys flinging stones and mockery at him from time to time because of his robes and turban, his stay in North America was marked by wonderful welcomes everywhere. He expressed deep gratitude and tenderness, with a personal note that was very unusual for him, in saying farewell to the American Bahá'ís:

My tongue falters at offering adequate thanks to God for having granted me such loving brother and sisters. I am reminded of a passage in the Gospels (Mark 10:29–30): ". . . and Jesus answered and said, 'Verily I say unto you, there is no man that hath left house, or brethren, or sisters, or father, or mother, or wife, or children, or lands, for my sake and the gospel's, but that he shall receive a hundredfold now in this time . . .'" Praised be God that in this glorious age all the verses of the Holy Books have come to pass.

Thirty-two years ago when I was leaving my hometown, I was still a Muslim, and my mother, sister and brothers gathered to say good-bye to me. Three years later when I entered this Mighty Cause in Tihrán, all my relatives abandoned me and left me friendless, helpless and alone in the world. Now consider the bounty and generosity of our Master who has fulfilled His promise and granted me hundreds of times over what was lost in His path . . . How can I ever adequately thank the Divine Bounties for having bestowed upon me such spiritual kin as you?[19]

Pauline Hannen was one of the spiritual kinswomen Mírzá referred to in his farewell, and she would communicate the welcoming feeling of amity to Louis Gregory, soothing his heart more than he could realize at the time. With her instant and subsequently consistent, daring embrace of human equality, she'd certainly became Mírzá's fellow "standard-bearer of oneness" in the two years that he was her teacher before he donned his fine, warm leather gloves, wrapped his fur-lined cloak around himself, and sailed away, back to the East.

6

Home

with Paul K. Dealy, Lua Getsinger, Pauline and Joseph Hannen,
Phoebe Hearst, Robert Turner

it is beginning oh
it begins now
breathes into me
becomes my breath . . .

—*Robert Hayden*

In a poem, Pauline Hannen's husband described Pauline as "a Lamp of Love" and said, "On this self-smitten earth you stand / Extending e'er the helping hand . . ."[1] When she first met Louis Gregory on that cold night in 1907 in the Corcoran Building and extended her hand, she'd already heard about him from his friend, the Southern gentleman, and perhaps had been praying for his guidance, that he would come to a meeting. She gave him a copy of the book that had transformed her, *The Hidden Words*; a small pamphlet; and a volume called *The Dawn of Knowledge and the Most Great Peace,* by Paul K. Dealy, who was one of North America's earliest Bahá'ís.

Paul was a Canadian who had spent years in Chicago—where he had become a Bahá'í—but was living in Alabama by the time Louis received his book; he used to walk miles in tropical heat to tell the people of Bay Minette, an all-black town, about the Bahá'í Faith. He would have been happy that his introductory book, with its exposition about the fulfillment of biblical prophecies, found its way into Louis' hands.

Soon after Louis met Pauline, two African-American Bahá'ís arrived: Millie York and Nellie Gray. They had both learned of the Bahá'í Faith through Pauline. Then Lua Getsinger, introduced by Pauline as "our teacher," came in. And that was it. Few folks were out and about on that frigid night.

Lua was a lovely woman with deep blue eyes, a pensive smile, and a pillow of golden brown hair. She was renowned among the Bahá'ís for her eloquence, which they said was a blessing bestowed on her by 'Abdu'l-Bahá during one of her lengthy stays in His household, when she taught English to the ladies and children of his family and they taught her Persian.

She had trained as an actress and had a beautiful voice for singing as well as speaking. She was also known for her constant traveling and teaching; she'd become a Bahá'í in Chicago over a decade before Louis met her and was already a legend. She would be given various titles, among them Disciple of 'Abdu'l-Bahá, Herald of the Covenant, and the ones carved on her tombstone in Egypt: Banner of the Cause and Mother Teacher of the West.

But we're meeting Lua in her prime as she sweeps into the room greeting Pauline, Carrie and Millie, meeting Louis, then taking a seat from which she can consistently see everyone present—that's her habit. Though only a few people are there, and Louis is the only one who isn't a Bahá'í, each pair of eyes is a book for Lua. She cherishes every soul. She speaks briefly and simply, telling of the early history of the Faith and the martyrdoms in Iran.

In Paris, at around the time when Pauline became a Bahá'í, Lua was personally petitioning the shah, who was staying at a luxurious hotel there, to cease persecuting the Iranian Bahá'ís. In doing so, she was 'Abdu'l-Bahá's ambassador, as she generally was in all she did. In 1898, she'd been in the first group of Western pilgrims to visit the

Master in the prison city, 'Akká, and He had recognized her courage and fervor, and chosen her to herald Him.

With her in that historic pilgrimage group was the first African-American Bahá'í, Robert Turner. Lua must have been thrilled when the Master enfolded Robert in a hearty embrace of welcome, for she had introduced Robert to the Faith. He was butler to the mega-wealthy philanthropist, Phoebe Hearst, widow of mining magnate George Hearst and mother of newspaper tycoon William Randolph Hearst.

Mrs. Hearst had huge households, the most immense being in Washington, DC, and San Francisco, and Robert was steward for all of them. He was highly intelligent, trustworthy, and competent. Having begun in the 1870s as a valet for Mr. Hearst, Robert was much respected by Mrs. Hearst, her family, and staff. Mrs. Hearst once noted that Robert could manage anything—he could extend and expand his capabilities to suit any circumstance.

Nevertheless, when Lua paid her first visit to Mrs. Hearst, Robert, following time-honored custom, retired into anonymity after tea was served. Lua began telling Mrs. Hearst about the Bahá'í Faith. Robert maintained the low (or no)-profile requisite for a servant, but Lua, who saw the divine Beloved in every face, observed him and sensed his interest in what she was saying. She beckoned him to come closer.

Robert became a Bahá'í. So did Mrs. Hearst. When she organized a party of pilgrims to go and meet 'Abdu'l-Bahá, Robert was among them. It seemed he was traveling as Mrs. Hearst's butler, but in his heart he was a Bahá'í pilgrim: Lua knew it, and so did the Master and the others.

The pilgrims stayed in Paris while awaiting 'Abdu'l-Bahá's permission to leave for 'Akká. Lua taught a study class for them, and Robert participated. It was quite rare for a group of upper-class white Euro-American ladies and an African-American man, a butler, to sit and study on an equal basis. They had to rise above a great deal of prejudice and other psychic baggage. Robert had been a slave as a child, and he remembered calamities of the Civil War and other perils he'd been through, while at least one of his fellow students, Harriet Thornbourg, a Southerner, also had traumatic memories of the Civil War.

When Louis Gregory later wrote a biographical sketch of Robert, he described Robert's first meeting with the Master. He said that when the women arrived in 'Akká and "entered the room of the Master they assumed that Robert Turner . . . would of course follow. After greeting them . . . 'Abdu'l-Bahá waited with His face turned toward the door, in evident anticipation. The ladies looked around and to their surprise they found that Robert was not in the room. The Master then went to the door, on the outside of which Robert stood in an attitude of deepest humility. At the sight of the Master he dropped upon his knees and exclaimed, 'My Lord! My Lord! I am not worthy to be here!'" 'Abdu'l-Bahá lifted him up and hugged him.

As the golden days of pilgrimage wound on, the ladies kept begging 'Abdu'l-Bahá to sit down, relax, and let Robert be the servant. After all, he was a butler. And he himself would have been happy to serve the Master. But 'Abdu'l-Bahá served every company He was in, and He refused to put Robert to work, except on "one occasion," Louis wrote, when "the honor was bestowed upon" Robert "of sharing the Master's servitude."

When she returned to the United States, Mrs. Hearst enlisted Robert's help with a reception in her Washington mansion for black educators; she later included African Americans in her push to start kindergartens for needy children. She always remained close to Robert, but she eventually became estranged from Bahá'ís because of the money-hunger of a few misguided souls. Robert, however, in his own words, "refused to let the world throw dust in his eyes."[2] Steadfast to the end, he was posthumously named, like his teacher, Lua, a Disciple of 'Abdu'l-Bahá.

However, Robert wasn't yet "posthumous" when Louis Gregory first met Lua and heard the name Bahá'u'lláh. Louis soon attended another get-together, this one at the home of Millie York and Nellie Gray, in a humble neighborhood. Pauline was the teacher, and she invited Louis to her house for further study. There, Louis met her husband, Joseph Hannen, a stalwart, pleasant-looking man with an inquiring mind, a true-hearted kindliness and "joyous disposition" that brightened every gathering he entered.[3] He became Louis' main lifeline to Bahá'í, his teacher and, soon, his brother in faith. Every Sunday evening, Louis was at the Hannens' house, sometimes bringing friends along with him.

Joseph Hannen had become a Bahá'í in 1904 after two years of study, and he often expressed gratitude to Pauline for her patience during that time. Like her, he'd been born in the Deep South. But he was raised in Washington, DC, from the age of seven. According to family lore, his father stepped out to pick up some milk for the baby one day and never returned. His mother, Mary Virginia Anthony Alexander, raised him on her own, except for a couple of step-fathers at intervals. Beautiful and lively, she lived in Pauline and Joseph's house, and she, too, became a Bahá'í, frequently helping with tasks and childcare so her son and daughter-in-law could have extra time for Bahá'í activities.

Joseph worked from home as an east Coast manager for Viavi, a company that sold a homeopathic remedy in various forms—drops, cream, salve, etc.—guaranteed to cure practically everything. Joseph and his family had great trust in it; his sister-in-law, Fanny Knobloch, was a salesperson for the company, and all the relatives used the potions. They must have recommended it to Louis Gregory and, later, to Louisa, because she mentions it in some of her letters. This line of work let Joseph make his own schedule at home so he could tend to the many needs of the Bahá'í community, and when he traveled for business, he could fit in Bahá'í activities.

The talents that sustained Joseph's commercial success—his bon-homie, trustworthiness, flair as a writer and speaker, and training in clerical duties—also gave him a sturdy handle on his chosen Bahá'í work. During conferences and talks he took stenographic notes; then he wrote reports for *Star of the West.* He also constantly and encouragingly reported on activities throughout the United States, in Iran, and in other parts of the world, because he maintained a stellar information network via what we now call snail mail. When he used it, however, it was state-of-the-art. From 1910 on, Louis' letters from cities, towns, rural outposts, and college campuses gave Joseph plenty of stirring material for news reports.

Joseph also helped found the Persian American Educational Society (his favored child, perhaps), and as correspondent-central for that organization, he forged personal links among Bahá'ís in Iran and North America. Bringing together Orient and Occident, build-ing racial amity in America—unity was Joseph's passion.

'Abdu'l-Bahá warned Joseph in 1906 that nothing would come easily to him on his path of faith, just as nothing came easily for the Apostles of Christ. 'Abdu'l-Bahá said, "Therefore, there is no doubt that you will become afflicted with trial, calamity and oppression in the path of the beauty of Abhá! But these trials are the essence of Bestowal and pure Bounty, and the proofs of your acceptance in the Threshold of Oneness." 'Abdu'l-Bahá told him that when he suffered the "contempt" of "the people of passion and desire," he could recognize the pain as proof that he was truly serving his Faith. "Consequently, when the fire of trials is ignited, celebrate ye in joy . . . Thy services in the Highway of the Kingdom are accepted, thy toleration of thy troubles are known and manifest and thy eloquent speeches in the assemblies of believers are heard and appreciated."[4]

So we can see why Joseph was posthumously named one of the nineteen Disciples of 'Abdu'l-Bahá. And now we've been privileged to meet three of those disciples—Lua Getsinger, Robert Turner, and Joseph Hannen—and an Apostle of Bahá'u'lláh, Mírzá Abu'l-

Faḍl—all in the circle of Louis Gregory, who, as we know, was named a Hand of the Cause of God.

It was a shining circle, indeed.

When Pauline and Joseph went as pilgrims to visit the Master, they were gone for several months, and Louis' interest in the Bahá'í Faith waned. (In fact, he felt most comfortable at the Hannens' house and didn't attend Bahá'í meetings in other places.) However, the Hannens didn't lose interest in Louis. Joseph spoke of him to the Master, asking 'Abdu'l-Bahá to heal Louis of an ailment. The ailment is unidentified by Louis in the letter where he refers to it.* 'Abdu'l-Bahá, "out of His Divine Wisdom refused" to proffer instant healing, Louis later recalled, "because it (this difficulty) would be the means of my entering the Cause." Apparently the Master did provide some advice, for Louis added that "through Divine Guidance, the Instructions of 'Abdu'l-Bahá, all turned out well."[5]

Louis later regarded the affliction as his "patrol," as in the Persian story of the lover lost in the night searching for his lady: the lover, chased by the watchman, jumps over a wall to escape and finds himself in the garden of his beloved. Seeing her there, beautiful in lamplight, he profusely thanks his enemy, the watchman. The affliction was, Louis said, "the driving force which made me set out on the journey to know God rather than end my own life!"[6]

This, with a couple of other references made by Louis to his feeling that only his Bahá'í beliefs made life worth living, point to an inner vulnerability of which he was well-aware, but which he almost never shared with anyone except his wife. From their correspondence, it's clear that they were sensitive to each other's needs and protective of each other.

---

* Possibly the ailment was tuberculosis. In other letters, Louis mentioned his tubercular tendency, and he seemed to worry about it. Some people viewed TB as a "taint" and didn't think that people who were, or had been, tubercular should marry.

In June, 1909, at the age of thirty-five, Louis Gregory became a Bahá'í. Around the same time, Robert Turner died in California. The Master had promised Robert during his historic pilgrimage that if he were steadfast in his faith, he'd be "a door through which his whole race would enter the Kingdom of God."[7]

During his final illness, Robert sent a message to 'Abdu'l-Bahá assuring him of his love and requesting prayers. The Master wrote to him, "Be not grieved at your illness, for thou hast attained eternal life and hast found thy way to the World of the Kingdom. God willing we shall meet one another with joy and fragrance in that Divine world and I beg of God you may also find rest in this material world."[8] Robert died with the Greatest Name, "Alláh'u'Abhá," on his lips.

While he lay ill, Pauline and Joseph, on the other coast, were teaching Louis the Greatest Name and helping him learn, he said, how to pray. The mantra *Alláh'u'Abhá*, meaning *God is Most Glorious*, is viewed by the Bahá'ís as a special gift. 'Abdu'l-Bahá said, "The Greatest Name should be found upon the lips in the first awakening moment of every dawn. It should be fed by constant use in daily invocations, in trouble, under opposition, and should be the last word breathed when the head rests upon the pillow at night. It is the name of comfort, protection, happiness, illumination, love and unity . . . The use of the Greatest Name and dependence upon it cause the soul to strip itself of the husks of mortality and to step forth free, reborn, a new creature . . ."[9]

No doubt sped by Robert Turner's last prayers, as well as the Hannens' prayers, and certainly by his own, Louis started on a mystical journey along with his mission as a race amity worker. Soon after becoming a Bahá'í he had a vision of Bahá'u'lláh with His head bent forward, right arm extended, "four layers of mellow golden light" flowing from his right side, "each layer containing numberless spirals and beautiful figures." When the glow vanished, Louis saw himself on a street "in which some enemies of the Cause of God were menacing the believers. I raised my right hand above my head and shouted, 'It is all true! Mine eyes have seen the Glory!'"[10]

In telling of his vision Louis referenced the Bible, Joel 2:28—looking that up, we read: "And it shall come to pass afterward that I will pour out My spirit upon all flesh; / And your sons and your daughters shall prophesy, / Your old men shall dream dreams, / Your young men shall see visions . . ." And Louis' echoing of "Mine eyes have seen the glory of the coming of the Lord," the first line of the "Battle Hymn of the Republic," links biblical prophecy to his own era, to the Civil War to free the slaves, fought just before he was born, and to the issuing of the Emancipation Proclamation in 1863, a few months before Bahá'u'lláh's announcement of His mission in Baghdad.

Louis' mystical awakening would be strengthened by all his interactions with the Master. When he was on pilgrimage and he told 'Abdu'l-Bahá of the vision, the Master likened the figures in the four layers of light to people of four kinds: those who join the Bahá'í Cause and labor for it; those who believe in it but remain quiescent; those who hear of it but don't accept it; those who haven't yet heard of it. Then there are those who "deny and oppose," and He told Louis, "You have already had experience enough to know what this means."[11]

Louis knew more and more of the dream's meaning as time went on. His mysticism was consistently fed by his tireless social activism. In him, mysticism and activism were one. He joined a small race amity army in which his friends the Hannens were, you could say, already captains. Louis was immediately an officer and quickly ascended through the ranks. The general was 'Abdu'l-Bahá himself; He gave Louis his marching orders.

As a fledgling Bahá'í, Louis did what all newcomers did in those days: he wrote to 'Abdu'l-Bahá. The Master's reply came in November, 1909: "I hope that thou mayest become the means whereby the white and colored people shall close their eyes to racial differences and behold the reality of humanity: And that is the universal reality which is the oneness of the kingdom of the human race . . ." He told Louis to ignore his physical and spiritual limitations, to concentrate on God's power and be resigned to God's will, "so that . . . thou mayest . . . become the cause of the Guidance of both races . . ."[12]

Louis committed the tablet to memory. He'd found the fulfillment of his heart's deepest desire, the longing that had entered him when he was a child in the midst of violent tragedy: I want to make the hate go away. I want to make the pain go away. I want humanity to be one, united in love.

He felt he'd found the answer to W. E. B. DuBois' impassioned cry: ". . . By the bones of our stolen fathers, by the tears of our dead mothers, by the very blood of our crucified Christ . . . Tell us the plan; give us the sign; whisper—speak—call, great God . . . show us the way and point us the path . . ."

Louis had found his way home.

7

And to Work

with Edith Chapman, Pocahantas Pope, Harriet Gibbs-Marshall,
Amalie Knobloch, Coralie Cook, George Cook

Know that love has chosen you
to live his crucial purposes. . . .
—*Robert Hayden*

Louis had gotten busy telling people about the Bahá'í Faith and arranging meetings even before he officially identified himself with the movement. To name two instances: in 1908, he set up talks for Joseph Hannen at the Howard University Literary Club; and, at around the same time, he supplied Edith Chapman, a close friend from his college days, with Bahá'í literature. She was an African-American educator who would, years later, become the first Bahá'í in Kansas City, Missouri.

Edith later wrote that she'd known Louis "since my girlhood days in Nashville, and was even then impressed with his sincerity; in fact, to me, he seemed to be at that early date of his life in another world." Was that because he was so tall and thin that his head seemed to be in the clouds, or because he was always yearning for something exalted? Probably both. And he and Edith no doubt became friends because, like him, Edith sought a truth she could recognize as her own. "At the early age of sixteen I tried to teach a class in Sunday School in Nashville," she said, "and soon realized I did not understand a great part of our Bible. Not long after, I began teaching in the public schools in this same city, and decided to give up trying to teach the Bible; however, with the firm resolve to investigate Truth to my own satisfaction, some day." But when she and Louis first discussed Bahá'í beliefs, Edith didn't understand. Alien name. Alien origins. Nevertheless, at least she didn't agree with friends who thought "Louis had lost his mind over some strange religious cult."[1]

Louis himself reported that "by far the majority" of his friends thought he'd become "mentally unbalanced" when he began calling himself a Bahá'í. Louis was an influential citizen, and leaders like W. E. B. DuBois had their eyes on him as an ally and colleague. Now people warned him that he was "blasting all hopes of a career" and popular leadership by his departure from traditional church ties, the bedrock of the black community. One friend and mentor, a professor of international law, almost wept over him. The *Washington Bee* had a field day, bashing him in two full columns to which Louis did not respond. Some of Louis' friends, knowing how "disputatious" he was, and how inclined to express himself in the *Bee* and other publications, said, "He must have religion since he does not answer that!"[2] Because he met insults and opposition with such patience, a few became curious about Bahá'í.

So Louis was immediately thrown into the hot pot. And all for love. As Robert Hayden said further in the poem quoted at the beginning of this chapter:

> Know that love has chosen you.
>
> And will not pamper you nor spare;
> demands obedience to all
> the rigorous laws of risk . . .[3]

Louis knew that love had chosen him, and he didn't seek pampering. He wasn't afraid of "rigorous laws of risk" or confrontation. But now he'd found his inner wisdom. And as it says in Proverbs 3:17, "Happy is the man that findeth wisdom . . . Her ways are ways of pleasantness, and all her paths are peace."[4] So, he *confronted* problems and *consulted* with people.

He jumped right in because there was a major problem in the Bahá'í community, and it took Louis to name it. He later wrote, "As soon as I became a believer . . . my colored friends got on my back and began to press me with troublous questions. If this were a new religion, which stood for unity, why were its devotees divided? Why did they not meet together in one place? Were the Bahá'ís not full of prejudice like other people?"[5]

Although African-American believers welcomed people of all hues in their homes, and Joseph and Pauline Hannen did the same, the Bahá'ís as a whole didn't sponsor integrated public meetings. They had separate meetings for "colored" and white, in accordance with Jim Crow law and social mores. Immediately after becoming a Bahá'í, Louis wrote to the Hannens asking to meet with them and have a talk about the local Bahá'í "attitude . . . toward the colored believers . . . It is with sincere regret that I find it necessary to bring the matter up, and only because some impressions are going abroad which I fear will injure our Cause among both white and colored."[6]

'Abdu'l-Bahá repeatedly, specifically instructed the Bahá'ís to integrate their meetings. And of course Bahá'u'lláh was very clear about oneness; to embrace this principle, Pauline Hannen had needed no instruction or urging other than her own purity and sensitivity. But many white Bahá'ís chose to ignore the principle that prejudice must be abolished. Or, they had theories—one person even seemed to think such a spiritual revolution was to occur in one thousand years, not right now. For Louis and his fellow African Americans, it couldn't happen fast enough. In fact, Louis had never chosen to go to any of the "public" (i.e., segregated) meetings before he became a Bahá'í—"I rarely attended a meeting but went to the home of the Hannens where my friends and I were always welcome."[7]

But now that he was a Bahá'í, Louis knew he had work to do. He didn't sit back and sigh because some of his fellow believers were blinkered, and he didn't let them disillusion him. The Bahá'í Faith was his credo and cause now. He would live by it as he understood it and serve it as he saw fit.

When he met with the Hannens, they told him that the matter of integrated public meetings "had never come up," and they arranged for Louis to meet with the Working Committee. That was the elected body that, at the time, headed the Washington Bahá'í community. Louis and the committee had a pleasant meeting, but it had no immediate results.[8]

Despite the committee's stodginess, Louis arranged a successful series of talks for Joseph Hannen at the Bethel Literary and Historical Society, of which he was the president. Bethel, formed under the auspices of the A.M.E. (African Methodist Episcopal Church), was the foremost African-American cultural forum in Washington, especially for debates on racial issues. Most likely it was a place where Louis had aired his views favoring "fiery agitation," earlier.

Louis took naturally to public speaking and large meetings— although he once told Joseph that he preferred the intimate communication of smaller gatherings. Doors opened for him and other Bahá'í presenters at his alma mater, Howard University, and at various prestigious spots. For support, there was already a nucleus of African American Bahá'ís in Washington who had been taught by Pauline Hannen and family.

—◆—

As soon as she became a Baháí in 1902, Pauline told her husband, sisters, mother, and mother-in-law about the Bahá'í teachings, and eventually they all followed her into the Faith. They didn't stop there, however. They enthusiastically joined her as champions of oneness. Pauline taught her black laundress, Carrie York, and her sister's seamstress, Pocahantas Pope. Soon the Hannens and Knoblochs (Pauline's family) were attending meetings in African-American homes and welcoming people of color to their personal gatherings.

In 1906, Pocahontas Pope was the first African-American Bahá'í in Washington. After she sent her letter to 'Abdu'l-Bahá, he answered her with a tablet in which He said, "Render thanks to the Lord that among that race thou art the first believer, arisen to guide others."[9] He may have meant she was first among the black community in Washington to become a Bahá'í, but some think He could have been referring to her Native American ancestry.

Pocahontas came from the Cha-Kay family in Halifax County, North Carolina, a region that several First Nation tribes call home. Given her name, her parents had obvious pride in that ancestry. Anyway, the Master also revealed a wonderful prayer for her—

> . . . *With supreme confidence and certitude, say: "O God!*
> *Make me a radiant light, a shining lamp, and a brilliant star,*
> *so that I may illumine the hearts with an effulgent ray*
> *from Thy Kingdom of Abha."*[10]

Pocahontas' husband was an African-American government worker, son of free-born Quaker parents from one of the most established families—black or white—in North Carolina; the Pope House Museum in Raleigh honors his historic relatives. As Quakers, the family would have upheld interracial ideals. Quakers led the anti-slavery movement, the establishment of schools for African Americans, and outreach in teaching their faith to African Americans. However, Quakers, like Bahá'ís, had trouble unifying themselves on a grand scale to create true amity, with inclusion for all, although certain of their local communities managed to lead the way at instituting integration.

The Popes held integrated Bahá'í meetings at their house, and integrated groups also gathered informally at the home of Andrew and Lydia Dyer. Little is known of the Dyers except that it seems they were an interracial couple—Lydia being the African American of the pair—and they were friends of Louis Gregory's. He'd introduced Pauline Hannen to them because they wanted to provide hospitality for the Bahá'ís.

The Bahá'ís of Washington also had integrated children's classes— the first Bahá'í Sunday School in the nation. 'Abdu'l-Bahá gave Pauline Hannen the mission of starting it when she and Joseph were on pilgrimage in 1908. She began with twenty-one children, including, of course, her sons. She recorded that she and Joseph "called on two . . . families, both living in the same house, not believing in any religion. They gave their consent for their children to attend the proposed school . . . Later we took in colored children with the white . . . What an inspiration, looking into the faces of these dear children, so eager, so free from prejudice, such open minds . . ."[11]

Joseph reported in the first issue of *Bahá'í News* (forerunner to *Star of the West*) that on March 6, 1910, the Washington Bahá'ís had their first integrated official community gathering, a unity feast, at the Hannens'. About thirty-five people came; Louis was the speaker, and some of the Sunday School children "chanted melodiously in Arabic." And Louis' immediate intervention in community affairs was bearing fruit: Joseph said the plan was for every fourth Nineteen-Day Feast to be interracial, and he added that such a meeting was "a radical step in this section of the country and is in reality making history."[12] This was true, but he would soon receive a Tablet from the Master reiterating that *every* Bahá'í meeting must be interracial.

That year, the Bahá'ís also began integrated public meetings at the Conservatory of Music and School of Expression run by the noted African-American concert pianist Harriet Gibbs-Marshall. Her school occupied a large mansion given to her by her father, Judge Mifflin Wistar Gibbs; among his other achievements, which included striking it rich in the California Gold Rush and being a business tycoon, he was the first black judge in the United States, in Arkansas.

Harriet's school was one of most venerable female-owned businesses in Washington, and her policies were progressive. For example, she hired married women as teachers at a time when married woman weren't even considered for most professional jobs. Harriet became the first Bahá'í to teach in Haiti when she went there with her husband—a most distinguished man—who had military duty to fulfill. She authored *The Story of Haiti*, founded the National

Negro Music Center, and helped found the National Association of Negro Musicians.

She and her conservatory were in their prime when the first integrated, public unity feast was held. It was a memorial for Pauline Hannen's mother, Amalie Knobloch. Pauline praised her mother: "The work among the colored people was really started by my sainted Mother and Sister, Alma (Knobloch), though I was the one who first gave the Message to Mrs. Pope and Mrs. Turner. My Mother and Sister went to their homes . . . meeting others, giving the Message to quite a number and started Meetings. Then my sister left for Germany . . . I then took up the work. During the Winter of 1907 it became my great pleasure with the help of Rhoda Turner colored (sic) who opened her home for me . . . to arrange a number of very large and beautiful meetings . . . (with) from twenty to forty colored people of the intellectual class." Pauline preferred to avoid public speaking. She said her work was "to run around and arrange the meeting . . ."[13] Pauline was always good at claiming the back seat when in fact she was a driving force.

But 'Abdu'l-Bahá, too, recognized the importance of Amalie Knobloch and was so pleased when He heard about her memorial that He said it brought joy to the angels in heaven. Amalie Knobloch was the matriarch of a rare family of race amity workers—still going strong to this day—and the Master revealed a visitation Tablet for Amalie which is read at her grave in Washington to ensure that her legacy of raising offspring who walk the path of oneness will live on.

Another outstanding African-American woman who became a Bahá'í in those early days was Coralie Franklin Cook. She hadn't been born a slave, but her forebears were slaves at Thomas Jefferson's plantation, Monticello, where he fathered children by one of her ancestresses. However, though Coralie had great leadership qualities, we can't trace her descent directly to Jefferson.

Her husband, George William Cook, noted professor and dean at Howard University, also became a Bahá'í. He had been born into slavery. In his boyhood, he began his education with a doctor for whom he worked. He was a lawyer, founder of Howard University's School of Finance and Commerce and business manager of the university. He was so linked with establishing Howard that a building there is named in his honor. Alain Locke wrote that Professor Cook was convinced "knowledge . . . makes men masters of themselves and sets them free. And for a person with such a faith, one can imagine no greater boon than to spend practically all his life in a school that grew in sixty years from a handful of unlettered freedmen to today's community of nearly three thousand college and professional students, and from a mortgaged farm property to a state supported university."[14]

The vision of Howard's founders really embraced global diversity. Students from other countries who were perhaps too brown to be admitted on the campuses of other U.S. schools attended Howard, and women of all hues could study there. Some of the first female doctors in the United States, including some white women, graduated from Howard.

George Cook was also "ever an advocate and counselor of political action and joined every campaign for the safeguarding of the Negro's political and civic rights . . . (he was) one of the main supporters and officers of the Washington branch of the National Association for the Advancement of Colored People."[15]

At the time, the Washington branch of the NAACP was newly established, and George Cook's immediate involvement shows the fervor of his activism. Like the Howard student body, the NAACP was and still is a prime example of America's other racial tradition, race amity. It was founded in 1909 when sixty people, seven of them black, issued a national call to peers summoning them to meet and formulate a plan to fight for social justice following the Springfield, Illinois, race riot and in response to the ongoing terrorism of lynching.

W. E. B. DuBois and Mary Talbert, of the Niagara Movement, became leaders in the NAACP. At first, all NAACP directors were white, with the exception of DuBois, who was the director of publications and research. He edited a magazine titled *The Crisis*, which is still highly influential today. The NAACP provides legal advocacy in the fight for equal rights and education toward the achievement of social justice, with one of its goals being to "eliminate race prejudice."[16] Today it is still a massive, powerful, active, institution with membership open to all, led by and identified with African Americans.

Coralie and George Cook were middle-aged, established community leaders when they became Bahá'ís. Among her other services, Coralie was a member of the Board of Education for the District of Columbia and superintendent of the Washington Home for Destitute Colored Women and Children, and she was chair of oratory at Howard University, where she also taught English. She was a nationally known speaker and writer, an activist for feminism and civil rights among white women as well as women of color, and she was especially outspoken on women's right to vote.

In "Votes for Mothers," written for *The Crisis*, she pointed out, "I wonder if anybody in all this great world ever thought to consider man's rights as an individual, by his status as a father? Yet you ask me to say something about 'Votes for Mothers,' as if mothers were a separate and peculiar people . . ." But she went on to say that mothers actually were special and highly equipped to judge "educational systems, charitable and correctional institutions, public sanitation and municipal ordinances" and that they deserved the right to help make laws. She said, "Disfranchisement because of sex is curiously like disfranchisement because of color. . . . I grow in breadth, in vision, in the power to do, just in proportion as I use the capacities with which Nature, the All-Mother, has endowed me . . ."[17]

At one point, when Coralie was overwhelmed by civic, family, and academic duties, she wrote to Pauline Hannen, "Dear sister . . . I must live my life where I am placed . . . Every atom of strength I have is used up every day. I am praying for patience and wisdom to live my life so that I may not bring discredit upon the Teachings that have brought such joy to my weary heart. If I do not see you I know that we are one in spirit working together, you such a strong brave spirit . . ."[18]

People sent the Hannens many such loving and grateful messages. Joseph received Louis Gregory's message of pure joy in 1910, when Louis hit the road for the first time as a Bahá'í itinerant teacher. He visited his hometown and four other southern cities and wrote to Joseph from Charleston, "Am just having the time of my life!" He'd had nonstop speaking engagements to very receptive audiences, but he felt he was in danger of getting too proud and told Joseph, "I am fortunate in having a dear good soul like you, to remind me ever and anon what a horrid, as well as dangerous thing, conceit is . . ."[19]

It probably occurred to Louis now that the vision he'd had in the mission center years before while listening to a choir sing about the unknown future, when he'd pictured himself "running to and fro, delivering a message like unto heavenly music," hadn't been "a creation of fancy" but a glimpse into his own destiny. His journeys, and his ability to impart the "heavenly music" as he heard it, only increased over time.

In late 1910, Louis received an invitation from 'Abdu'l-Bahá, in Ramleh, to visit Him in the spring. He must have felt that blessings were overflowing. As 1911 began, he was elected to the Working Committee to temporarily replace a member who was unable to serve. He told Joseph that he was happy at this integration effort but that he didn't feel worthy of representing his race. This was an unexpected statement from a brilliant and accomplished man who said he had to fight against pride and conceit, but it certainly spotlights the inner and outer pressure African Americans felt to be the most impossibly perfect of the perfect so that they could overcome prejudice against them.

On March 22, 1911, Louis went to a weekly meeting at the Dyers' house and found over fifty Bahá'ís of various colors, all there to fete him with a surprise farewell dinner before he left on his pilgrimage. "Mr. Gregory was given the seat of honor," Joseph Hannen reported in *Star of the West*, "at the head of the long table, and his chair was surmounted by a horse-shoe of flowers. While refreshments were being served, speeches were made . . . Mr. Gregory responded in a feeling manner to the good wishes expressed."[20]

Pauline was moved and shaken by Louis' prospects. "Our pupil was now to meet his Great Test," she later recalled. "Would he turn out to be the answer to our prayer? Mr. Hannen was toastmaster. I asked him not to call on me, as I was so deeply moved I felt it would be impossible to articulate. After all, however, he thought it best to get me to my feet and prepared the way with a toastmaster's joke. Then among other things he said: 'One is present who is the spiritual mother of two big sons, one white and one black.'" (Joseph was referring to himself as the white one, for Pauline had been his Bahá'í teacher and so his "spiritual mother.")

"I trembling rose," Pauline wrote, "and these were the potent words of my response: 'Mr. Gregory, you are on the eve of meeting your Greatest Test. When you return to us you will not be the same. You will be changed. You will be a different Mr. Gregory, *never again the same.*"[21]

With our aftersight, it's easy to forget that Pauline was unaware of Louis' destiny, but of course she didn't have a crystal ball. And she knew that the experience of being in the Master's presence could be a test as well as a blessing. Would Louis recognize 'Abdu'l-Bahá's Christlike spirit? Would he *not* see it and so be disappointed and lost to the Bahá'ís? Would he feel it as a challenge to himself and strike out tragically against it, becoming an apostate?

Pauline really was his spiritual mother, and she worried as any mother worries! With her anxious prayers accompanying him, Louis traveled to New York City, where the Bahá'ís also feted him. On March 25, a lively group of them accompanied him to his ship, a German liner presciently named *The Louise*.

8

Happiness

with Louisa Mathew, Mírzá Abu'l-Faḍl, Ghodsea Ashraf

A day so happy.
Fog lifted early, I worked in the garden.
Hummingbirds were stopping over honeysuckle flowers.
There was no thing on earth I wanted to possess.
I knew no one worth my envying him.
Whatever evil I had suffered, I forgot . . .
—*Czeslaw Milosz*

Louis quickly made friends on the liner *Louise* and was happy to share with them the seasickness remedies people had given him upon saying bon voyage. Never having gone to sea before, he'd thought he might need them, but he proved a good sailor. He wrote to a friend, "I haven't missed a meal, that is, no regular one." He thought it would be "unwise . . . to eat every time these jolly Germans are willing to feed us, six or seven times a day!" He told everyone he could about Bahá'í, including two German nuns, one of whom confidently predicted that he'd end up a Roman Catholic priest. On April 4, 1911, he wrote, "We land at Alger (sic), and for the first time I set foot on the shore of Africa, my ancient Fatherland. Have much fun in party of Americans and Italians, trading with natives. It is a French possession, but a small boy wishing to sell his wares calls after me in endearing English tones, 'O black man! O black man!'"[1]

Since Louis' grandmother, stolen from Africa in girlhood, was a great storyteller, Louis had no doubt heard African lore from her and had a deep feeling for the continent. He, too, was a great storyteller, with a fund of homey, old-time tales and a marvelous, ringing laugh.

When he arrived in Ramleh, Louis made sure to ask 'Abdu'l-Bahá's "special consideration" for "the African tribes." The Master told him, "You must be a leader to them. Guide them to the truth."[2*]

We've glimpsed Louis' meeting with the Master, but unfortunately we've come across no notes by his future wife, Louisa Mathew, describing her own first encounter with 'Abdu'l-Bahá. However, pilgrimage goals transcended even that meeting. 'Abdu'l-Bahá stressed that the sacred tombs in Haifa and Bahjí—the shrines of the Báb and Bahá'u'lláh—were the main goals, just as they are today.

So, let us join the travelers from the West—Neville Meakin, Louis Gregory, and Louisa Mathews, "three pilgrims about to leave the illumined Presence of Abdu'l-Bahá for the Holy City"—as they call on the Master to say farewell. At His house, they meet Shoghi Effendi and one of his cousins, both about fifteen years old, who greet them affectionately.

Of course the pilgrims don't know that Shoghi Effendi will be the Guardian of the Bahá'í Faith after the Master's death. He doesn't know it himself. When, as a very young man, that mantle falls upon him, Louis and Louisa will remember him as a teenager and wholeheartedly give him their allegiance—as will others, some of them familiar with him since his infancy. But some will question, waffle, and even oppose the new Guardian for that very reason—familiarity. It's hard to see past the mask of familiarity, to bow one's head before greatness when it's close up and personal. Familiarity has blinded others to the greatness of 'Abdu'l-Bahá. That's another reason, perhaps, that Pauline Hannen, back in Washington, is praying

---

* Sadly, Louis was unable to return to Africa after his first visit, but the Master's remark has played out in many of Louis' spiritual children and grandchildren bringing the Bahá'í Faith to Africa, telling the story of his life there, naming schools for him there, and more. That, plus the quantity of people who heard of and became members of the Baha'i Faith in the United States through Louis, also confirms 'Abdu'l-Bahá's statement that the steadfast Robert Turner would be a door through which African Americans would enter the Faith. This heritage continues to grow and has yet to attain its complete fulfillment.

so ardently for Louis' spiritual success as a pilgrim. She wants him to see the ineffable grandeur of the Master. As we see, her prayers are receiving positive answers.

During the farewell visit, Neville says they hope to find the Master at home when they return, and Louis adds, "Another year, we hope to see You in America!" 'Abdu'l-Bahá's eyes twinkle. "Will you bring an aeroplane and steal Me away?" He asks. Then He blesses them as they take their departure, and He says, "I hope that your insight will become so clear that you will not need a teacher; but the Holy Spirit will guide you in all things." And He asks them to pray for him in Bahji where his Father is interred. Whenever He's away, it saddens Him that He's unable to visit the shrines.[3]

The three sail from Ramleh to Alexandria and, on April 17, take a ship across a rough Mediterranean to the port of Jaffa. While docked there, Louis strolls through steerage among travelers of diverse hues and nationalities. A boy approaches him and speaks to him in English. Surprised, Louis asks, "How did you know that I speak English?"

"Because you are an American."

"How did you know that?"

"I am a student at the Syrian college at Beirut. My professors are all Americans; and so I could tell by even glancing at you that you are an American."

Louis soon discovers that said professors are all white. By his own description, Louis is "dark brown" with "nothing in my dress to distinguish me from most Europeans." He remembers that during the Spanish-American War, the Spaniards identified black troops as Yankees, lumping them in with white troops—though the troops themselves, sons of American Apartheid, might have called each other by different names. He concludes, "The number of things that Americans have in common appear to impress the rest of mankind, despite details of color which impress only within the country."[4]

The incident—along with his welcome by the Master, fellow pilgrims, and then by the Master's family in his household and the

Bahá'ís of Haifa—reinforces Louis' sense of confidence not only as a world citizen but as an American. Now and for the rest of his life, this assurance is part and parcel of the positive, transforming energy he imparts to others.

The ship leaves Jaffa, sails northward "along the coast of Palestine and in full view of its picturesque mountain range," and reaches Haifa Bay as night falls. "In darkness, by the aid of a small boat," they land. The next morning, resident Bahá'ís guide them up Mount Carmel to the tomb of the Báb, "half way up the mountain side . . . stately in proportion . . . The famous cypress trees, where Bahá'u'lláh liked to rest in the shade, rise nearby, dark green, ancient."[5]

'Abdu'l-Bahá has advised Louis to "lecture at Haifa." Louis has been wondering how to do that, surrounded as he is by older, knowledgeable Bahá'ís whose personal histories are deeply linked with that of their Faith—whose heroism is, in fact, part of that history. But when evening comes, he finds himself with a group of about twenty-five men at the Master's house easily "giving a talk" while answering their questions about "the progress of the Cause in America and . . . racial conditions."[6]

On April 21, the first day of the Festival of Riḍván (Paradise), when Bahá'ís commemorate Bahá'u'lláh's announcement of His mission, Louis and Louisa, with Neville Meakin, go by carriage about nine miles down the beach from Haifa to 'Akká. Louis and Neville leave the carriage and walk through the city to see where the Master and His Father—with some seventy followers—suffered imprisonment in the barracks. Then they view the dwellings where the two were held for long years under house arrest. But Louisa stays in the carriage with an elderly Persian friend.

Perhaps Louisa is feeling too frail that day for the dank, crowded, very narrow, stony streets of 'Akká. She is one of the many sufferers from tuberculosis in that world of 1911. To overcome the illness, 'Abdu'l-Bahá—Who Himself had TB as a child—has recommended that she follow a diet of mostly chicken and fish. This proves so efficacious that she'll basically follow it for the rest of her life. There are some indications that she may have been a vegetarian before, but if so, those days are gone. 'Abdu'l-Bahá will later tell her, "I found you almost dying in Egypt," and add that if she hadn't followed his advice she would have gotten "worse" than Neville Meakin—he's also tubercular and, sadly, will die four months after his pilgrimage. Louisa will remark in a letter a decade later, "'Abdu'l-Bahá saved my life and therefore it belongs to Him to use for the Cause."[7]

In 'Akká, Louis and Neville have the privilege of viewing, in one of the buildings where Bahá'u'lláh had been confined, portraits of Him and the Báb. Since Louisa's itinerary is different from Louis', she'll doubtless be able to view those faces at another time. She proceeds to Bahji with Louis and Neville in the carriage, and they gather with other pilgrims for lunch in the courtyard outside the shrine before entering the sacred precincts.

They can't enter the mansion where Bahá'u'lláh lived the last years of His life in rural tranquility, because that tranquility has been breached—the place is in the hands of the *nakazeen* (Covenant-breakers), members of Bahá'u'lláh's family and their allies who, in their envy of the Master, have become His deadly enemies. According to Mírzá Abu'l-Faḍl, ". . . the violation by the nakazeen . . . is one of the most astonishing events which human prejudice has ever created in the world . . ."[8]

Use of the word prejudice here is interesting for us in our society today, because we usually connect it with those who reject the "other" because of obvious differences—skin color, nationality, age, gender, etc. But Mírzá Abu'l-Faḍl referred to the deep emotional reality of prejudice: it is born of envy, fear that the "other" is better than the envier and a desire to destroy the "other," to wipe his or her feared superiority off the face of the earth.

What could cause such prejudice in the hearts of relatives and one-time acolytes? Isn't it natural for them to love one another with a united-we-stand-divided-we-fall kind of mentality? Mírzá said it was "on account of jealousy and selfishness that they violated the

Cause of God," not merely turning against the Master but doing their utmost to destroy His followers and instigate His assassination. Think of Judas, then multiply him.[9]

At the time of Louis' pilgrimage and for some years afterwards, if left to themselves, the nakazeen hurl insults, imprecations, and worse at pilgrims. The Master won't make them homeless, but He takes measures to contain them. He sends pilgrims with a guard from the local government so that when the pilgrims enter the tomb of Bahá'u'lláh, they can pray in peace.

The nakazeen of the early twentieth century came close to success in their ruinous campaign, but they ultimately failed, and now there are few traces of them left. Yet we still need to be on guard, to pray for protection and to keep watch over our own hearts and minds, for the seeds of what ailed them—egotism, envy, ambition—are alive and well in all of us. The closer we come to sacred sites and persons and lofty insights, the more we need "to take refuge with God" that He may "guard us, ever, from the recklessness of the insistent self."[10] This was yet another reason Pauline prayed so hard for Louis, her spiritual "big son"!

Louis records that the nakazeen maintain invisibility and all is as it should be while his pilgrimage group is at Bahji. Just as we would find it if we entered it today, the shrine is fragrant with flowers and adorned with greenery and blossoms. It may be a tomb, but it's the least tomblike of places, with its shining windows letting in the bright Mediterranean sun whose warmth releases the roses' perfume onto the balmy air. The pilgrims pray silently, and Louis focuses his prayers intensely on unity among the Bahá'ís. Then Louis and Louisa revel in the harmonious mingling of pilgrims from Christian, Islamic, and Zoroastrian backgrounds as they have tea on a small island, the tiny Riḍván Garden, in the beneficent shade of huge mulberry trees and among rosebushes heavy with bloom, where Bahá'u'lláh brought His grandchildren for picnics as recently as nineteen years before.

We could say the old trees are reminiscent of the Tree of Life in the verse of Bahá'u'lláh's about the "true and radiant morn" when humanity gathered about Him beneath its shade. "Have ye forgotten? . . ." He asked. The full verse is:

O My Friends! Have ye forgotten that true and radiant morn, when in those hallowed and blessed surroundings ye were all gathered in My presence beneath the shade of the Tree of Life, which is planted in the all-glorious paradise? . . .[11]

This harks back to the primal covenant of the Creator with humanity. As the fragrant air stirs softly under the mulberry canopy, primal collective memory stirs, too, within the pilgrims. Perhaps they had forgotten His presence, but all their lives a feeling of loss and want niggled at them until now, when at last they remember and feel it—happiness.

———

The next afternoon, Louis sails for Egypt, having promised to write to Louisa; she'll later mention corresponding with him from aboard the steamship *Cedric* while she's on her way, with the Master's entourage, to New York. In Haifa, she apparently spends more time in the Master's household with the women of His family. In Cairo, Louis visits Mírzá Abu'l-Faḍl, of whom he's no doubt heard much from Pauline Hannen, all of it complimentary. And he's not disappointed, for he has two private interviews with Mírzá; in them, Mírzá expresses deep interest "in the race problems" and is "gratified to know that 'Abdu'l-Bahá had approved intermarriage as the most effective means of effacing racial differences."[12]

Louis asks Mírzá about the ancient Ethiopians and whether they had a great civilization; Mírzá answers that they did, as recorded by Greek and Persian historians. He also says that the people of central

Africa were "once high in the scale of civilization . . ." Louis also enjoys the company of other Bahá'ís in Cairo, one of whom gives him a citywide tour. And, although Louis has felt regretful at not hearing of the Bahá'í Faith earlier in his life, he's glad to hear Mírzá say, "It is a great thing to live in this day and know 'Abdu'l-Bahá."[13]

Soon Louis is back in Ramleh with the Master, with a few more days before he must sail away. He brings the Master greetings from Mírzá and the other friends in Cairo, Haifa, and 'Akká. The Master responds, "You must visit Persia,"* and directs him to go to "Stuttgart, Paris, London, and various points in America." He has already told Louis, "I want the friends to know you." Louis finds the Master looking "hard-worked and weary," and cannot help but feel he's unworthy as 'Abdu'l-Bahá lavishes great affection on him.[14]

He's made the Master happy by bringing him the news that Mírzá, whose health is more fragile than ever, is holding his own. No doubt 'Abdu'l-Bahá misses Mírzá, for on Mírzá's return from America, He'd settled him in Ramleh in a house surrounded by date palms, and later recalled, "Whenever I felt depressed or sad, I called on him, and soon afterward I was in a happier frame of mind."[15]

'Abdu'l-Bahá loved to tell amusing anecdotes about Mírzá. He once sent Mírzá a cook who was also supposed to be a health aide / companion. When he went to see how the arrangement was working out, he found the servant seated submissively, and Mírzá waiting on the servant.

Mírzá didn't like the idea of people waiting on him; by serving the servant he was proving that he could still take care of himself. He was also too much of an introvert to enjoy the constant company of a helper. An Irish Bahá'í, Isabel Fraser, wrote, ". . . sick or well, the old philosopher was a hermit. He loved his circle of friends, and

---

* This was a desire of the Master's that Louis couldn't fulfill, although he did try several times in later years to go to Iran. But each time, the Guardian told him he was more needed in the United States.

he also loved his hours of solitude and contemplation. He was not used to having anyone around administering to what he regarded as merely trivial needs . . ."

Isabel said that Mírzá's rooms "resembled an un-kept library. There were books on every conceivable shelf and table, and even the floor was littered with volumes and papers. His place was a rendezvous for the learned sheiks and Muhammadan (sic) mullahs of the ancient city of Alexandria . . . His favorite outing was a visit to the house of 'Abdu'l-Baha's secretaries which was just around the corner, and which . . . was used as a guest-house for visiting pilgrims . . . Here he would sit on the spacious veranda; the news would go forth and soon a little group would be gathered around him . . ."

She described Mírzá's "peculiar personal charm," saying, "With all his book learning he was not at all 'bookish.' Gifted with one of those rare minds that explore all the channels of life with equal grace and facility—the same dignity and impressiveness with which he discussed a verse of the Koran with the learned sheiks, he put into the meeting of some sojourning American; often finishing with a personal pleasantry, for he was a ready humorist and made his guests instantly at ease. He had the placidness of a child and the air of one who was never in a hurry and had plenty of time to make radiantly happy the place where God had placed him."

When Mírzá was in Ramleh, 'Abdu'l-Bahá came to visit him just about every day. If the Master wasn't at home, people immediately looked for Him at Mírzá's house or in the nearby rose garden where he liked to work, answering His correspondence. One day Isabel Fraser was present at Mírzá's along with "about twenty sheiks . . . One who seemed to be the leader was a very learned and gorgeously attired young sheik . . . the editor of a magazine." He'd come to interview Mírzá, and he and the others had been listening to Mírzá for upwards of an hour. Mírzá's "sharp eye would glance from one face to another to see if his point was understood . . ." and "his talk was interspersed with an occasional jest . . ."[16] Then 'Abdu'l-Bahá came in. Mírzá stopped speaking, bowed his head, quickly arranged a seat for the Master, whispered the topic of discussion to Him, and fell silent. The Master spoke.

Another time, some Western Bahá'í ladies came to see Mírzá. Perhaps they brought him questions about their dreams or their futures, which he did not care to answer. Or it might have just been that it was morning, Mírzá's time for writing. They knocked and knocked on his door and finally heard an elderly voice through the keyhole say in English: "'Abu'l-Faḍl not here."[17] They realized it was Mírzá himself, and they dissolved in laughter. From within the house, they heard Mírzá laughing, too.

He probably let them in, in the afternoon. That was when he received visitors, and served them tea brewed and sweetened by himself, poured by his own hand. He would have it no other way. One can assume that Louis Gregory also enjoyed Persian tea made by Mírzá, and that 'Abdu'l-Bahá rejoiced in the image of the two of them, His beloved friends, together.

One afternoon, Louis is in the room while 'Abdu'l-Bahá reveals a Tablet on racial oneness for a black Bahá'í in Washington who wrote to him "that there were several meetings of joy and happiness, one for white another for colored people." The Master reiterates that all must gather "into one assembly" and also "intermarry . . . (for) the result of this will abolish differences and disputes between black and white . . ." Louis observes, "After dictating this Tablet Abdu'l Baha took a vessel containing blackberries and gave some of them to each of the friends present, serving us with His hands."

That evening, Louis is alone with 'Abdu'l-Bahá, except for a translator. Louis stands ". . . at one end of the room while 'Abdu'l-Bahá in Majesty" walks back and forth, as is his habit. He is rarely still. Louis finds the silence "deep but not oppressive," for he can't help but be happy in the presence of the Master, "This living Temple of Love."

At last, from across the room, the Master gently addresses Louis in English, "Speak to me, Mr. Gregory."

Louis tries to think of something to ask, but all his questions are answered, his needs satisfied, his cup "full and running over." He's leaving in the morning, and it occurs to him that "in order to receive larger gifts I must go out and work, that in His Providence the Giver of all might grant larger capacity."

'Abdu'l-Bahá strides over to him and strikes him several times "upon the breast, using the palm of His Hand." He says, again in English, "My Gregory! My son!"

Louis feels "a thrill of joy." He asks permission to come the next day to say good-bye. "Come, my dear, come," the Master says in indulgent, fatherly tones, and the two part "with an embrace of great affection."

When Louis returns to the Master in the morning, the reception room is crowded and He's dictating Tablets while conversing with His guests and distributing handfuls of fragrant dried roses. He gives double to Louis and tells him, "Scatter them among the friends."

After two hours, Louis must leave. The Master goes out into the hallway with him. "Although I desired to speak with you, the time was taken up. Go forth and speak of the Cause of God. Visit the friends. Gladden their hearts. You will be the means of Guidance to many souls. The Divine Bounties will be with you. You are always in my mind and heart."

As the translator escorts Louis back to the Hotel Victoria, he tells him, "This morning 'Abdu'l-Bahá spoke of you to me and told me to say to you, 'Keep your face turned toward the Kingdom and fear nothing.'"

With his enviable psychic balance, Louis, unlike most pilgrims, is not prostrated with grief by the leave-taking. He feels, "Thus parting with 'Abdu'l-Bahá need not be sorrowful, because in reality (it is) not a parting. The Reality of 'Abdu'l-Bahá abides with the friends."[18] Indeed it will always abide with, and within, Louis. Everywhere he goes throughout his life, he'll bring the presence and love of the Master in his very essence and demeanor. 'Abdu'l-Bahá knows it.

Louis visits European Bahá'ís en route home, including Pauline Hannen's sister, Fanny Knobloch, who has been establishing the Bahá'í community in Stuttgart, Germany, since 1907. Later, a German Bahá'í writes to the Master, praising Louis, and He replies that during the pilgrimage Louis "received another life and obtained another power. When he returned, Gregory was quite another Gregory. He had become a new creation. This man shall progress." It's as Pauline Hannen said it would be—during his pilgrimage, Louis has been transformed—and her prayers have been answered, for he is truly happy.[18]

Louis also spends four days in London. A British Bahá'í, Arthur Cuthbert, perceives him as "a great soul . . . an inspiration," especially because he is "wise enough to be proud of his colour."[19]

'Abdu'l-Bahá informs the white Bahá'ís of Washington that "Mr. Gregory is at present in great happiness . . . He will return to America very soon, and you, the white people, should then honor and welcome this shining colored man in such a way that all the people will be astonished."[20]

⸺•⸺

But Louis' homecoming on June 3 went mostly unheralded because of someone else who arrived on the same day. In fact, she arrived with Louis. She was a twenty-two-year-old Bahá'í named Ghodsea Ashraf, and she was the first Iranian woman to come to America to study. Louis had been in England, had left from Southampton with Ghodsea aboard the *Mauretania*, and had chaperoned her during the trip, so he'd come to regard her as a little sister. It didn't bother him when she got the big reception dinner in Washington, press coverage, and interviews. She was brilliant, talented, and poised, worthy of the attention, and besides, Louis didn't trouble himself with such things, especially after his halcyon pilgrimage.

Ghodsea had studied at the American School for Girls in Tehran, where she'd learned English with special zeal—she'd already been privately tutored in Arabic and Persian. She taught in Tehran, but in her hunger for knowledge, she asked her parents to send her to the United States to study, and they agreed. They were a Bahá'í family, but, nevertheless, such daring was unusual. They, and their daughter, must have been inspired by the example of the poet Táhirih, who, as a true dawn-breaker, passionately heralding Bahá'u'lláh's revelation, brooked no obstacles in her determination to live as a free person on equal terms with men.

Within two weeks of her arrival in the United States, Ghodsea gave a public talk in English about the progress of Iranian women, addressing the first annual conference of the Persian-American Educational Society, the association running Bahá'í schools for girls and boys in Iran. It had Joseph Hannen's unstinting devotion and service, the support of Dr. Susan Moody—she was practicing medicine among the women of Iran—and a stellar crew from east and west. It was linked with the Bahá'í-inspired cultural exchange group, the Orient-Occident Society.

Rudyard Kipling had sung—

Oh, East is East and West is West, and never the twain shall meet
Till earth and sky stand presently at God's great Judgment Seat . . .[21]

The Bahá'ís, believing that they were living in the Day of Judgment, the time of the New Revelation, were working to bring the twain together.

Emotion ran high when Ghodsea, head-covering parted to reveal her earnest little face and round spectacles, spoke in English at the conference and then as a guest of honor at a reception at one of the Washington Bahá'ís' favorite gathering spots, Rauscher's Hall, the only restaurant in the city that would serve integrated groups. Pictures of Ghodsea—some showing her without her glasses, looking very cute in a fashionable, flowery hat—and interviews with her appeared in many newspapers. In one interview, she emoted that she was probably the only Persian woman not going veiled in public.

"Talk? Do I mind talking?" she answered the interviewer's opening salvo. "About why I came, and when, and how long, and to do what? I love to talk. I talked at home, to everybody I knew. And I came to America to talk . . ."[22]

It's too bad she missed the Internet Age, but she did very well with the means at hand. On June 19 she attended the twenty-fifth wedding anniversary of President Taft at the White House. Then she traveled to Chicago, with attention from the press all the way, and began school in the Windy City so she could earn U.S. high school credits and start university studies.

She later went back to Iran and lived to a ripe old age, "developing programs for the education and advancement of women, specifically programs designed to prepare women for involvement in realms from which they had hitherto been excluded." As a nurse, she pioneered public health programs in Iran and South America, where she "waded through the thick vegetation and toiled up steep hills, championing, with the aid of indigenous interpreters, the education and health care of women and youth in isolated rural areas." Back in Iran, she worked with tribespeople, creating medical faculties, libraries, and more. In her obituary, *The Washington Times* noted, "Throughout her life, Ghodsieh Ashraf repeatedly observed, not without pride, that her material belongings could be packed into one suitcase. Though she may not have been an easy taskmaster, she was served by an unflagging *joie de vivre* and cut a figure distinct from the traditional models of her times."[23]

We can see why, even at a young age, she bowled people over. As for Louis, he had a whole new bag of stories from his pilgrimage to add to his repertoire, and he wasted no time getting some of them down on paper. He published "Impressions of 'Abdu'l-Bahá While at Ramleh" in *Star of the West*, September, 1911.

He returned to all his work—career and Bahá'í activities—with new enthusiasm. Soon he learned, to his great delight, that the Master would fulfill His promise to journey westward. In a personal letter, 'Abdu'l-Bahá told Louis He looked forward to seeing him in Washington and "renewing the Covenant of the ancient love . . ."[24]

9

Planting the World-Tree in the U.S.A.

with Louisa Gregory, Edith Sanderson, Agnes Parsons,
Robert Abbott, Alan Anderson and others

*Straight and far-stretching path etched by your own light through
urban hearts and sweet hill country:
you are the path the pilgrims take as they carry water to the world-tree,*
laboring that each deep
interconnecting part of the tree may be fed, that she may stand, diffusing
fragrance east and west,
north and south, her royal head reposing against the stars,
and crowned with stars.*

—*Janet Ruhe-Schoen*

Louis' pilgrimage had been adventure and confirmation. Now, with the Master in North America, Louis would receive the structure and pattern for his life, and his importance in the Master-plan (so to speak!) would be further clarified. On April 20, 1912, less than a year after Louis said good-bye to Him in Ramleh, 'Abdu'l-Bahá arrived in Washington.

It wasn't His first view of the Western world. He'd spent four months with the Bahá'ís of France and England, returned to Alexandria for a rest, then traveled from Naples aboard the steamship *Cedric* to New York, docking there on April 11. Nevertheless, despite all

---

* "Straight and far-stretching path" from 'Abdu'l-Bahá's prayer for the Bahá'ís of the Central States, *Bahá'í Prayers*, p. 215. World-tree and its interconnecting parts from 'Abdu'l-Bahá, *Selections from the Writings of 'Abdu'l-Bahá*, p. 1.

He'd seen of the gothic towers of Paris and London, He'd chuckled at the New York skyscrapers when He sighted the famed Manhattan skyline. "Those are the minarets of the West," He remarked.[1]

Traveling with Him were several Iranian aides, including a witty elderly cook who would be one of the delights of the Bahá'í community during his sojourn, teaching interested parties how to make a particularly festive style of Persian pilaf. (Louis was among those who became expert at it.) A small entourage of Westerners also traveled with Him, among them Louisa Mathew, who would, unbeknownst to herself and to Louis at the time, remain in the United States as Louis' wife.

Oneness, particularly the oneness of the human race and its expression in racial amity, was the major focus of 'Abdu'l-Bahá's nine-month sojourn in North America. It was, indeed, the hallmark of His message to the world. As He saw it, realization of fundamental human oneness is the primary requisite for the establishment of real and lasting world peace. It can't just be an intellectual realization. It needs to be a conversion within the heart to belief in oneness, such as the moment of newborn faith and vision that transformed Pauline Hannen immediately and irreversibly from a frightened, prejudiced child-woman to a courageous, open, mature woman. "The gift of God to this enlightened age is the knowledge of the oneness of mankind and of the fundamental oneness of religion . . ." the Master proclaimed in England during the first public talk of his life, given from the pulpit of the City Temple in London, September, 1911.[2]

During the spring of 1912 in the United States, 'Abdu'l-Bahá focused especially on interracial amity, giving talks on the need for integration and harmony every day for eight days, beginning on April 20 when he arrived in Washington unexpectedly. 'Alí Kulí Khán was by then the *charge d'affaires* of the Persian Legation. On that April afternoon, the phone at his ambassadorial residence rang as he and his wife, Florence, sat at lunch with their children. An agitated voice announced in Khán's ear: "Hurry! The Master's train is arriving at the station in half an hour!"

The Master's fluid interpretation of train schedules, and other schedules, was always exciting for His hosts! But He had His reasons. In this case, He hadn't wanted a big group meeting Him at the station. When He and His small entourage were gathered into the three autos that had managed to arrive at the gates just in time to receive Him, Florence Khán cried, "Where's Marzieh?" Her daughter, Marzieh, was two. Florence needn't have worried. She soon sighted Marzieh perched on 'Abdu'l-Bahá's lap in one of the autos. Marzieh had noticed how the Master's hair fell in a curl on his shoulder. Her hair did that, too, only hers was brown and His was silver. She was entranced and never wanted to leave Him.

That evening, the Master spoke about world peace at an Orient-Occident-Unity Conference in the Washington Public Library Hall, which was filled far beyond its capacity of four hundred people. He spent time the next morning with Agnes Parson's little son, looking at the boy's toys and books and going up to the roof of the Parson house with him to enjoy the view. He was interested in everyone's lives, their surroundings, and the details of their days. No one was too important or unimportant for the Master. He had an open heart and an inquiring mind. When He could snatch a moment, He took in sights—the Museum of Natural History in New York, the Library of Congress in Washington, Lincoln Park in Chicago, and other spots. He took the elevator up to the top of the Washington Monument and stood for a while at every window, absorbing the views. But more than anything, He doted on rural vistas, especially mountainous green landscapes.

At one point, traveling through New York State to a peace conference at Lake Mohonk, He was so exhilarated by the countryside that He burst into song. Another time, gazing at a panorama that reminded Him of His Father's forested home province in Iran, He wept, remembering how Bahá'u'lláh loved the outdoors and how He suffered, deprived of the gift of greenery in the fetid, stone prison-city of 'Akká.

The Master was highly emotional and emotive, spontaneous and authentic, never stiff. He could be serene and silent, but always with the sense of vibrant life, never with the dullness of reserve and constraint. He was at home in every gathering, whether speaking one-on-one with a distinguished scientist or statesman, in the salon of a lady of fashion, before an audience of two thousand people, at a children's party, at a picnic, with alcoholic men at the Bowery Mission. But Joseph Hannen noticed that ". . . when both white and colored people were present, 'Abdu'l-Bahá seemed happiest."[3]

So He was very happy on the morning of April 23, when He addressed an integrated crowd of about sixteen hundred people at Howard University. One of Washington's new African-American Bahá'ís, Coralie Cook, who was in that audience, was so deeply affected by Him that when she wrote to Him two years later, she began by saying that as soon as she picked up her pen, she seemed to be "ushered" into His "very presence."[4]

It was a festive occasion, with a band playing. Among other things, the Master told the audience at Howard, "There are no whites and blacks before God. All colors are one, and that is the color of servitude to God . . . The world of humanity . . . is like a garden, and humankind are like the many-colored flowers. Therefore, different colors constitute an adornment . . ." He said that African Americans must be grateful to the white Americans who fought to emancipate them, and the whites must love people of color, help them progress and respect their dignity. "I pray that you attain to such a degree of good character and behavior that the names of black and white shall vanish. All shall be called human . . ." But he counseled that oneness would be "impossible except through love . . ."[5] The crowd applauded often as He spoke, and when He left the auditorium, they formed two lines, one on each side of Him, bowing and waving their hats and handkerchiefs.

—·—

The rhetoric of love and gratitude wasn't unfamiliar to people at the time, especially because they were still close to the Civil War era and the Abolition Movement. The heroism of many whites helping slaves escape to freedom via the Underground Railroad and fighting in the Union Army—and then in not deserting the Union Army after the Emancipation Proclamation was issued in 1863 (an outcome Abraham Lincoln feared)—truly deserved praise. Of course, African Americans fought for freedom and equality from their earliest days on U.S. soil, and they would go on fighting. At the same time, they manifested incredible patience, gentleness, humor, and love. All of that, plus their sense of their own dignity, and their incontrovertible brilliance—evident, for example, in their musical and oratorical eloquence, along with the shrewd business and other associations they formed to help themselves get ahead when they were not welcome into white-run associations—commanded respect, if whites would take time to get to know them.

Sometimes 'Abdu'l-Bahá used other popular rhetoric, considered healing by race amity adherents, along the lines of William Blake's well-meant but sorely limited: "I am black but O! my soul is white . . ." from *Songs of Innocence*. The cliche about having a pure, white soul was echoed by many speakers, preachers, writers and singers, including African-American ones. But the metaphor equating black with bad and white with good is obnoxious to many of us now, no matter our skin tone. Even stories of the Master lovingly holding a dark chocolate to the cheek of a black boy or saying of a black child, "Here is a black rose," may be misinterpreted as patronage, at least by some people. But in 1912, such actions were revelatory. And when the Master gently unfastened a little black girl's hat from her complicated hairdo and delightedly tweaked every braid on her head, her grandmother dined out on the tale for years. She loved it, because she'd felt His love.[6]

The Master's simplicity and purity came from constantly living His Father's counsel: "We fain would hope that the people of Bahá may be guided by these blessed words: 'Say: all things are of God.' This exalted utterance is like unto water for quenching the fire of hate and enmity . . ." He believed that "When human brotherhood is founded upon the Holy Spirit, it is eternal, changeless, unlimited." And because His life had been one of willing sacrifice for the greater good, He knew that "Until a being setteth his foot in the plane of sacrifice, he is bereft of every favour and grace; and this plane of sacrifice is the realm of dying to the self, that the radiance of the living God may then shine forth."[7] That's what's needed to abandon the righteous anger and the feeling of revulsion against the "other" arising from entrenched, bitter, biased opinions—the anger and grudge-bearing that so intoxicates the self that it can't see beyond its own nose. Only self-sacrifice, "dying to the self," can dissolve the unforgiveness that hardens hearts and brings untold sadness to all of us.

The Master's every glance and gesture was motivated by and manifested universal love. And He often used interracial metaphors from the writings of Bahá'u'lláh that humans of any hue could understand visually and viscerally: We are flowers of one garden, the garden brought to the peak of its beauty by our diverse colors and kinds. We are waves of one sea, fruits of one tree.

Along with bedrock belief in human oneness, courage is needed, of course, to overcome virulently enforced boundaries. The Master had courage in abundance and, when He wanted to, He took radical action to prove his points, as He did at the regal residence of the Kháns' on that April day after leaving the Howard auditorium to attend a formal lunch with nineteen dignitaries—all white.

And here I can't help but interject: Were the Master, Khán, and others of the entourage considered "white" by the racially obsessed Americans? Journalists described 'Abdu'l-Bahá in various ways, one alluding to His dark complexion, another to His brown hands. Florence Khán recalled her brother quizzically remarking that despite her Iranian husband's three-piece suit, his derby hat, and his walking stick, there was just something . . . With their abás, fezzes and turbans, the Master and his suite were definitely exotic to the American eye, but not, perhaps, non-Caucasian. Not exactly Caucasian, either.

Asian. As a matter of fact, although African Americans were guaranteed U.S. citizenship, Asians could not become citizens at the time, and that was because of their color. It took a court to determine who was white and who wasn't: was a Syrian white? a Punjabi? an Arab? Native Americans, the original inhabitants of the continent, couldn't attain U.S. citizenship until 1924 and even later. African Americans who looked white were considered black unless they chose to pass for white, which could be for them a guilt-fraught, dangerous, and often tragic business.

Even the heavily accented first generations of fair-haired immigrant groups—Irish, Norwegian, Polish—were races apart in society's view, especially if they were Catholics. Not to mention Italians. Greeks. Jews. Come to think of it, who, or what, was white? Perhaps it came down to this: I'm white, and you're not.

Of course, nationalism also played a part. Toward the end of the Master's trip in the United States, war broke out between the Balkan States and Turkey, and the United States sided with the Balkans. "It is the main topic in all the newspapers," one of the Master's secretaries wrote, "and people look upon these visitors in their Persian garments with eyes full of prejudice. We have even been refused accommodation by some of the large hotels because they thought we were Turks."[8] (How painfully ironic, considering that 'Abdu'l-Bahá had been a prisoner of the Ottoman Empire.) Despite the fact that, for whatever reasons, people, especially children, sometimes mocked the Bahá'í travelers in their Persian garb, the only place where the Master made His entourage change completely to European suits and go without turbans was in Suttgart, Germany, in 1913. He Himself, however, retained His usual Iranian abá and headgear.

The Master always spoke and acted with freedom no matter how others viewed Him. He often expressed sentiments matching Richard Lovelace's classic lines:

Stone walls do not a prison make,
Nor iron bars a cage;
Minds innocent and quiet take
That for an hermitage;

If I have freedom in my love
and in my soul am free,
Angels alone, that soar above,
Enjoy such liberty.[9]

So the Master, before the luncheon at Khán's government mansion, sent for Louis Gregory, saying He wanted to talk with him. They met in a small parlor, and 'Abdu'l-Bahá conversed until he could no longer evade the fact that lunch had been announced. He led the distinguished guests to the long, glittering table with its carefully laid places while Louis stayed quietly in an anteroom, waiting for an opportunity to unobtrusively leave. In the dining room, 'Abdu'l-Bahá took his appointed seat—a throne-like armchair—and the guests all sat down. Then 'Abdu'l-Bahá stood up. "Where is Mr. Gregory? Bring Mr. Gregory!"

Khán found Louis and brought him into the dining room. Florence Khán had set the table with much deliberation according to Washington's diplomatic protocol, but the Master quickly rearranged the settings with a place and chair for Louis. He assigned his "throne" to Agnes Parsons, chose another chair, and seated Louis by his side, at his right hand. Remarking that He was very happy to have Mr. Gregory there, he proceeded to give a talk on human oneness.*

Louisa Mathew was not at that luncheon. Tellingly, none of the Bahá'í guests at the meal, including the artist and diarist Juliet Thompson and the influential Agnes Parsons, recorded the sudden inclusion of Louis. Agnes merely wrote, "There was some delay in

---

* President Theodore Roosevelt had scandalized Washington over a decade before by having a private dinner at the White House with Booker T. Washington. In 2012, Deborah Davis' book about that dinner, *Guest of Honor*, was published. The continuing relevance of the issue is also illustrated by Beverly Daniel Tatum's book, *Why are All the Black Kids Sitting Together in the Cafeteria?* which has gone through five editions since it first came out in 1997.

the luncheon, as 'Abdu'l-Bahá saw fit to rearrange the places of some of the guests."[10] Louis was too modest to report it in any of his own writings. It remained to Louis' dear friend, Harlan Ober, who wrote the "In Memoriam" for Louis, to tell the story.

And before the Master went back to his own quarters that afternoon—after another reception that included Alexander Graham Bell, Admiral Robert Peary, an Italian duke, the head of the American Red Cross, and others—He shook hands with each of the legation's African-American servants and spoke with them. He was consistently egalitarian with servants of all hues, tipped them generously and shared flowers, fruit, and other gifts with them.

That night, the Master spoke at the Metropolitan African American Episcopal Church to a hall full of some 2,300 people. One among them was a black woman named Leila Y. Payne, from Pittsburgh, Pennsylvania. It was her first Bahá'í meeting, and she was won over. She said 'Abdu'l-Bahá's talk was "soul-stirring," and "left its imprint on my memory forever."[11] She and her husband, who was an undertaker, had a funeral home, which area Bahá'ís later used as a meeting hall—it gave their gatherings a rather unique atmosphere!

When the church took up its usual collection, the Master contributed. He always gave during collection time, and He always gave to beggars and buskers in the street, as well as spearheading larger philanthropical projects, such as growing and storing grain to distribute in the Holy Land when famine came. But He never accepted donations to help with His own expenses or commitments.

During His Western travels, the Master generally spoke publicly several times a day, from morning through evening. In Washington, He gave a talk at 5:00 p.m. each day in the home of Agnes Parsons. She was an extremely wealthy southern lady, doyenne of white Washington society, and her husband headed the rare prints department of the Library of Congress. She had the inbred prejudices of her class and caste. But now she was a Bahá'í, and the Master was with her, so her house was open to guests of all skin tones and nationalities. At the end of the that week 'Abdu'l-Bahá spent in Washington during April, 1912, the *The Washington Bee* reported, "Its (the Bahá'í Faith's) white devotees, even in this prejudice-ridden community, refuse to draw the color line. The informal meetings, held frequently in the fashionable mansions of cultured society (such as, the homes of Alice Pike Barney and Agnes Parsons) . . . have been open to Negroes on terms of absolute equality."[12]

Agnes' husband tolerated her activities and admired 'Abdu'l-Bahá but never became a Bahá'í himself. He confided in 'Abdu'l-Bahá that he really wished all the black people would just go back to Africa, thus solving the "Negro Problem" once and for all. The Master dryly replied that in that case the Parsons' beloved African American butler must lead the exodus.

On April 24, the Master's first gathering was with children and their parents at Studio Hall, the capacious residence of Alice Pike Barney. Many of those present regularly participated in Pauline Hannen's integrated Sunday School at Studio Hall; the parents also had a class, studying Biblical prophecy and various Tablets by Bahá'u"lláh.

'Abdu'l-Bahá gave a short address and closed it with a prayer. Usually when He spoke, someone made shorthand notes that were later transcribed, and most of the talks he gave in the United States and Europe have been published in books. But this time, He asked the stenographers not to write down the prayer. He didn't want it recorded. He wanted it fully felt.

The children sang to Him, and Pauline's sons Carl and Paul were excited because they had a special job. They brought a box of semiprecious stones that Pauline called "agates of various colors, generally designated as cateye pearls" to the Master and asked Him to accept them. The Master did, and "handed the beads to Mírzá 'Alí Kulí Khán, to be given to all the children and adults alike."[13] Before Khán could do that, a young African-American woman with a babe-in-arms rushed to the front of the room and held out her child for 'Abdu'l-Bahá to bless and name.

She was the wife of Alan Anderson, who had become a Bahá'í shortly after Louis Gregory did; he and Louis were good friends.

Alan was a Pullman car porter, and he'd had the good fortune to be working on the same train that carried the Master from New York to Washington. He also spent time with the Master at Agnes Parsons' house. He'd received a Tablet from the Master saying,

> O thou who hast an illumined heart! Thou art even as the pupil of the eye, the very wellspring of the light, for God's love hath cast its rays upon thine inmost being and thou hast turned thy face toward the Kingdom of thy Lord.
>
> Intense is the hatred, in America, between black and white, but my hope is that the power of the Kingdom will bind these two in friendship, and serve them as a healing balm.
>
> Let them not look upon a man's color but upon his heart. If the heart be filled with light, that man is nigh unto the threshold of his Lord: but if not, that man is careless of his Lord, be he white or be he black.[14]

Bahá'u'lláh Himself had compared dark-skinned people to "the black pupil of the eye surrounded by the white," and the Master often employed the metaphor. He'd written to Robert Turner that he was like the pupil of the eye, "dark in color, yet it is the fount of light and the revealer of the contingent world." At another point He said, "In this black pupil is seen the reflection of that which is before it, and through it the light of the spirit shineth forth."[15]

Alan Anderson, honored recipient of the Tablet, later said, "I have no special Bahá'í talent, but I understand very well the Bahá'í Message and teachings."[16] He also said that 'Abdu'l-Bahá received him at Mrs. Parson's house and gave a Persian name to his baby daughter.

In Pauline Hannen's telling, Mrs. Anderson's babe-in-arms was a boy. "The assemblage was quiet as a mouse during the impromptu ceremony," she recalled. "Partly hidden by floral decorations were cages of canaries which warbled lustily."[17] 'Abdu'l-Bahá named the baby Mubarak, meaning happy or joyful.

Child: boy or girl?

Setting: Alice Barney's house or Agnes Parsons' house?

Presenter of child: Mr. Anderson or Mrs. Anderson?

Do we have two different versions of the same story, or did the Andersons have two children, a tiny girl and an even tinier son, and did they bring them to the Master on separate occasions? One could write two different novels on the subject . . . But the theme of both would be the same: Blessing. Affirmation of the beauty of the black family and foreseeing a positive future for its descendants.

Pauline reported that after the meeting, she was exhausted, "nearly dead, and wanted to rest, but this big boy of mine (her elder son, Carl) just hugged and kissed me over and over again, in thought going over the whole Meeting again and again with such evident Joy, that his Joy rested me. Have never seen Carl like that."[18]

That was what 'Abdu'l-Bahá wanted. Much of His mission was to awaken our spirits and gladden our hearts. No one did it better. He was never still when speaking; He walked about, His long robe moving with Him, gesturing upward with His open hands as if to say, Come up! Rise up! That evening, He spoke to about one hundred people at the home of Andrew and Lydia Dyer. He arrived there feeling too tired to address the meeting, but the group was genuinely interracial, and that lifted His spirits. He said the assembled guests reminded Him of "a string of gleaming pearls and rubies."[19] He left feeling very happy and went to a meeting at the home of Alexander Graham Bell that included the Treasurer of the United States, Lee McClung. The next day He was feted at the Turkish embassy by the ambassador, who had become very devoted to Him against the wishes of the government in Istanbul. President Taft invited the Master to the White House but then had to cancel the visit when other duties loomed.

Whatever His surroundings, the Master didn't lecture; He didn't thunder forth law or jeremiads. As Louis Gregory put it, He encouraged people and "pointed out the oases rather than the deserts of their environments," envisioning "a new sociology for the world in general and America in particular."[20]

Part of people's growth past anger and into awareness would occur, according to the Master, when they recognized the international implications of their striving toward equality and amity. He said that African Americans were fortunate to be able to strive for "equal attainments with the white race," fortunate to be able to publicly assemble at all.[21] In the world of 1912, democracy—constitutional government, freedom from monarchy and oligarchic, imperialist rule—was rare, not just for people of color, but for any people. The rights to assemble in large groups and to form associations for protest and self-improvement were not granted by many governments. 'Abdu'l-Bahá sometimes reminded his audiences that He Himself had only recently been able to leave the prison-city of 'Akká after a lifetime in exile under despotic rule because revolution had toppled the sultan.

Gayle Morrison explains in *To Move the World,* "'Abdu'l-Bahá addressed Himself to the hopes for the future shared by His black audiences, rather than to their fears. He knew that in general blacks still held to the American dream and to a faith that whites would share that dream with people of color. He was also well aware that pervasive injustice threatened to undermine both the optimism of blacks and the American dream itself . . ."[22]

In other words, the Master didn't wear blinders. He predicted many times that race war would ensue if prejudice and resultant terrorism against people of color continued. In a letter to a Bahá'í in Chicago, He wrote that "the realm of humanity will not find rest" until prejudices are abolished. "Nay, rather, discord and bloodshed will be increased day by day, and the foundation of the prosperity of the world of man will be destroyed." A year before He died, He said to Dr. Zia Bagdadi, one of His entourage in the United States and a great friend to African Americans, that He hadn't wanted to sadden the hearts of His hearers in America, so He limited His warnings to telling them that they must be united because only unity could forestall bloodshed. "I did not say more than this . . . But, indeed, there is a greater danger than only the shedding of blood. It is the destruction of America . . ."[23]

Louis Gregory heard the Master's dire warnings along with His optimistic encouragement. He knew with every fiber of his being the pain of those warnings and the hope that would flame up, against all odds, with the encouragement. He said, "If this room were filled with darkness we could not remove that darkness by intensifying the darkness, nor can we remove discord from the face of the earth by increasing discord." He wanted to be like the Master, "able to make all things fruitful."[24] For the rest of his life, Louis did just that. It's impossible to underestimate the amount of willpower he summoned up within himself, his depth of prayer and emotional discipline.

As for the Master, He required Louis' presence as much as possible. There were certain Bahá'ís whose composure, purity, and genuine modesty comforted the Master, and Louis was high on that list. Louisa later remembered times when Louis wasn't present at a meeting, thinking he wasn't needed and that he'd better try to get some of his professional work done, and the Master would tell her to go and get Louis. Since the Master's next stop after Washington was Chicago, Louis had no excuse not to be there: the Bahá'ís would be having their national convention, and Louis was to give an address.

––•––

The train arrived in Chicago at night when city lights were impressively blazing. A large crowd of Bahá'ís awaited the Master; more and more of them had gathered all day long, for they hadn't been sure of his arrival time and had greeted every train from New York, in case He was on it. Cries of jubilation went up, and later 'Abdu'l-Bahá was quite indignant at fanciful newspaper reports about Him and His Father's Cause, especially one that said He wore a red-and-white-striped robe. He said He would never wear such a thing.

His first talk in Chicago was to an integrated audience at Hull House, the famous shelter for immigrants started by the pioneering social reformer, Jane Addams, who was also a founding member of the NAACP. The reception at Hull House was actually part of the Fourth Annual Convention of the NAACP. Jane Addams welcomed the Master and introduced Him to the crowd that overflowed the auditorium. Robert Sengstocke Abbot, soon to be the leading African-American newspaper editor and publisher in the United States, was one of the audience members who approached 'Abdu'l-Bahá later.

Robert, the hardscrabble son of slaves, had been struggling since 1905 to build up his African-American newspaper, *The Chicago Defender*. His office was in the neighborhood called "the jungle," the stockyard area on the city's south side. His press runs were, at first, only three hundred copies each, and he was his own paperboy, reporter, and editor, distributing *The Defender* while gathering news. In 1912, *The Defender* began to be sold from newsstands. Though it was still the size of a handbill and each issue was just a few pages long, it was getting more influential because of muckraking reporting on the Levee, the red-light district bordering the African-American ghetto.

When Robert Abbott greeted 'Abdu'l-Bahá, the Master "placed his hand on Abbot's head and said, as Abbot recalled years later, 'He would get from me some day a service for the benefit of humanity.'"[25] During the 1920s, when Robert became a millionaire as his newspaper flourished, he and his wife, Helen, were on the Chicago Bahá'í community membership list. After the Roaring '20s, during the Depression, Robert lost some of his wealth, but that didn't affect his spirit. In the midst of the Depression, in 1934, he formally became a Bahá'í. *The Chicago Defender* is still a vital news organ and voice for justice, in print and digitally.

The *Defender* reported that, from Hull House, the Master went on to address another session of the NAACP convention at Handel Hall. He "showed the folly of discrimination on account of the only point of difference between men, that of the color of the skin. A garden of flowers, all of one color, would be monotonous and by no means beautiful."[26]

Among the black leaders who met the Master at that convention were W. E. B. DuBois and Ida B. Wells—they were also among the founders of the NAACP. Du Bois put the Master's photo on the front cover of *The Crisis* in May, featured him as a "Man of the Month" and published a report of some of his talks in June. Ida Wells, born a slave, was an eloquent, fearless journalist crusading against lynching and for women suffrage. She would become a Bahá'í in around 1919, but it wouldn't be a lifelong commitment.

From Handel Hall, 'Abdu'l-Bahá went across the street to address the closing session of the National Bahá'í Convention, where Louis Gregory had just been elected to the Executive Board of the Bahá'í Temple Unity. The vote was a tie, and the white Bahá'í who split the vote with Louis withdrew from more balloting, so the national Bahá'í administration had its first African-American member.

In all, it was a happy, exciting time. The Bahá'ís were exhilarated by the Master's presence, the amazing ground-breaking ceremony on the shores of Lake Michigan for the first Bahá'í House of Worship in the Western world, and their own progressiveness. But an unhappy result of all the effervescence was that Zia Bagdadi got evicted from his dwelling. Although Chicago boasted more venues open to integrated meetings than Washington and was a northern city remembered for protecting escaped slaves during Underground Railroad days, racism abounded. The diarist Mahmud noted, "One day, Dr. Zia Bagdadi invited Mr. Gregory . . . to his home. When his landlord heard about this, he gave notice to Dr. Bagdadi to vacate his residence . . ."[27]

However, that happened after Louis had left Chicago. While there, no doubt he was cheered, inspired, and, because he was Louis, humbled, by being elected to the nine-member Board of the Bahá'í Temple Unity. Louis little knew that he was also about to take a wife.

'Abdu'l-Bahá

Ghodsea Ashraf

Mírzá Abu'l-Faḍl

Coralie Cook

Louis Gregory

Robert Abbott

Joseph Hannen

Lua Getsinger and Mírzá Abu'l-Faḍl

Zeenat and Zia Bagdadi

Zia Bagdadi

Pauline and Joseph Hannen

Willard McKay

Louis Gregory

Louis and Louisa Gregory

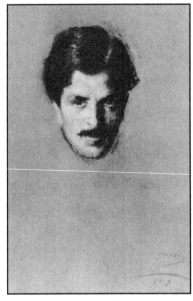

Ali Kuli Khan

Mírzá Abu'l-Fáḍl

10

A Marriage of Equals

Black is the color of my true love's hair
His face so soft and wondrous fair
The purest eyes
And the strongest hands
I love the ground on which he stands . . .

— Traditional Folk Song

In 1912, Louisa* Mathew was a quiet, middle-aged woman
who had never married and didn't expect to. She'd encountered the
Bahá'í Faith about four years before, embraced it, and wanted nothing more than to dedicate her life to it, especially since she felt her
life had been saved by 'Abdu'l-Bahá.

Though she was introverted, she wasn't timid. In fact, she was
dauntless, traveling in Europe, supporting herself by teaching languages to young people as well as adults, often volunteering her time
to help needy children. Her family in England was large and affluent,
good tradesmen and businesspeople. They came from farming
stock, but she'd been raised in town in genteel circumstances and
had studied French, German, economics, and voice.

During one of her European sojourns, in around 1908, Louisa
was in Paris cultivating her "beautiful lyric soprano" and her command of French, that musical tongue, when she met Edith Sanderson, an American of about Louisa's age who had accompanied her
mother and sister from California to Paris so that her sister could

---

* Friends and family, including her husband, knew Louisa Mathew as Louise,
but we're sticking to Louisa here, because the names Louise and Louis are so close
they can confuse the reader.

become an opera star. Tragically, Edith's sister died soon after starring in Jules Massinet's opera, *Thais*, in a role written especially for her. Edith, though fragile-looking, had more staying power. She became a Bahá'í in 1901 through May Maxwell, learned fluent Persian and maintained a salon of celebrated philosophers and mystics. They were attracted to the "rarified atmosphere" that surrounded her.[1]

When Louisa embraced the Bahá'í message, she wrote to 'Abdu'l-Bahá from Paris, and He responded, "Thou must with all thy heart be grateful to the servant of God Miss Sanderson, because she has been . . . the means of life eternal for thee. Thou hast become born anew . . ."[2] Louisa had asked if she could come to Haifa that year, and He said yes. But she had to postpone her trip.

She was mostly in continental Europe but also spent time in England with her family—at one point she asked for 'Abdu'l-Bahá's prayers for her father, who was ill—and with the Bahá'ís, among them Jean Stannard and Ethel Rosenberg, two leading lights in Britain. She wasn't given to public appearances and wasn't fond of large gatherings, but her one-on-one Bahá'í teaching encounters were highly effective. 'Abdu'l-Bahá praised her, ". . . you have given the Message of the Manifestation of the Kingdom to many people . . ."[3] She longed to meet Him.

As we know, when she finally attained His presence, her visit coincided with Louis' because he, too, had been constrained to change his plans. Later, realizing the coincidence, Louis and Louisa decided it was divine intervention. However, when they initially met in Egypt, although they were "greatly attracted to each other," as Louis later said, they considered it the attraction of friendship and never imagined their destiny.

As we have seen, in making statements on integrating the Bahá'í community, 'Abdu'l-Bahá frequently declared the efficacy of interracial marriage. Along with this firm opinion, He had intuitive trust in Louis and Louisa and had observed them closely. Also, He did delight in certain matchmaking efforts over the years. The idea of weddings made Him happy.

And Louisa and Louis did become partners in faith and in fact. They shared their lives fully, and she must have told him stories of her childhood, but unfortunately, so far as is now known, she didn't write them down. Not much is known of her early life except what we can glean from census records and local histories. She was born in 1866 in Penge, England. She had two older sisters and a younger brother. Her parents were Michael Mathew and Emma Collins, who married in 1859. Michael was a grocer. His father, also named Michael, had owned the Crooked Billet Pub. He died shortly after Louisa's birth, and his widow Maria, her paternal grandmother, ran the business after that. The Crooked Billet still exists; there's been a pub by that name on Beckenham Road in Penge since the 1600s.

Louisa's great-grandfather had run the 250-acre Copers Farm near Beckenham; after the railway demanded that terrain, he ran Stone Farm. His father had also been a farmer. There were Mathews in the area since at least the beginning of the eighteenth century. Later, the family became coal merchants, and one owned a garage. Her mother lived to be eighty, and others in the family lived longer. Louisa, despite nagging health problems, apparently inherited those genes; she was in her nineties when she died.

So Louisa came from a hardy family rooted in a part of County Kent that's now one of London's wealthiest boroughs. Around the time her parents married, trains started running through Penge and adjoining areas such as Beckenham and Bromley, where she also resided at times with her maternal grandmother, the widowed Betty Collins. Also, the famous Crystal Palace, built in Hyde Park for London's 1851 Great Exhibition—that paean to the Industrial Revolution—was relocated to Penge and enlarged; people came from all over England and other parts of the world to see it. They went shopping on busy High Street, and many no doubt supped at the Crooked Billet.

So, as Louisa grew up, her world became more cosmopolitan. The Crystal Palace was in a park full of elaborate pools and fountains, with a concert bowl, Italian gardens, Italian terraces where famous fireworks displays occurred, an orangery, a boating lake, a sort of sculpture garden of dinosaurs (models of "prehistoric monsters," as the Victorians called them), and more. Suffice to say that something was always happening at the Crystal Palace, not the least thing being the Crystal Palace School of Arts, Science, and Literature, which was mostly for ladies. Its engineering school, by contrast, only accepted gentlemen. Crystal Palace students attained certification for employment by taking Oxford and Cambridge examinations.

Louisa's "In Memoriam" writer, Joy Earl Hill, thought Louisa went to Cambridge University and earned a Certificate of Education there, but, so far, no records have been found of her attendance in the Cambridge women's colleges. It seems likely that Louisa studied at the Crystal Palace School, sat for the Cambridge examinations, and received a Cambridge Certificate qualifying her to teach English as a second language.

Whatever the exact story of her teaching degree, we know her as an educated, cultured woman accustomed to making her own decisions. She once wrote to Pauline Hannen, "Personally . . . I have been out of orthodox thought on religion since I was 16, been through so many stages from agnosticism to Theosophy . . ."[4] She knew what she was looking for by the time she reached her forties and became a Bahá'í. However, as we've seen, she was extremely ill by the time she met 'Abdu'l-Bahá, so she must have felt vulnerable.

———•———

After the pilgrimage, she and Louis began corresponding with each other. She may have been in England when Louis stopped there and met up with Ghodsea Ashraf to escort her to America. And perhaps she saw the Master again when He came to France and England in 1911. We know that she took a train from Paris to be in Naples when His ship docked there en route to New York, and she asked Him if she could travel with Him.

"Why not go later?" He said. "You will have difficulties." He reminded her that, previously, when He'd suggested that she take a trip to America, she'd said she didn't want to go because it was too far. "But as soon as you hear of my going," He added, "it gives you strength to go." He looked at her for a moment, gauging her health, and made a decision. "You are better, you may go, but I warn you, you will have difficulties."

"I would rather have the difficulties," Louisa said, "and go with you."

"I will strengthen you," 'Abdu'l-Bahá assured her.

While aboard the *Cedric*, Louisa wrote to Louis and reported that conversation. Louis replied, "I feel impressed strongly that 'Abdul-Bahá meant you to go to America . . ."

But—marriage? That was another story. "I had no thought of marriage when I came to this country," Louisa later wrote to a leading Washington Bahá'í, Agnes Parsons, "and from a physical point of view was entirely unfit for marriage being in a very weak condition . . ."

'Abdu'l-Bahá didn't mention marriage to Louisa while on shipboard. At one point, He invited her to walk on deck with Him and remarked that He had seen "a seed" in her heart. He added, "Now is the watering time." And, further, "I saw one seed. I wish it to produce many seeds."

She thought He was referring to the seed of faith and spiritual growth.

She told Agnes Parsons that it was only after two years of marriage that she understood: "The seed I realized was the attraction between Louis and myself, the watering time the ripening of this feeling into love leading to marriage—its fruit; the 'one seed producing many seeds' the attraction of the hearts of the white and colored races to be produced by our love and marriage."[5]

After ten days in New York of nonstop public and private gatherings and interviews, the Master proceeded to Washington, and

Louisa was again part of His entourage. Louis may have gone to New York, eager to see the Master, or he may have stayed in Washington, but, whatever the circumstances, she and Louis met again, spent time in each other's company, and, because of 'Abdu'l-Bahá's continued encouragement, got married five months later.

On April 29, when 'Abdu'l-Bahá left Washington on the train for Chicago, Louisa was with Him, and He asked her, "How are you and Mr. Gregory getting along?"

"What do you mean?" she queried. "We are good friends."

With a mischievous smile 'Abdu'l-Bahá said, "You must be *very* good friends."

Then, one Chicago morning, the Master gave Louisa a white flower and told her to give it to Mr. Gregory. After that, she told Mrs. Parsons, love began to grow in her heart for Louis. Being a very forthright person who never scrupled to say exactly what she meant, Louisa later asked 'Abdu'l-Bahá if she understood correctly: Did He want her and Louis to marry?

He said yes.

Louisa intimated that, as a woman, she could do nothing to bring the marriage about.

"Do you love Him? Would you marry him if he asked you?"

Louisa said she would.

"If he loves you, he will ask you."[6]

Later, 'Abdu'l-Bahá summoned Louis. "I would be very pleased if you and Miss Mathew were to marry," He said.

Louis was stunned. He stood motionless, speechless.

"What's the matter?" the Master inquired, "Don't you love her?"

"Yes, as a friend."

"Well, think about it, and let me know . . . Marriage is not an ordinance and need not be obeyed but it would give me much pleasure if you and Miss Mathew were to marry."[7]

Louis left the Master's presence deeply shaken and walked around Chicago for hours, pondering this new and unlooked-for path. In some states, interracial marriage was a felony and could result in imprisonment. In most, it could expose a couple to mob violence and other dangers, not to mention daunting criticisms, taunts, major insults, and inconveniences such as the impossibility of renting or buying a house or apartment together or sharing the same hotel room while traveling.*

Louis was deeply sensitive to public opinion; he hated to offend others, and he strongly felt he must always be meticulously tactful and courteous. Most people, black as well as white, would hardly consider it tactful for him to be married to a white Englishwoman. And it wasn't as if he couldn't say no to the Master. People did say no to some of 'Abdu'l-Bahá's matchmaking schemes; Juliet Thompson comes to mind, finding herself utterly unable to marry the architect Mason Remey despite the Master's urging. And indeed, at the time, 'Abdu'l-Bahá told Juliet that he was not giving her a spiritual command: "'This is different; this is material, and, in regard to it, I am not commanding, but suggesting . . .'"[8]

On the other hand, besides being receptive to the Master, Louis was completely committed to the principle of human oneness and proud of being a black American. In fact, to him, there was romance and adventure in being African American, struggling against long odds day after day. He had no fear of adventure and struggle, and, in his faith, had developed a wholeness—his own inner oneness—that nothing could shake. He was also very fond of Louisa.

Soon they were betrothed. In July, after taking a trip to fulfill a speaking engagement, he wrote to his fiancée, "Of course it was a sacrifice not to be permitted to see my beloved Louise this weekend, but as you unite with me in this sacrifice of our personal desires you shall also share, God willing, its precious fruits. May God cement our souls together and make us richer by the Divine outpouring of His Spirit of Love."[9]

---

* The U.S. Supreme Court didn't overturn states' statutes against interracial marriage until 1967. In the year 2000, Alabama was the last state to repeal its ban on interracial marriage.

So Louis traveled to propagate the Master's philosophy even while 'Abdu'l-Bahá was in the United States. He didn't cling to 'Abdu'l-Bahá, he didn't become His satellite or shadow; instead, he released himself to act with ever-increasing assurance and independence, following 'Abdu'l-Bahá's example and acting in accordance with His wishes.

On September 19, Louis wrote to Pauline Hannen, "My marriage to Miss Mathew will occur at noon on Friday, Sept. 27, in the parsonage of an Episcopal Church, NYC . . . My fiancée and I find ourselves growing into wonderful harmony and are seeking Guidance to higher spirituality. Last year we visited 'Abdu'l-Bahá and the Holy Tomb at Akka and although greatly attracted to each other not even dimly realized its future bearing. Last Sunday we prayed for guidance at your mother's grave, after reading the visiting (sic) Tablet. The Light grows brighter and brighter. We are happy and content in the Will of God."[10]

However, Louisa had great trepidation. She was forty-six, and shortly before the wedding date, a doctor examined her and told her that if she became pregnant, probably she and the baby would die. Louis wanted a child. Louisa wrote to Zia Baghdadi and asked him to tell the Master what her doctor had said. 'Abdu'l-Bahá's message in return was, "Do not fear. It will be all right." She understood him to mean that she'd never have a child, while Louis took it to mean that she'd survive having a child. She felt, "The wonderful thing about this answer was that it satisfied both . . ." Later on in their marriage, Louis understood, and was content—as was his wont!

And though Louisa was highly sensitive and introverted, so that she needed to rest and seek privacy frequently, she was iron when it came to upholding Louis, his teaching and traveling, their marriage, and the status of African Americans in general. Louis once wrote to a friend of "the vile reproaches of people of both races" that descended upon him when he and Louisa got engaged, and all their lives they suffered critical, biased scrutiny even from those who should have been nonjudgmental. There were exceptions, such as Ali Kuli Khan and his wife, Florence Breed Khan.* Louis said that when he was engaged to Louisa ". . . the Khans showed me such real Bahá'í love and understanding as I hope never to forget in time or eternity. Of course there were other friends . . . yet none too many . . ."[11]

With a handful of those friends present, including Louis' fellow-Washingtonian Alan Anderson, Louis and Louisa were married on September 27, 1912. They wed in New York City because 'Abdu'l-Bahá advised it. He also told them to wed quietly, with no fanfare. Louis wrote to Pauline Hannen that the wedding took place "at noon, at the residence of Rev. Everard W. Daniel"** and "just nine persons were present, including the minister and his wife, the bride and groom." There was a Church of England (Episcopal) ceremony, Louis and Louisa spoke the Bahá'í marriage vows, and there were readings, including an extract from 'Abdu'l-Bahá's first Tablet to Louis in which He expressed the hope that Louis would "become the means by which the white and colored people shall close their eyes to racial differences, and behold the reality of humanity."

After the ceremony, all gathered for a wedding breakfast. Louis reported, "In the small company were represented Christian and

---

* Florence Breed Khan was a daughter of Boston high society, and her wedding to 'Alí Kulí Khan was the talk of the season when they married, and for quite a few seasons thereafter. Theirs was the first Bahá'í marriage between an Iranian and a North American (but definitely not the last!). It wasn't one of 'Abdu'l-Bahá's match-making efforts, but a dazzling love-at-first-sight romance. Their daughter, Marzieh Gail, has written fascinating memoirs of them, the most complete being the books *Summon Up Remembrance* and *Arches of the Years*.

** Reverend Everard Daniel was the African American curate at St. Philips Episcopal Church in Harlem, one of the oldest, strongest African-American congregations in the United States. He also ran the church's sports club, and his basketball team, the Red and Black Machine, was legendary, especially during the early 1900s. (http:// www.blackfives.org/Reverend Everard Daniel)

Jew, Bahá'ís and non-Bahá'ís, the white and colored races, England and America, and the three Bahá'í assemblies of New York, Philadelphia, and Washington.

"During the ceremony there was a light rainfall. This, Mrs. Nourse says, was a Bahá'í sign, the Bounty of God. After the ceremony the skies cleared, the sun shone, and everything and everybody seemed to be happy. The same afternoon we arrived here (in Atlantic City) on our honeymoon. We find ourselves very harmonious and very happy . . ."[12]

Elizabeth Nourse, their hostess in Atlantic City, was a white woman who had lost her high social standing because she became a Bahá'í. But her husband, though he didn't share her beliefs, stood by her. She had several children, was Lua Getsinger's close friend and confidante, and had weekly Bahá'í meetings in her house for people of every hue. Louis and Louisa felt very welcome in her company.

They were proud of their marriage, their chosen Faith, and each other. Years later, Louis pointed out in a letter the Guardian's mention of their marriage in *God Passes By*. Listing the highlights of the Master's American journey, Shoghi Effendi included, ". . . the exemplary act He performed by uniting in wedlock two of His followers of different nationalities, one of the white, the other of the Negro race."[13]

Shoghi Effendi's insight here is instructive. For most people, Louis and Louisa's differing skin tones drove out other considerations, but another great difference they had was that she was British and he was American, a definite cultural divide. And then there was the ten-year age difference, which Louis didn't want Louisa to disclose to people when they first married. Not only that, but neither of them—he in his thirties, she in her forties—had previously demonstrated any overwhelming desire be tied to another person, yet now they had to love and understand each other in the crucible of marriage.

11

"The Difficult Part of Peacemaker"

with Hallie Queen, the Martin Family, Mírzá Abu'l-Faḍl,
Coralie Cook, Roy Williams

Your shoulders are holding up the world
and it's lighter than a child's hand.
Wars, famine, family fights inside buildings
prove only that life goes on
and not everyone has freed himself yet . . .
—*Carlos Drummond de Andrade*

When 'Abdu'l-Bahá left North America in December 1912, He'd
so inspired and challenged the Washington Bahá'ís that they seemed
well on their way to being a truly integrated community. They were
already the most diverse group of Bahá'ís in the United States, and
Louis Gregory and other African-American believers continued to
take leadership roles.

In August, 1913, Joseph Hannen wrote to 'Abdu'l-Bahá about a
Unity Feast that was attended by over eighty Bahá'ís and their guests
of various skin colors, nationalities, and religions. He enclosed a
letter from "Miss Hallie Queen, the Colored Believer whom Thou
directed to return to her school work in Puerto Rico last Season."
Apparently Hallie met the Master when He was in Washington, but
we can't say whether she became a Bahá'í before meeting Him, or if
the meeting itself converted her.

However it happened, she was deeply motivated. She wrote,
"During the year 1912–13 I have endeavored to add an humble
mite toward the spreading of the Bahai (sic) Principle in Aguadilla,
Puerto Rico, where I was stationed." She said she was hampered by

the "intense" Catholicism of the country: limited literature in Spanish, and the English literature having "so many Persian figures that most of the teaching had to be done orally;" and the fact that she was "a beginner, striving to work out my own personal problem of salvation, and scarcely fit to take up God's work."[1]

Despite her doubts about her qualifications as a saint, she was a highly qualified educator—at that time, she was one of the few black women to graduate from two of the most demanding universities in the United States. She had a bachelor's degree from Cornell and a master's from Stanford. After teaching English in Puerto Rico, she went on to teach German, French, and Spanish at Howard University, to translate and interpret for Latin-American consuls in Washington, and to publish articles in *The Crisis.*

In her letter, she told the Master that since she couldn't directly give them Bahá'í instruction, she tried to "instill the *teachings*" in her pupils through social action projects and consciousness-raising. "What little I have been able to do," she said, "I lay at the Master's Feet." She organized a "welfare society" to take fruit baskets and clothes to needy women, collected $42.00 to send for flood relief to a stricken area of Ohio, and "held weekly discussions on the Beauty of Universal Peace and the horrors of war." One of her pupils wrote an essay on the life of Táhirih and entered it in a national contest, where it won first prize. Among her own achievements she recognized that "I myself learned how not to be afraid of life."[2] Perhaps that's the basis for becoming a world citizen: be unafraid of life, as the Master immediately taught Louis when he was a pilgrim, and as He kept teaching him.

In July, 1913, 'Abdu'l-Bahá sent Louis instructions for the North American Bahá'ís to petition the shah of Iran to stop the once-more renewed persecution of the Bahá'ís in Iran. By 1914, Joseph reported to the Master that 510 Bahá'ís from twenty-one localities had signed the petition and that it had been addressed to the shah's regent and sent through the Iranian Minister of State, per 'Abdu'l-Bahá's directions.

Louis also expanded his program of travel-teaching that would soon become his life. In 1913, the Bahá'ís of Cleveland, Ohio, invited him to speak, following up on the Master's visit to their city. There were already some black Bahá'ís there, and the *Plain Dealer* newspaper and other local press had given a lot of space to 'Abdu'l-Bahá's encouragement of interracial marriage. Louis gave a fireside talk at the home of Tom and Lethia Fleming. Among the guests were the Flemings' neighbors, Mary Brown Martin and her husband, Alexander H. Martin. The two women were dynamic educators and civic activists, while Alexander was a young lawyer like Louis and their host, so they all had a lot in common. Mary later remembered seeing Louis, from her vantage point in the soprano section of the choir, attending services at her church on three Sunday mornings. About a year later, the Martins and all their children became Bahá'ís, and the family became a bulwark of the Faith in Cleveland. Their daughter Sarah Martin Pereira grew up to be a particularly fine linguist, a noted Bahá'í administrator, and beloved counselor.

A Dec. 31, 1913, unity feast given by Louis and Louisa at the Washington Conservatory of Music had "an audience of nearly 100 persons," Joseph Hannen wrote the Master. "The presence of white and colored people, as well as a Buddhist from India, was a notable feature . . ." Joseph anointed all the guests with attar of rose from a bottle sent by a Persian friend to honor "the Unity of the East and the West."[3]

Soon after that, Louis was part of a distinguished group entertained for dinner by one of the Washington Bahá'í community's leading ladies, Miriam Haney. Joseph was also there, along with Dr. Neval Thomas, Howard Colby Ives, and Professor George Cook. Guest of honor Neval Thomas was known as the "great warrior president" of the Washington branch of the NAACP, and he was also a member of its national committee.[4] Among his many achievements: getting the military academies West Point and Annapolis to admit African-American students.

In early 1914, the Washington Bahá'ís in unity sent the Master a letter of condolence after the death of his great friend Mírzá Abu'l-Faḍl, who died of a heart ailment in Cairo on January 21. His last word was "*Khoda!*"—the Persian word for *God*. The Washingtonians, who had benefited so much from Mírzá's presence among them, knew well why 'Abdu'l-Bahá loved him so much. "He was most sincere, most straightforward," 'Abdu'l-Bahá had said of Mírzá, "he had not the least hypocrisy or deceit in his nature . . . If he expressed publicly his love for some particular person, in his heart he loved him more; if he eulogized him, in his heart he praised him more; if he was attached to him, in his heart he was more deeply attached to him . . . If he was displeased with a person, he could not hold conversation with him."

'Abdu'l-Bahá was in Alexandria when Mírzá passed away. He received the news in a telegram as he sat at lunch, and he left the table without eating and spent the long afternoon alone in his room. Later, he went to the telegraph office and sent a reply, "Verily the eyes have shed tears and the hearts have burned because of this great affliction. Be ye possessed with the beauty of patience in this mighty calamity."

Later that evening He addressed the Bahá'ís. Speaking with His eyes closed, emotion flooding Him in waves, He said Mírzá Abu'l-Faḍl "was a standard-bearer of the oneness of the world of humanity. In the servitude of the Holy Threshold of Bahá'u'lláh he was my partner and associate. During the hours of grief he was the source of my consolation. From every standpoint I trusted him . . .

"During all the days of his life I never heard from him the use of the word 'I'—'I said so,' or 'I wrote so and so.' He would say: 'This servant requested them,' or 'This servant begged the believers.' He never made a display of his knowledge, nor wished to impress upon the mind of any person that he knew such and such a subject, or had locked in his mind such and such information. He was evanescent and lived in the station of nothingness. He was self-sacrificing at the Holy Threshold. No one inhaled from him the odor of superiority.

"Now the consummate wisdom of God hath deemed it wise to take him away from amongst us. The only way left to us is patience. *How often one man has been equal to one thousand . . .*"[5]

The Bahá'ís of Cairo carried Mírzá Abu'l-Faḍl in his coffin to "the cemetery on the hill" and laid him in a tomb owned by one of them; it was "a large room . . . and fragrant narcissus blossoms were scattered on his resting place . . ."[6]

At a February memorial for Mírzá, the Master said of him, "Strange, passing strange, that there was not a breath of self-desire in this person. . . . He lived in order to dig out of the rich mine of his heart and intellect nuggets of brilliant proofs, conclusive arguments and glorious expositions of the ideals of the Kingdom and establish the validity of the Cause of God . . . From the moment that he was ushered under the shade of the Blessed Tree, he forewent every pleasure and cut his heart from every worldly station . . . He lived afar off, above the thoughts of conflict and supremacy which are waging war on the battlefield of the minds and the hearts of many people . . ."[7]

It's as if the prayer about "luminous realities" and "supernal grace," revealed by 'Abdu'l-Bahá, was revealed in honor of Mírzá. We don't know what or who exactly prompted its revelation, but here are excerpts:

> O God, O Thou Who hast cast Thy splendor over the luminous realities of men . . . and hast chosen them out of all created things for this supernal grace . . . shedding upon them the resplendent lights of knowledge and guidance . . . help Thou Thy loved ones to acquire knowledge and the sciences and arts, and to unravel the secrets that are treasured up in the inmost reality of all created beings. Make them to hear the hidden truths that are written and imbedded in the heart of all that is. Make them

to be ensigns of guidance amongst all creatures, and piercing rays of the mind shedding forth their light in this, the 'first life.' Make them to be leaders unto Thee, guides unto Thy path . . .[8]

Since his wisdom and love made a portal for his seeking students to pass through toward the embrace of their mystic Beloved, it's fitting that one of the entrances to the Shrine of the Báb on Mount Carmel is named for Mírzá 'Abu'l-Faḍl.

———◆———

And it seemed all was going swimmingly in Washington, as if Mírzá's students there were living up to his standard of oneness. But on March 5, 1914, Joseph Hannen reported that Mrs. Aseyeh Allen had sent around a letter to the Washington Bahá'ís that most of them considered "a violation of the Covenant . . ." Then she called a meeting of "The Washington Evangelizing Committee of Baha" and also announced a series of events to be held at the Pythian Temple called "white group meetings for inquirers."[9]

Joseph's letter included a supplication from Pauline for "forgiveness for Mrs. Allen; for deep in her heart she (Pauline) feels that this sister would not knowingly violate what she believed to be Thy Will . . ."[10] He also enclosed a strongly worded letter on the problems of being black in America, written to the Master by Coralie Cook on March 2, 1914. Pauline, with Miriam Haney, had asked Coralie to put her thoughts on paper.

Coralie said, "'Race relationship, in the Southern States especially, but more or less thru out the country is in a deplorable condition. In many instances where friendship, mutual sympathy and good will ought to exist, hostility and venom are manifested by the whites and are met by distrust and dislike on the part of the colored people. To cite the contributing causes which have led up to this direful situation—culminating recently in acts of certain public officials, leading toward segregation and discrimination among the employees of the federal government itself—would be to write a book.'"[11]

She was referring to many incidents, calamities, and tragedies. To name a few: the 1906 Brownsville Raid and Atlanta Riot; the 1908 Springfield Race Riot (a few blocks from the birthplace of Abraham Lincoln); and a brutal attack on Booker T. Washington in uptown Manhattan. As that venerable elder stood searching out his friend's name in the directory of an apartment building, a white kennel owner accused him of trying to break in, beat him with his fists, then grabbed a walker from a passerby and beat him with that.

The segregation in the federal government that Coralie referred to had begun in the U.S. Post Office and the Treasury Department. Black workers were reassigned to basement offices without windows or to desks behind screens so whites couldn't see them. They had to eat in their own cafeterias and use their own restrooms. Meanwhile, the government didn't hire as many African Americans as it had before and began demanding that applicants for the Civil Service submit photos of themselves. The NAACP and National Equal Rights League protested with petitions and rallies. Religious groups from all over the world wrote letters of protest to President Woodrow Wilson. He didn't do anything. The segregation of the Civil Service wasn't an executive order, but it was imposed without opposition by Wilson or by the secretaries of the Treasury and other departments, and it became policy along with segregation in many other areas.

———

If Louis had started working in the Treasury Department then, he certainly wouldn't have been seated between his two white friends from Massachusetts and Maryland. But, by that time, he'd stopped working in the Treasury and was in his own law practice, understandably enough.

He and Louisa, as ambassadors of oneness, were life-givers to the increasingly divided Washingtonian Bahá'ís. In Louisa's words, they had to constantly act "the difficult part of peacemaker, explaining the difficulties of the white people to the colored and the point of view of the colored people to the white." Yet they felt "increasingly isolated" and "separated from most of the other Washington Bahá'ís by a profound gap in understanding." On the plus side, Louis' law practice was quite profitable, he'd started a real estate business, they owned a house, and, most importantly, they enjoyed each other's companionship.[12]

Their marriage had immediately been subject to severe strains aside from the endless social pressures born of racism. About a year after they married, Louis became very ill while teaching at Storer College (Coralie Cook's alma mater) in Harper's Ferry, West Virginia. He had a high fever that got worse and worse. Louisa rushed to his side and the doctor privately told her "he feared typhoid fever . . ." In a letter to Pauline Hannen she said, "If you write to Louis don't let him know you heard his illness was serious . . ."

Pauline and friends in Washington immediately sent flowers and bed linen. Louisa hadn't been able to hire a person to do the laundry, so: ". . . I washed all the things myself finally as well as I could in cold water and naptha soap and I had no means of ironing so had to let them rough dry. You can imagine then how rich I feel with all you have sent . . ." Soon afterward she wrote, "Louis is steadily improving though he often has a good deal of pain . . . I hear him now talking to nurse in quite his natural voice . . . Letters do him much good when I read them to him. He needs a good deal of cheering and encouraging as he is mostly very depressed, quite contrary to his usual nature, but he is entirely unused to pain and does not at all understand it . . ."[13]

Louisa had chronic migraines and other afflictions, so she did understand pain, probably more than she would have wished to, but she didn't let it stop her in her drive to be of service. She wrote Agnes Parsons, proposing first a home, then a fund, for unemployed and indigent Bahá'ís; she worried about "putting myself forward too much as a newcomer" but said, "I find I sometimes get intuitions which I must act on and that it is best then to consult no one as I rather easily lose faith in myself if my ideas are disapproved of." She added, "My husband very much approves of the idea of a fund."[14]

Louisa, always generous, was often very personal in her philanthropies, doing things such as finding an affordable room for a needy person and helping to furnish it. Her bequest from her family in England was modest, and she was practical in her giving and in her thinking, but she never stopped giving. She and Louis gave consistently to the Orient-Occident Society's scholarship fund for students of the Bahá'í-run schools in Iran, often to the point of sacrifice.

The community's splintering affected its ability to function in many ways, including financially. When it couldn't pay off an outstanding debt, Louis and Louisa were among those who helped. 'Abdu'l-Bahá recognized their generosity and interracial bridge-building, writing to them: "I am most pleased with your philanthropic activities, especially your contribution toward the final payment of the debt of the Orient-Occident Unity. I know also that your thought and mention by day and by night is the guidance of the *souls*—white and black. Therefore be ye most happy, because you are confirmed in this great matter."[15]

Louisa also took teaching trips of her own. We find her writing a letter in May, 1914, to another itinerant teacher, Albert Vail, about Kalamazoo, Michigan, where she "stayed two days with a very delightful family of colored people," spoke at a small meeting, and "telephoned to Mr. Patterson of 'The People's Church' and took it upon myself to say that you may be coming . . . and to ask if he would care to have you speak . . ."[16]

Just as Louis and Louisa found struggle everywhere, they also found friends. Despite intense opposition to intermarriage in both white and black communities, there was some support for it, usually because of belief in the principle of oneness no matter what the supporter's politics or religion. In clubs for interracially married people, such as the Manasseh Clubs in the Midwest, members provided each other with social life, legal advice, etc. In her letter to the Master, Coralie Cook quoted Theodore Roosevelt as saying that intermarriage "is the accepted mode of race adjustment in Brazil . . . and is provocative of no race friction whatsoever, but on the contrary establishes harmony and good will."[17]

——•——

Coralie cited the New Abolitionists* in her list of friendly forces and mentioned the Southern Sociological Congress, which had held an integrated conference for the second time in Atlanta in 1913. She added, "So far as the matter of amalgamation goes here in the United States, it is settled past undoing. 250 years of domestic slavery with the female slave at the command of her master has bequeathed to the country hundreds yes thousands of mixed bloods ranging in type from a dark rich brown skin with curly hair to the perfect blond with golden hair and blue eyes all classed as negroes and all—if known to have a drop of negro blood—subject to the same restrictions, insults and persecutions." (We recall that Coralie herself may have been related to Thomas Jefferson.) She went on to list famous geniuses who were descendants of slave-master—slave alliances such as Fredrick Douglass, W. E. B. Du Bois, Alexandre Dumas, and Aleksandr Pushkin.

She spoke for the progress African Americans had made "during their fifty years of freedom," saying it "has astounded the world and incited the envy and hatred of those who prophesied their extinction and argued their inability to work for themselves. In the midst of unfriendly surroundings they have accumulated $7,000,000,000

---

* Over the years the world has seen various New Abolitionist groups. I haven't been able to identify the one Coralie mentioned, but currently there is a New Abolitionist Movement to eliminate trafficking in human beings, slavery, which still exists in many forms.

worth of property . . . Coming out of slavery with 95% of their whole number unable to read or write . . . that number is reduced to only 30%, an advance surpassing that of whites during the same period."

She pointed out that such progress seemed only to inspire white lawmakers to institute more Jim Crow statutes. "Back, back and everywhere back!" she said. "'Be ye hewers of wood and drawers of water only! Come thus far and no further!' . . . until the average person of color is almost in a state of desperation." If he looked to the churches "for protection and championship," he found that "one by one they have given in to the mandates of the Race Problem or Prejudice that is enclosing the white race almost as much as the black . . . At one time . . . the Seventh Day Adventists* . . . were in perfect harmony and fellowship" but finally "divided on racial lines, and the same thing is true of the Salvation Army. Where then is the black man to turn. The Bahá'í Cause is his last hope." She said that to draw a color line among the Bahá'ís would break the hearts not only of black adherents but of white ones who were their true brothers and sisters: ". . . The colored people and their brave friends feel this is the most crucial period in all the Nation's History. I pray to God that no one who has ever embraced the Faith will step aside to so contribute to the Nation's shame and so abandon the Cause . . . To any one of the Bahá'í Faith to whom the tempter says 'temporize' or let the matter work itself out I say beware. When was ever a mighty Principle championed by temporizing or delay? I know some must suffer both black or white, but who better able to wear the mantle of suffering than the real Bahá'í?"[18]

---

* Various evangelical Christian groups, like certain Quaker circles, were militant abolitionists when they began and also gave women the right to speak from the pulpit (and other places). In fact, abolitionists started the Holiness Movement and ran Oberlin College, a pioneer in accepting African-American and female students. The Wesleyan Methodists were also abolitionists—that's why they were called *Free Methodist*. One of their bishops advocated interracial marriage.

Coralie's long, impassioned screed was one of many letters the Master received. Sadly, quite a few of those letters were reactionary, not enlightened and forward-looking. And all of the letters were the continuation of an argument that had been going on for a long time, as we have seen.

'Abdu'l-Bahá delayed His answer, but finally wrote in a general letter, "I know about everything that is happening in Washington. The sad, somber news is the difference between the white and the colored people. I have written to Mr. Hannen requesting him, if possible, to arrange a special place of meeting for the white people only, and also a special place of meeting for the colored people, and also one for both the white and the colored, so that all may be free . . . I can see no better solution to this question."[19]

So, 'Abdu'l-Bahá seemingly gave in. Before anyone could write to Him for clarification—to ask if, perhaps, he was only referring to whites-only meetings for inquirers deemed not "ready" for integration—World War I disrupted global communications. Although the United States didn't enter the war until 1917, the Bahá'ís were cut off from 'Abdu'l-Bahá starting in 1914.

A so-called Bahá'í in Washington went so far as to voice racist views at the "white" weekly meeting in the Pythian Temple, an immense, pretentious edifice erected by the original Knights of Pythias, an all-male secret society which was, in practice, during that Jim Crow era, racially segregated. Anonymous letters touting that person's opinion winged their way around Washington and other parts of the United States. Meanwhile those who met at the Pythian building formally denied having prejudice and said their meetings were educational.

The Wednesday meeting at the Dyers' house and meetings at Harriet Gibbs Marshall's music school were labeled "colored." African Americans stopped attending. Someone facilitated a "mixed" meeting but few people went; the hostess wasn't exactly welcoming to people of color. In fact, Louisa went to see her and confronted her with the difficulties posed by her attitude, but she remained unbudging.

Louisa wrote to Agnes Parsons, ". . . the unfortunate state of affairs here . . . is bringing the Cause into disrepute to the outside world as well as troubling the believers . . ." She felt the Master had meant that any whites-only meetings should be in private homes for inquirers unable to get past their own interior color line but that all public and official community meetings must be integrated. "Both my husband and myself . . . foresaw the disastrous consequences to the teaching (of) the Cause to the colored people, in fact we foresaw all that has happened now—for the work here is practically at a standstill among the colored people and many who were believers or on the brink of becoming so will have nothing to do with us."[20]

So the Bahá'ís of Washington mirrored the racial strife that rent the United States. Another insult adding to ongoing injury was the release, in 1915, of the world's first epic movie, D.W. Griffith's *The Birth of a Nation*, which romanticized Klu Klux Klansmen as crusader knights waging gallant war against black rapists running wild. Good guys in white hoods. Bad guys in blackface—because white people in blackface make-up played African Americans in the film. Despite this obvious fakery, the film incited race riots, and in Lafayette, Indiana, a white man murdered a black teen after seeing the movie. *The Birth of a Nation* also reawakened the Klu Klux Klan itself. The white supremacist terrorist group had been languishing, but with the movie hype, it resurged rampantly. In fact, into the 1970s, the Klan used the film to recruit new members.

The NAACP campaigned to take the movie out of circulation. A 1916 letter from George Cook thanks Joseph Hannen for writing to the District Commissioner to ask that Griffith's film not be shown in the capitol. Some cities banned the movie, but Washington wasn't one of them.

Louis and Louisa remained optimistic despite all odds. Louisa was writing "The Most Great Peace," a tale set in the future (1963!)

in a united world "with an old grandmother who tells the story of her life" recalling early Bahá'í history—the history that Louisa was living through. She'd told the plot to 'Abdu'l-Bahá, and He'd encouraged her to write it. She dreamed of starting a children's magazine and "a school where no racial lines shall be drawn or recognized . . . to leaven the loaf of Humanity with the Principle of Oneness . . ." While sailing to America, 'Abdu'l-Bahá had told her that "when the school was built on Mount Carmel" she'd teach in it. Hopefully, one day there will be a Louisa Mathew Gregory school on Mount Carmel![21]

Always open and honest to the point that Louis sometimes worried she might offend the ultra-sensitive Washington Bahá'ís, Louisa doughtily went to the aid of her African-American friends. In 1916, after the community made yet another decision based on bias, she wrote to Agnes Parsons, "The colored people have a real source of grievance because they were not really *represented* at that meeting for consultation . . . What was done does not meet the wishes of the majority of the colored believers . . . the separate meeting . . . has practically stopped all work among the colored people in the teaching of the Revelation . . . That the 'colored Bahá'ís' are 'not expected to attend' was the part of that explanation that wounded most I think . . ."[22] And she didn't just write; as we've already seen, reserved and introverted though she was, she went to see people and discuss situations with them face-to-face, with varying results.

Louis wrote that the NAACP openly denounced the Bahá'ís of Washington "for offering segregation in the name of religion." (The NAACP, at the time, counted six thousand members in the District of Columbia and had large branches throughout the United States). Louis was neither blinded nor intimidated by the terrifying interracial violence that broke out all-too-often across the country. At one point, he summed up the situation between black and white Americans with an old saying: "If the devil ain't loose now, he's got a devil of a long rope." But he saw sweet promise: ". . . Progressive orders everywhere," he said, "seem to be trying very hard to get free from the old order of things . . . North and South, there is a very decided trend toward unity, cooperation and harmony among the various elements."[23]

He knew that open-minded people seeking truth needed hope. Capable of courage and boldness themselves, and longing for interchange with folks long stigmatized as "other," whether black or white, these open-minded seekers were frequently disappointed by rejection and failure, and they badly needed the Bahá'ís to be courageous, bold, and united. Since any association of people tends to splinter and become rancorous, the potential unity of the Bahá'ís once they all became firm in their Covenant was desperately needed—and firmness in the Covenant demanded a commitment to actions predicated on and defending the oneness of humanity.

As an open-minded and frequently disappointed pair themselves, Louis and Louisa could at least take comfort in certain friendships, such as that of Roy Williams, a new young black Bahá'í. In Washington, they often went to Roy's grandmother's house for dinner.

"My grandmother was a very excellent cook," Roy remembered, "and Mr. Gregory always liked to . . . visit especially on the days when Grandma would cook her famous hot rolls. Being a southerner born Mr. Gregory was accustomed to wholesome southern type food and enjoyed the type of cooking that my grandmother so gladly offered . . . He was a very affable man and . . . he could tell simple, homespun stories . . . that would keep the other people present (and there were always others present) roaring with laughter." Much of Louis' charm, according to Roy, was in his "humility, his utter disregard of arrogance and ostentation, his smiling happy face—no complaints, no criticisms, no idea of the superiority of his position as an excellent lawyer, a graduate of Howard University."[24]

Roy added that Louisa hadn't learned to cook in her girlhood and ate as heartily as everyone else at Grandma's table. She did eventually learn to cook some of Louis' favorite dishes, and perhaps Roy's grandmother was one of her early teachers. Louis was surely Roy's great mentor and example, the closest Roy could get to the presence of the Master, for he never met the Master face to face. He did see him, however.

In 1912, Roy Williams was a young workman in Washington, and he later recalled rushing around a street corner as he ran to catch a train, glancing up and seeing a group of men in Oriental garb walking toward him. He recognized 'Abdu'l-Bahá as the "oriental sage" whose picture had been in all the papers. But that was as far as it went.

He had no idea that his mother, Bertha Marie Joyce, was a Bahá'í. She didn't tell him, he said in his reminiscences, recorded when he was in his eighties, "but she lived the life and attended all the meetings." In the summer of 1914, he went to visit his mother in New York. She was a fine seamstress who made costumes for Broadway plays and worked with some renowned stars. In fact, when Sarah Bernhardt was in the United States, Marie helped her with her English.

Roy recalled that his mother invited him to walk with her to a meeting "on the east side of Harlem. I refused to go, though I walked with her to the building. She went up and I told her I'd sit down on the porch . . . and wait for her. It seemed to me that she was unduly long in this meeting and I got tired of that. So I got up and walked up some stairs. It was summer and doors were open and I could look in on the meeting. And there was a young Irish girl and she was speaking to these people and reading from a book.

"I walked in there and I walked right on up to her and said, 'Give me the book . . .' I took the book and walked on out and went downstairs and returned to our apartment. I forgot all about my mother because of this book. It was the story of the man from San Francisco who went to the World Conference of Religions in 1893 . . . (and heard mention of a certain) Prisoner in 'Akká. The story was very vivid. He went back home and he couldn't forget what he'd heard. So he took a boat, and he went to Haifa, and he met 'Abdu'l-Bahá. That was the first Bahá'í in America, Thornton Chase."

Roy didn't stop reading until he finished the book. Then, lying on his bed, he saw "this brilliant white light and it seemed to me that it was beckoning." Eventually he got up and went into another room. His mother was there—she'd come home under her own steam. "I said to her, 'I am what I am.' And she looked up at me and she said, 'You know what you are. I've been waiting for you to tell me.'" From that day Roy was a Bahá'í.

Roy was born in 1888 in Washington, DC. Because his mother worked, his grandmother raised him in her home along with seven other children. Like his mother, he became a fine craftsperson, but in a different field. He said, "I wanted to do something with my hands so I studied furniture building and repair. One of my customers was the wife of the man who had the Campbell Soup Company. I had many like that. They all floated around me but at the same time I kept in touch with this Faith until the call came that I must go out."

One of Roy's chief early Bahá'í instructors was a white court stenographer named Hooper Harris. He had been "sent by 'Abdu'l-Bahá to India to teach the Faith, returned to America and became a strong leader and advocate of the Faith . . . In New York I studied with him when he wasn't very busy in his court work . . ."

Roy met Louis in Washington, and we've seen how they enjoyed being together at Grandma's. He also remembered how well Louis impressed him when he first saw him officiating at a Bahá'í National Convention—"He was always pleasant but was businesslike in his approach, well acquainted with the official means of conducting the affairs of the convention."

But Louis was spontaneous and improvisational, too. As a result, Roy had what he considered the most momentous experience of his life. There was a deadlock on a vote that needed to be unanimous. Zia Bagdadi and Louis turned to Roy. "They beckoned to me. I didn't know what they wanted. They kept saying, 'Come, come.' They said we want you to repeat for the convention in the original Arabic the prayer of the Báb until we feel that we can proceed—or not proceed."

Roy stood up and began to chant in Arabic, "Is there any Remover of Difficulties save God? Say: praised be God! He is God! All are His servants and all abide by His bidding!" At first he didn't have everyone's full attention, but gradually they quieted. He said, "I continued until I heard the sound of weeping from somewhere in the audience and I addressed the chairman to bring the convention to order. The first time there was no response. The second time the whole convention arose like one man" in unity.[25]

By 1916, the lie being lived by the people in Washington having "Bahá'í" meetings for whites-only had mostly played itself out. In the beginning of 1917, Joseph Hannen could write to Agnes Parsons of a lecture series on Bahá'í: "The attendance is always in the neighborhood of 50 to 75 each Sunday evening; there are always strangers present . . . several are coming regularly . . . The meetings are being advertised in the four newspapers . . . At all times both races attend . . . and we have had at times fully one-half of the colored people in a single audience."[26] With help from Katherine Nourse, Louis and Louisa's friend in Atlantic City, the Bahá'ís had also reestablished the Sunday school in Studio Hall.

Around that time, Roy and Louis began traveling and teaching the Bahá'í Faith all over the South in response to the only tablets from 'Abdu'l-Bahá that managed to reach America during the war. They were the first five Tablets of the Divine Plan, addressed to the Bahá'ís of the different regions of the United States and to the Bahá'ís of Canada and Greenland. Joseph Hannen received the one for the Bahá'ís of the Southern States. In brief, it summoned each Bahá'í to travel through the South, sowing seeds of faith and establishing new Bahá'í centers, and if they couldn't perform this service, they were to send another in their stead.

After the Tablets arrived, Louis was in Harlem and he and Roy met again. All the Bahá'ís were talking about the Master's teaching Tablets. When Roy heard that Louis was going to take a trip through the South trying to fulfill 'Abdu'l-Bahá's desire, he said, "I'll go with you. We'll try to change the attitude of the people . . ."

It was the beginning of long years on the road. Roy said, "We were tackling a problem that was too deep for one man or two men. We had the cooperation of others. We had the cooperation of such a soul as Dr. Bagdadi of Chicago, who came down to the south to help—and others. This journey seemed rather hapless and haphazard to us but as we picked up the trail to our astonishment we . . . kept out of harm's way and out of trouble with the people . . . I do not know now how we managed to do these things. I do not know how we managed to survive."[27]

12

Into the Maw

with Roy Williams, James Elmore Hays, James Oakshette,
George Henderson, Zia Bagdadi

Racism is not intelligence.
I can not reason these scars away.
Outside my door
there is a real enemy
who hates me . . .
I do not believe in a war between races
but in this country
there is war.

—Lorna Dee Cervantes

"How long are ye silent and speechless? . . . 'Abdu'l-Bahá is not satisfied with a meek voice and depressing lamentation! He seeks the passionate tumult and joyous clamor and he roars and cries at the top of his voice so that the realities of things stir into movement and action . . ."[1] So Louis Gregory quoted the Master in a 1916 report of his teaching travels written for *Star of the West*.

At another time, writing to a female Bahá'í in Paris, 'Abdu'l-Bahá said, "Roar like unto a lion and exhibit such ecstasy and love among these few souls (the small Bahá'í group in Paris) that praise and glorification may continuously reach thee from the divine Kingdom . . ."[2]

Louis was among the Bahá'ís who took the Master's exhortations to boldness very seriously. He wouldn't let fear deter him nor rage infect him; he schooled himself to be a gentle lion, like 'Abdu'l-Bahá. He had to wrestle for turf with the monster of hatred and prejudice, had to go right into its maw, so he frequently went to bed gnashed-at and wounded, but he always woke up ready to go on, unbowed. Where others saw dissolution and despair, he saw potential solidarity and hope. Of course he felt pain, probably more than most people, for his vision embraced all people—but he also won the gift of jubilation.

He wrote, "In one meeting, held in Memphis, Tenn., over fifty persons . . . after hearing the message and proofs, arose and said the Greatest Name . . . The strongholds of orthodoxy were taken by the fire of divine love . . . The time has come to declare the message from the housetops."[3]

Louis let nothing stand in his way. Therefore, nothing much *could* stand in his way, although Roy Williams recalled, "In the South of that time it was often impossible to get an interracial group together. The black people were anxious to hear what we had to say, but the white people were aloof and had to be dealt with very kindly. The measures that we used were always adaptable to the time in which we moved. In cities like Houston, Texas, before we could speak to anybody we had to be interviewed by the police department. We said what we had to say and said it without any fear."[4]

Louis and Roy had helpers, although the pickings were slim. Some white Bahá'ís who went to live in the Deep South and teach before and around the arrival of the first five Tablets of the Divine Plan included Dr. James Oakshette, Fred Mortensen, and Paul K. Dealey. Because of Jim Crow laws, not to mention social taboos against blacks and whites associating together, some of their meetings had to be clandestine.

James Oakshette, generally called Dr. Oakshette, was an Englishman who had been a congregational minister in England, Canada, and the United States, and he knew Greek, Latin, Sanskrit, Hebrew, Gaelic, and German as well as the rolling rhetoric of Shakespeare. He learned about Bahá'í from Lua Getsinger while he was living in Chicago, moved to Atlanta in around 1912, and was the first Bahá'í there. He apparently supported himself as a Liberal Catholic priest, following a philosophy from England based on the actual meaning of the word *catholic*—all-inclusive or all-embracing—serving people who were disenchanted with traditional churches. This was before western Bahá'ís disassociated themselves from other religious congregations. Dr. Oakshette used Bahá'í prayers and taught Bahá'í principles, and in the 1920s, when one young man came to him and said he, too, wanted to be a Liberal Catholic priest, Dr. Oakshette said there was something better in store for him and gave him a copy of the book *Bahá'u'lláh and the New Era.*

Louis Gregory worked with James Oakshette in Atlanta and said, "He had a marvelous comprehension of the Teachings and of the stations of the Great and Holy Ones." Roy Williams said, "During my first teaching trip (in 1916) I met Dr. Oakshette . . . in his office . . . This had to be done very secretly but he never showed any fear and we spent many happy hours discussing ways and means and contacts he knew among colored people. I have never met a more charming and lovable character . . . Dr. Oakshette personified the best of ideals of the Cause under all conditions . . ."[5]

Louis and Roy also worked with James Elmore Hays, the first native-born white Georgian to become a Bahá'í. In 1915, Louis said that Elmore (as he was usually called) later confided in him that he'd been frightened when he heard that Louis was on his way. But he managed to summon up his courage, and he worked publicly, consistently, with Louis in Atlanta.

There was no reason why Elmore shouldn't have been scared; that was the year "Colonel" William Simmons, inspired by *The Birth of a Nation*, marched up Stone Mountain, near Atlanta, with some old buddies, burned a cross and revived the Ku Klux Klan, which had been put to rest in the 1870s by ex-Union soldiers who were sick of attacks against them and newly freed African-American southerners. Now the Klan adopted the knight-in-shining-armor romanticism of the movie, dedicating itself to protecting white womanhood against what it deemed the greatest evils—Jews, Catholics, people of color. The ghostly white regalia and fiery crosses that had been featured in the movie became terrorizing trademarks of the Klan.

Elmore forgot his fear to such an extent that he ate with Louis at the "colored Y.M.C.A." and, despite a night shift job, abandoned his sleep schedule to accompany him to as many speaking engagements as possible. These included Atlanta University, Morehouse College, and Morris Brown University. He aided Louis on subsequent trips and also accompanied Roy Williams, who said of him, "This Bahá'í was like a shining sun—strong of physique and equally strong of spirit. He was entirely devoid of any racial prejudice . . . The amusing albeit very dangerous methods he employed to spend an hour or two with me always live in my memory. Under cover of darkness walking across the city sometimes very late at night, he would come to our house at 2 Beckwith Street, and sit, eat and talk for hours . . ."[6]

In Nashville, during his 1915 trip, Louis met another man of great promise, the African-American educator and businessman George Henderson, who was running the school of commerce at Roger Williams University. Professor Henderson became a Bahá'í and gave up his job at the university so he could devote himself wholly to the Faith. He fell severely ill, which led to depression. A native of Knoxville, Tennessee, he'd started out as a shoeshine boy and had few resources other than his own energy and motivation. Louis received some sad news of his illness and breakdown before things began looking up, but soon, with a capital of $2.20 and two typewriters, and an enrollment of six students, the professor started Henderson Business College in Memphis; it became a flourishing institution.

On another trip south, a six-week jaunt, Louis had, as always, Louisa's unconditional support, and he also had a dream that 'Abdu'l-Bahá was with him. He considered his trip a pilgrimage. From Tallahassee, Florida, he wrote to Joseph Hannen "that he'd spoken to almost 5,000 people" of diverse backgrounds with "practically no opposition." Further speaking engagements in other places brought the total of people who had heard him to "probably more than fifteen thousand . . . most of them students." He said "opportunities" to reach people in the South with the Bahá'í message seemed "limitless." When he returned to Washington, he closed his law practice and newly begun real estate firm and refused an offer to teach law at Howard University. Pauline Hannen reported in *Star of the West* that "Louis Gregory has closed his home and given up his business" and started on "an extended teaching tour."[7]

Louisa concurred with her husband in these decisions, and at her suggestion, they began the process of selling their house to fund his travels. "My dear little wife," he said of her in a letter, "the Flame of whose spiritual love is aglow . . ."[8]

Unfortunately, flames of racial strife were also aglow as Louis, with Roy Williams in his train, journeyed on. In July 1917, East St. Louis, Missouri, suffered four days of riots so lethal that six thousand African Americans fled the city. In August, mob violence wreaked havoc in Houston, Texas, after a black soldier who tried to stop white police beating a black woman was beaten to the ground himself. African Americans not only resisted persecution but also protested it. In New York City, ten thousand African Americans rallied by the NAACP marched down 5th Avenue protesting the devastation in Missouri. The procession must have made a striking portrait of a people, for the men all wore black, while the women and children wore white.

Louis and Roy rode Jim Crow in the uncomfortable rear seats of trains and buses where they choked on diesel fumes and coal dust. Sometimes they found nowhere to sleep or eat comfortably because their skin color barred them from accommodations; now and then they had to sleep in police stations, the only places that allowed them in. Because Jim Crow laws and customs changed from place to place, one never knew what would apply where.

Perhaps a black person didn't have to step off the sidewalk while passing a white person in one town, but if he didn't step off the sidewalk in the same situation in the next town, he could be reviled, hit, or worse. Since Louis and Roy couldn't possibly know all the little local ways, the best thing to do was step off every sidewalk, everywhere. They'd been raised to be constantly aware of the threat of insult, injury, and violence, but now that they were on the move, their awareness had to be even sharper and their tempers under even stricter control. They solved this problem not only by being extra-vigilant, but by a trust in the power of prayer that gave them a sense of security even in the midst of danger.

Louis, who apparently had the Midas touch when he applied himself to money matters, was also suspected of being insane, fanatical, or both by old college and professional friends who knew the opportunities for financial gain and prestige that he'd rejected. Those friends often arranged for Louis to speak from important podiums and pulpits. Louis said of one of them that he'd consider it "the nth degree of insanity" if he ever found out Louis didn't charge lecture fees or at least pass the hat on his own behalf.[9] Louis had to have complete detachment from the world and its opinions, infinite patience with the world, total faith in the good outcome of the work he was doing, and complete reliance on God and on the core of strength, integrity and wholeness—*oneness*—within himself.

Although expectations of Roy Williams were not as high because he didn't have the same professional qualifications, he also had to develop tremendous faith and independence from external judgment. He was younger than Louis and very unlike him. He was a force of nature, with a turbulent personality and dramatic style. He had far more potential than Louis for getting into trouble! Also, he was a skilled craftsman who had built furniture-to-order for stylish customers and had supported himself quite well. Now he sometimes ended up in worse circumstances than Louis because he lacked similar family resources, and the two didn't always travel together, for they could often get more done working in different spots. Roy frequently found himself without bus fare to go on to his next destination; then he would be rescued by $5.00 coming to him in the mail from Louis, or $25 from Agnes Parsons.

Louis' pockets were nearly as empty as Roy's, but he didn't allude to or describe material difficulties in his letters. Roy did. At one point, when Roy had no overcoat and nothing more than the clothes on his back, which were getting quite disreputable-looking, Louis sent him some money because "he thoroughly agreed with me," Roy wrote to Joseph Hannen, "in the matter of presenting a reasonable appearance because of the hardship that some souls have in accepting when the real poverty of the friends is shown and like myself, he felt that the indigence of the teachers should be kept out of sight as far as possible."[10]

When Louis supplied Roy with a few dollars out of his personal funds, it became much harder for Louis to make ends meet along his own route, especially because, Roy explained, "one cannot calculate even to pennies on these trips because of the unusual always cropping out in the way of assisting others and doing charitable works which are necessary to establish the principles of the Cause."[11] For example, Roy and Louis always tried to be the first to contribute when collection receptacles made the rounds at churches where they spoke.

To afford such beneficence, they often went with just two meals a day and gave their rousing talks on empty stomachs. During a visit to Austin, Texas, Roy addressed three hundred people in a Baptist church, and although he'd told the pastor he didn't want reimbursement, the pastor insisted on taking up a collection. "In a few minutes," Roy said, "the sum of seven dollars lay on the table and then I was truly in a fix. However, I suddenly remembered that a rally was on in the church and rising and calling for seven leaders of the campaign . . . I distributed the collection among them equally. It is indescribable the commotion and effect that this single act had upon those people who had never known a speaker to refuse money and in such a fashion and . . . they stood in the streets talking about it after dismissal . . ."[12]

With his tempestuous nature, Roy admired Louis' composure and his ability to keep his clothing "immaculately clean . . . unstained and in order." If Louis only had one suit, his training as a tailor enabled him to take care of it, and his shirts "were always pure white, starched." Roy said Louis' clothes were "of moderate and conservative design and appearance . . . He was always prepared to meet any weather condition that would prevail that day. Most of the time he was always seen with his tightly rolled up umbrella hanging on the crook of his arm. . . . He always wore black shoes. The last thing he did before going to sleep at night was to blacken and polish his shoes until you could see your face in them.

"His hair was a little longer than most men wore their hair, worn in what we used to call pompadour style, high in the front. He had trouble traveling on the railroad trains with all the dirt and dust, trying to keep his hair combed and brushed." In his old age, Roy chuckled over Louis' struggles with his hair, remembering that Louis became a fan of Madame C. J. Walker's famous hair care products, managing "to endure the torture and trouble of it" to make his hair behave.

Being such an orderly person, Louis "always had the day's affairs outlined and ready to pursue." As a speaker, "he had a very sweet and personable magnetism . . . and attracted attention so you wanted to listen to him. His speech was soothing to the ear and the heart of the listener.

"I don't remember that he had any trouble sleeping," Roy went on. "He rose early before sunrise and put on the floor a clean sheet of the daily newspaper or whatever he could obtain as a prayer rug. He would bow down and utter the prayer of praise and glorification. His mind was at peace, his heart was at peace, his conscience was unscathed."[13]

Like Louis, Roy was a true acolyte of 'Abdu'l-Bahá, Who wrote him some treasured letters, and he also had the good sense to perceive Louis' greatness, to subdue himself and follow guidance. He wrote to Joseph Hannen, "These have been the happiest days of my existence, accompanying this blessed soul, Louis, in the journey for the sake of God. Many wisdoms and lessons of judgment invaluable to this work have been gained through him . . ." He embraced teaching the Bahá'í Faith in the South as a personal mission, so that even when he went north to work in a steel mill to earn money to continue traveling, he had no desire to settle down. He said, "This is the work—this is my work—my life—my joy—my aim—my happiness—I must go on—I cannot keep still nor silent . . ."[14]

In September, 1917, Louis visited Memphis and found a Bahá'í community of sixty people, mostly African American, including Professor Henderson and eight Bahá'í teachers at the business college. While Louis was there, the entire student body wrote a letter to 'Abdu'l-Bahá.

The same month, Louisa, not satisfied with staying home, visited Berkeley Springs, West VA, and wrote to Joseph Hannen, "I have been able to give the message to the visitors here and the butler (colored) . . . The butler seemed . . . interested. I am to go and talk to his family and friends on Monday if the wife is back from a visit away somewhere . . ."[15]

Like all of Louisa's letters, this one was full of homely details—please look for her white sweater in the hall closet; look in the pocket of Louis' blue jacket for bus tickets that they (the Hannens) can use if they want to; the best ways to contact certain people would be by pushing a note under the inner door. Louisa always wrote fully and at length!

But letters from Louis to her at this period add to the story: "Your letter . . . told of your being alone in the house and having a lonesome feeling. At such a time, my darling, you must feel that you are very close to the Beloved of all hearts, 'Abdu'l-Bahá, and that His Great Love sustains you . . ." And also, "Be happy, O my Darling, in the sacrifice you have made in the Path of God. It may be the means of Guidance to many souls . . ."[16]

It seems Louisa might have turned to traveling in part to relieve her loneliness during Louis' absences. But we remember that she'd been on the go for some years in Europe, teaching languages, before she became a Bahá'í, so we also know she didn't like to sit still. In an effort to add to her and Louis' income, she began giving language classes again; French was in demand in the United States. In November, 1917, Louis wrote to her, "I am now pleased that you have taken up that work since it occupies your mind with pleasant thoughts . . . It was at first difficult to reconcile my mind to it, because I feared you would overtax your strength . . ."[17]

At the time, Louisa was boarding with a Mrs. Fanny Gregory, matriarch of a venerable Howard University family that may or may not have been related to Louis' stepfather. Fanny was an eminent community activist and educator herself, and her son, Thomas Montgomery Gregory, inaugurated and ran the university theater department, starting with his establishment of the Howard Players. Louis said, "I know she (Fanny) takes good care of you, my darling, else your letters would not show happiness." He signed, "With my heart's best love and a tender caress . . ."[18]

In December he wrote to Louisa from Chicago, where he was "well and comfortable" with Zia Bagdadi, his wife and their new baby, "I hope and pray you will manage to keep warm. If necessary ask Mrs. Gregory to put the gas stove in your room . . . I think I saw one in the room of Mr. Montgomery Gregory. I hope you will not suffer too much my darling . . ."[19]

A month later, Louis heard from Professor Henderson that Memphis was hemorrhaging Bahá'ís because of the Great Migration (also called the Exodus) of black Southerners to the north and also because of army conscription, since the United States had entered World War I. On the other hand, there was steady enrollment; the professor said that new Bahá'ís who were "servants in aristocratic families" were "shaking Memphis mightily."[20]

By 1918, Louis and Louisa had spent their savings from the sale of their house, but Louisa received a surprise legacy of $1,000 when one of her elderly relatives died, and she passed it on to Louis for his teaching work. That was the way it worked out for them; every time they were really in dire straits financially, one of Louisa's long-lived relatives passed away and Louisa came into a pittance, just enough to meet their modest needs as they carried forth their joint mission.

The next year, with World War I at an end, mail was coming through from overseas, and the Bahá'ís received all the teaching Tablets from 'Abdu'l-Bahá, so they formally launched the Divine Plan at the 11th Annual Temple Unity Convention in New York City. Louis was a member of the Temple Unity board at the time and was very active in organizing and running the gathering.

Joseph Hannen described it this way: "The immense banquet hall of the McAlpin Hotel . . . on the 24th floor . . . has accommodations . . . for about 500 persons . . . It was overcrowded . . . (with) friends from all over the country, with some from foreign lands; people of various creeds and religions, of different races and nationalities, yet they all joined in this wonderful feast . . ." The Bahá'ís and their guests, including many of the clergymen who had welcomed 'Abdu'l-Bahá to the city, celebrated their unity with flowers, food, music, speeches, and prayers. Then they "passed into the audience room, where the first session of the congress was held and the first of the Great New Tablets unveiled . . ." after which a speaker disclosed its contents.

Joseph said, "The arrangements for the unveiling of the Tablets were exquisite. The inscribed originals had been beautifully framed in gold and blue frames, with appropriate designs in the Persian style. Silken curtains covered each in turn, in the center of the platform, and at the appropriate time these curtains were drawn aside by beautiful young girls, who then reverently stood aside while sweet music discoursed, and all held breath, as it were . . . Above the framed Tablets was the Greatest Name, and below were placed illuminated maps of several regions covered by each Tablet, giving to the eye a picture of the work to be done."[21]

Unfortunately there was also discord at the convention because Zia Bagdadi and others felt suspicious about the credibility of the above-mentioned speaker, and indeed he soon proved to be one of the nakazeen. Troubles like that, along with frequent recurrence of Bahá'ís thinking it would be creative and innovative to have racially segregated meetings to make the white inquirers "comfortable," were just a few of the complications Louis Gregory had to deal with. But deal with them he did, and he only became stronger in his faith and never weakened.

Soon afterward, Louis received a Tablet from 'Abdu'l-Bahá praising him for his travels before and after the Convention as well as his work at the Convention itself, serving "beyond thine own endurance." He added, "Convey on my behalf the utmost kindness . . ." to Roy Williams, and said of Louisa, "I never forget her." Louis had received another Tablet from the Master, previously, one that had been long-detained by wartime mail snarls, in which 'Abdu'l-Bahá praised his teaching trips and encouraged him to keep on: "Do not ask for one moment of rest. Strive by day and by night. If it is possible take thou a trip to the Southern States of the U.S. . . ."[22]

Such were Louis' marching orders, and he was following them before he even got them. Added to them were words from the Divine Plan itself, in which the Master likened Bahá'í traveling teachers to the Apostles of Christ, especially if they clung steadfastly to the unifying Covenant and journeyed in a spirit of detachment, shaking the dust from their feet as they left one place to bring fresh spirit to a new place. Gayle Morrison has written of Louis that from the time of his pilgrimage, "The power of the covenant pulsated within him. Its radiance illumined his face . . . until the last moment of his life, he . . . revealed in the essence of his being the effects of that added, indefinable, cosmic dimension of the Covenant."[23]

'Abdu'l-Bahá said that souls firm in the Covenant were luminous as candles, bright and life-giving as the sun, emanating light, revitalizing "all beings." And he described Louis as "luminous," "shining as a bright light," "pure gold."[24]

So, overflowing with enthusiasm and eagerness, Louis and Roy headed out again to continue their work, right into the maw of the season of race warfare that came to be known as the Red Summer of 1919. Over twenty race riots instigated by whites tore up U.S. cities. To name a few: May 10, Charleston, South Carolina; July 3, Bisbee, Arizona; July 7, Philadelphia, Pennsylvania; July 11, Longview,

Texas; July 19, Washington, DC; July 27, Chicago; August 21, New York; September 28, Omaha, Nebraska; October 1, Elaine, Arkansas (this riot was also called the Elaine Massacre).

In Jacksonville, Fla., a riot was narrowly averted, and Roy arrived there to find people "in a state of terror" so that he could do little. He went to southern Florida for a time, returned to Jacksonville, and gave quite a few talks. Because of his efforts, a group of people became Bahá'ís. In October of 1919, he wrote to Joseph Hannen from Montgomery, Alabama: ". . . On arriving here I found almost the replica of the state of affairs in Jax, Fla. (sic) of several weeks ago, that is, that a triple lynching had just taken place and the running out of the city of some of the best colored citizens and the threatening which continues at present, and the determination of many to leave . . . and go northward, makes the condition very turbulent and no gatherings are held . . ."[25]

Most of the riots lasted several days; deaths were almost all African American and numbered into the hundreds; the wounded numbered a lot more, and property damage by white vandals in black neighborhoods was immense. The Chicago riot (ironically in the North, not the Deep South) was judged the worst. It began when a seventeen-year-old black youth unknowingly swam into the so-called white part of Lake Michigan—this in an area of the United States with no Jim Crow laws per se. Whites hurled rocks at him, and he drowned before he could swim to shore. The resulting riot went on for two weeks; over five hundred people died. Over one thousand black families became homeless because whites set fire to their neighborhoods.

A mob dynamited the home of a Bahá'í couple, Mary Byron Clarke and her husband (his full name isn't known). The same mob made sure the Clarkes were arrested and thrown into jail. In the beginning of 1920, homes belonging to the Clarkes were again bombed; Mrs. Clarke was a real estate agent, and it's likely that the attackers wanted her to move out of her predominantly white neighborhood. They may or may not have known of the interracial

Bahá'í meetings that had often been held at the houses. The famous anti-lynching crusader Ida Wells offered her house for Bahá'í meetings, and several were held there. Louis Gregory's good friend, Dr. Zia Bagdadi, won wide respect and admiration because in the midst of the Chicago riots, he drove through mobs and flames to bring food and comfort to stranded black families. He was indeed a rare soul, not only because of his courage and lack of prejudice but for the fact that he was one of the few people Bahá'ís could meet who had actually been in the presence of Bahá'u'lláh.

13

Sir Happy

. . . Youth, flaming like the wild roses,
Singing like the lark over the plowed fields,
Flashing like a star out of the twilight;
Youth with its insupportable sweetness,
Its fierce necessity,
Its sharp desire;
Singing and singing . . .

—*Willa Cather*

Zia Mabsut Bagdadi was named by Bahá'u'lláh. His first name means *light* and his middle name means *happiness*. He was a buoyant, handsome, cherubic-looking man with a splendid mustache. As a child, when he was at Bahji* during the last year or so of the Prophet's life, he must have been even more buoyant and cherubic—sans mustache, of course.

"I had the great honor and privilege to see Bahá'u'lláh and sit at His feet many days and nights in this mansion," he recalled. "Here he used to hold my hand while walking to and fro in His large room, revealing Tablets, chanting the prayers with the most charming and melodious voice, while one of the attendants took them down. Here I saw Him teaching and blessing the pilgrims who came from all lands. On hot days He would take me with Him to the outer alcove of the Mansion where it was somewhat cooler. I would stand in a corner with folded arms, my eyes fixed on His incomparable counte-

---

* The place called *Bahji*, or *Delight*, was in the countryside, outside the walls of the prison-city.

nance, while the gentle breezes blew on His soft jet black hair which reached almost to the waist, flowing beneath the taj, like a crown, that covered His head and a part of His broad, full, high forehead.

"From His light-colored garments which were similar to those of all the ancient prophets, I had always inhaled the fragrance of the pure attar of roses. At times, He would spend half an hour in the alcove, and my eyes would remain fixed on His majestic face. But whenever He glanced at me with His brown, piercing, yet most affectionate eyes, then I had to turn mine away and look down at the floor.

". . . On my first visit to Him, when He inquired about my health, I replied in Arabic, 'Mabsut' (I am happy). He questioned, 'How is your father?' I answered, "Mabsut.' And, 'How is your mother? He asked. 'Mabsut,' was my reply. He laughed heartily and after that He always called me Mabsut Effendi."[1] (Mr. Happy or Sir Happy)

Zia's father, named an Apostle of Bahá'u'lláh, had ridden in the entourage of the heroine Táhirih when he was a youth alongside his own father,* who had been the personal representative in Baghdad of one of the two visionaries** who taught Shiite Muslims new interpretations of millennial prophecy and its fulfillment in the years leading up to 1844. While Táhirih was in Baghdad under observation by government authorities and awaiting word as to her fate, she stayed in the home of Zia's paternal grandfather for a time. Then she was sent back to Iran, and he and his son rode in her caravan across mountains and deserts. In fact, a spirit of fiery youth that turned thought and intent almost instantly to action characterized Zia, his father, and grandfather, and it was enhanced and made immortal by their hearts' connection to their faith.

Zia's father, Mustafa,† first met Bahá'u'lláh in Tehran, long before He formally announced His mission. He became a companion

---

* Shaykh Muhammad Shibl.

** Siyyid Kazím-i-Rashtí.

† Mirzá Muhammad Mustafáy-i-Baghdadí.

of Bahá'u'lláh's and followed Him into exile in Baghdad. Eventually, he became a leading Bahá'í there and was also an influential businessman, known as the "Merchant of Baghdad." Years later, after suffering persecution and imprisonment in Iraq, he went to Bahá'u'lláh in the prison-city, 'Akká, and asked if he could live near Him. Bahá'u'lláh sent him instead to Beirut, where he established an import-export business, so he could be of aid to Bahá'í travelers.

After Bahá'u'lláh's death, Mustafa continued to serve the Master devotedly; in 1899, he and Zia helped transport the remains of the Báb to their final resting spot on Mount Carmel. The casket had been hidden since 1850 in the town of Rayy, Iran. Over the years, it was transported in secret stages closer and closer to the Holy Land. Zia remembered that "the body of the great martyr, the Báb, was kept in our home before it was delivered to 'Abdu'l-Bahá in 'Akká by a company including my father and myself."[2]

Mustafa was a big, strapping gallant, a poet who eventually went blind yet remained radiant, often chanting his own verses in praise of the Master. He had three sons, all outstanding Bahá'ís. Zia's mother was also a large person, weighing 240 lbs., very heavy for a woman of her time and place. She was frequently ill with diabetes and other ailments. Zia recalled how the practice of hijab (veiling) circumscribed her life. When the family doctor came to attend her, he had to sit in an anteroom trying to make a diagnosis while Zia's father examined her in the sickroom, calling out her symptoms. In extreme situations, the doctor entered the room to take her pulse, but she had to wear gloves so as not to expose her hands and wrists to his eyes.

As a young man, Zia studied at the famous American University in Beirut and helped his father serve the Bahá'í pilgrims, often not a mere matter of providing hospitality: "Once I went to meet a Bahá'í pilgrim at the harbor of Beirut," Zia said. "I saw the poor man being dragged by two officers with guns and bayonets in hand. I inquired politely what was wrong and they told me that the man had a book in English from the Bahá'í literature. As I objected for dragging the man to jail (sic), they said, 'Very well, then you come with us too.' And they locked me up with him."[3]

No wonder Zia was tough, dauntless, and authentic. He learned from such experiences, and from his father and grandfather's examples, that he had nothing to lose by fearless presentation of himself and his views, and all the gifts of faith to gain. In fact, his paternal grandfather had originally learned about the Báb from a man who was just like that, one of the first followers of the Báb and the first martyr in His path.

Louis Gregory recalled in a letter to a friend, "Dr. Bagdadi . . . once suggested to me that an interracial party of Bahá'ís tour the South and call the attention of all the people to the fusing power of the Cause of God. He says that if we all get lynched it will make the Divine Cause spread faster and faster. In fact, he wants us to speed things up a bit." With his usual wry humor, Louis commented, "Well, there may be a difference of opinion about such a procedure . . ."[4]

But that was Zia Bagdadi; he must have had to rein himself in often so he could work compatibly with others! However, graced by his nearness to Bahá'u'lláh and the Master, he continued, despite the potentially withering effects of age and experience, to be Mr. Happy.

In 1909, Zia came to the United States to further his studies of medicine. He was an energetic member of the U.S. Bahá'í community and set up his residency in Chicago. He passionately supported racial amity, as we have already seen. He was a fervent worker for the construction of the first Bahá'í Temple of the Western world. And he edited the Persian section of *Star of the West* while also contributing richly to its English content. For several years, he wrote the Persian section by hand in his fine calligraphy, which was then photographed, reduced, and etched on zinc to make page-sized plates for printing.

During the Master's tour of North America, Zia was in His entourage and rendered Him some signal services. Like his father,

Zia was a gallant. Once, when 'Abdu'l-Bahá requested some candy for a child He was holding on His lap, Zia leaped down a flight of stairs to a refreshment table two steps at a time and leaped back up the same way, bearing sweets for the Master. But the story of Zia and the Persian rug is the famous one.

'Abdu'l-Bahá was at Lake Mohonk, a fabled resort in the mountains of the Hudson Valley in New York, at an annual peace conference. He had been the keynote speaker, and while preparing to take His leave, decided He wished to present a Persian rug to his host, Albert Smiley. The only problem was that His Persian rugs were in an apartment in New York City. It was night, and 'Abdu'l-Bahá was to leave at 10:00 the next morning. Mohonk was in horse and buggy country, so the trip to the city and back was longer than an overnight. Nevertheless, Zia volunteered to get the rug and return with it in time.

'Abdu'l-Bahá gave Zia the key to the apartment. Unfortunately, by the time Zia made his way to the train station it was 9:00 pm, and there were no passenger trains. But a freight train came chugging down the tracks, and Zia jumped aboard the caboose. The conductor objected, but when he saw on Zia's business card showing that Zia was a doctor, he let him remain on the train. Zia tactfully didn't mention Persian rugs.

It was 2:00 in the morning when Zia got to the apartment, awakening Grace Ober and her sister, who were staying there. He declined their offer of tea, selected a rug, sprinted to the station, managed to find a train, and was back in the mountains with an hour to spare. How could he reach Mohonk in an hour? He came upon a mailman in a horse-drawn conveyance, and the mailman agreed to take him.

As 'Abdu'l-Bahá stood shaking hands with Albert Smiley, saying good-bye, Zia raced into view, bearing the rug, which the Master received and handed to His host, who exclaimed, "Why, this is just what I have been seeking for many years! You see, we had a Persian rug just like this one, but it was burned in a fire and ever since my wife has been broken-hearted over it. This will surely make her very happy."[5]

Zia remained in the United States after the Master returned to the Middle East, but he was always among the Master's most trusted attendants—viewed by Him rather as a son of His household. Because of that, and also as an editor of *Star of the West,* he often received Tablets with especially delicate information to be disseminated among the Bahá'ís regarding the nakazeen. Zia was definitely someone who had seen their machinations close up and could help protect the Covenant.

For example, Dr. Amin Fareed, a good-looking and personable young man with every appearance of piety, had been in the Master's entourage in North America. He made himself much admired among many Bahá'ís but was actually a liar and a thief. He stole the Master's signet ring (the seal that He used to authenticate His Tablets) out of Phoebe Hearst's house in California, and he would tell people—with his hand out—that although 'Abdu'l-Bahá did not publicly accept money for His expenses, He actually needed it and would accept it privately. Some were gullible enough to give, and, of course, Fareed kept that money.

Marzieh Gail wrote, "Fareed's efforts to destroy the Master (who had seen to his education from childhood) make a page of triple darkness . . ." When the Master's long Western journeys came to an end and He returned to Haifa, He went into His wife's room and in that sanctum said brokenly, "Dr. Fareed has ground me down."[6] He then sent a Tablet to Zia Bagdadi saying that He'd forgiven Fareed four times during His travels, but He would not forgive him any more, and the Bahá'ís must be told.

The Master was very pleased, however, with the conduct of a certain young woman whose father* was the Master's attendant, detailed to Him by Bahá'u'lláh since the days when They had been

---

* Hassan Aqá Tabársí.

imprisoned together in the 'Akká barracks. Her name was Zeenat Khanum.

Zeenat grew up in the Master's house, and He said, "I have trained Zeenat Khanum, and having confidence in her, therefore, I sent her to America." He sent her to Montreal to marry Dr. Zia Bagdadi in the home of May and Sutherland Maxwell. It was another of the Master's matchmaking efforts, and he wanted it to take place at the Maxwell residence so that it would be the first Bahá'í wedding in Canada. The Master said He hoped Zeenat would "become the 'Zeenat' (adornment) of America."[7]

The marriage brought forth a daughter, mentioned as a newborn by Louis Gregory in the letter quoted earlier. Their home was a place of hospitality for many, including the noted Native-African American journalist, poet, playwright, teacher, and theater director Olivia Bush-Banks. In her deep identification with her Algonquin Indian roots as taught her by her uncle, who was a shaman, Bush-Banks did much to preserve snippets of Montauk language and customs; she also wrote of her experiences as an African American and was a contributor to and supporter of the Harlem Renaissance.

She wrote about Zia Bagdadi in *The Collected Works of Olivia Ward Bush-Banks,* mentioning his skill as an artist, describing a calligraphic rendering of the word Allah that he'd given to her, saying he was "a fine Persian Idealist who believed absolutely in Universal Brotherhood." She recalled his "strikingly beautiful" home in Chicago, his gracious wife, the luscious Persian cuisine, and the lovely chanting of sacred verses by the daughter of the house. She also noted his devotion to the Temple project (its construction was ongoing from 1912 into the 1950s), and included in the book her poetic tribute to "the Temple that is to be" honoring human oneness.[8]

Robert Abbott, publisher and editor of *The Defender,* was another outstanding African American befriended by Zia. The two met at Hull House when the Master spoke there, and their friendship dated from that time. They consulted and worked together on race amity projects in Chicago, and later the Guardian said Zia was Robert Abbott's spiritual father.

He also said Zia was "exemplary" in his "faith, audacity, unquestioning loyalty," and his "indefatigable exertions" were "unforgettable." These qualities imbued Zia's speech as well as his actions. After he died of a heart attack in Augusta, Georgia, in 1937, Bahá'ís at his memorial service in Chicago remembered his presentation on the Covenant given at the National Convention of 1919. "Although he had been ill for three days, he arose to astonishing heights and depths of understanding in this address . . . a dramatic appeal that was arresting and soul stirring . . ."[9]

His writing also had a spark. In a circular letter about teaching among African Americans in Chicago (he spearheaded much of it along with some remarkable co-workers), he noted that "only a few souls" were doing the race amity work—those "who believe that results come from backbones, not from wish-bones."[10]

In that letter, he mentioned the visit of two carloads of black business students from Memphis who came with Professor Henderson to visit the Temple and the Chicago Bahá'ís. The letter signified progress from earlier days when things were so divided and shaky that Chicago Bahá'í administrators advised against integrating the Sunday School, and a special committee existed to decide which whites were fit to be invited to attend meetings that included African Americans.

By the 1930s, integration among Bahá'ís was more the norm in Chicago, and Zia and his family moved to Florida to establish new Bahá'í groups in the Deep South and strengthen interracial bonds. When he couldn't get a medical license in Florida, he moved to Augusta, Georgia. He opened a practice and forged ahead to win his Bahá'í goals. He was in his fifties when his heart stopped, which was not an abnormal age for a man to die in that era, but his death seemed definitely premature to those who knew and loved his evergreen spirit and welcomed his joyous presence to buoy them. So vivid was his soul that we can almost feel him, still actively teaching among us.

14

Red Summer, Rough Ground

with Sadie and Mabry Oglesby, Agnes Parsons, Roy Williams

Red was the midnight; clang, crack and cry of death
and fury filled the air
and trembled underneath the stars when church spires
pointed silently to Thee . . .

—*W. E. B. DuBois*

To return to our litany of woes, which we left with Zia Bagdadi driving into the flames in Chicago: No place was safe for any African Americans and friends who ventured to help them during 1919's tragic season of race riots. Even if they were within doors at home, or riding a tram, whites went looking for people of color and dragged them out into the street. In most places, police refused to intervene, and black people fought their own battles, often against armed militia units, but in Bisbee, Arizona, police attacked the 10th U.S. Cavalry, an all-black unit in existence since 1866.

Causes of the riots varied. Some arose because of white accusations of rape and / or murder against black men, but in Norfolk, West Virginia, a white mob attacked a celebration welcoming black soldiers home from World War I. Six people were shot, and the police had to call in the navy and the marines to quell the brutality.

So, the season was called the Red Summer because of the blood and fire, but not only that. Some authorities and pundits accused Bolshevik agitators of involvement. The revolution in Russia had overthrown the czar, and the United States was in the midst of its first really bad Red Scare. People were sure that communists were invading America and would conquer it. They reasoned that African Americans would be easily won over to socialism—didn't they have plenty of reason to be disaffected? Weren't they already discontented? A *New York Times* headline read, "Reds Try to Stir Negroes to Revolt."[1]

Add this to the fact that communists were known as the only group (other than Bahá'í, a much smaller and more obscure portion of the population) that encouraged interracial marriage, and Louis and Louisa's problems multiplied. Not only could they be seen as beyond-the-bounds-of-propriety—perhaps they were rather fast and frequented the swinging Black and Tan jazz clubs that were becoming a trend?—they could be rumored to be communists.

The Master had "specifically disapproved" of "fanfare" about their marriage or "crusading on their part in the cause of intermarriage . . . They were simply to be a potent demonstration of the Bahá'í position on race."[2] They heeded this advice and also tried to be canny about where they chose to be seen together and where they took up residence together. They apparently did quite well, because at the end of his life Louis remarked that they had never been physically attacked during their forty-year marriage because of their different skin colors.

During this time, leftists agitated for the unionization of workers, and they had cause. Laborers worked under inhumane conditions. Black laborers bore the added post-traumatic stress of slavery and the ongoing inescapable fact of their skin color, which made it so hard for them to get beyond their past. Communist publications compared the Chicago and Washington riots to the situation in "Soviet Russia, a country in which dozens of racial and lingual types have settled their many differences and found a common meeting ground, a country which no longer oppresses colonies, a country from which the lynch rope is banished and which racial tolerance and peace now exist."[3]

Never mind that such claims, premature at best, soon turned out to be completely false (ask any Russian Jew). They were enough to attract many people desperate for justice. And whites were extremely scared by calls for action such as this one, quoted in the *Times*: "Negroes must form cotton workers' unions. Southern white capitalists know that the negroes can bring the white bourbon South to its knees. So go to it."[4]

Yes, the ground was rough, the going very tricky. In July, Louisa wrote from Green Acre, in Maine, to Joseph Hannen, "I heard only yesterday of the terrible riots. I remembered how 'Abdu'l-Bahá said there was danger of a race war but Bahá'ís could avert it . . . (Bahá'ís) would do well to consult colored believers at this crisis . . . as well as consulting with the leading Bahá'ís in general unless 'Abdu'l-Bahá can be reached. Hope you will excuse suggestions from me but times are so serious, experiments may prove disastrous if a wrong step is taken . . ."[5]

Around the same time, from Louisville, Kentucky, Louis reported to Joseph that a white Bahá'í named Emma Stott was all smiles as she helped his efforts, introducing him to ". . . people of wealth . . . among the social leaders of the city . . ." He added, "Fortunately I have never stood much in awe of wealth and high social standing, as human nature seems just about the same in that realm as on a dead level. But the humility of these dear souls did fill one with surprise . . . Our meeting lasted two and a half hours and they . . . are eager to get in touch with 'Abdu'l-Bahá . . ."[6]

He was more impressed that a pawnbroker in Louisville became a Bahá'í and closed his shop two days in a row to attend Bahá'í functions. He mentioned a new Bahá'í, an African-American woman, who "kept very busy helping Mrs. Stott to arrange meetings. It is very clever management to put the new souls to work . . ." He recalled how Joseph and Pauline got him working right away "in the early days, for which I can never be too grateful . . ."[7]

An interracial congregation at the "Apostolic Church or Pentecostal League" also impressed him. "In introducing me the minister expressed doubt that a lawyer could find anything to say to 'saints' . . . (and) they say they have no trouble over the unity of races as the Holy Spirit has united them. In this meeting for the first time I saw 'white folks' shout and Hallelujah! and cry 'Glory to God' at the top of their voices as 'cullered folks' are wont to do in camp meetings. I thought I knew you 'white folks' but now I see I am not onto all of your ways . . ."[8]

From Ashville, North Carolina, Louis wrote to Joseph: "In this time of world crisis I am trying by prayer and effort to prevent my thoughts from crystallizing around particular events, as I find that *I must be happy in order to do effectively the work to which I am directed.*" He enclosed a letter from a chief of police refuting the rumor (repeated by one of the Bahá'ís) that a "recent race riot was caused by an attack of a Negro on a white woman . . ." He concluded, "*Truth at some time must have a hearing, tho it seems a long time to those who wait.*"[9] (Italic emphases by the author.)

But he added that "to adopt the expedients of people around us is to give ourselves over to the devastating fire which now consumes the world. The times are indeed troublous and full of unrest . . . The Bahá'í teacher must maintain a state of happiness if he is to do his work effectively. And this seems possible only by constant prayer and, as far as one can, ceaseless activity. Otherwise, the well-authenticated reports of cruel injustices and crimes against defenseless peoples would entirely absorb the powers of concentration . . ."[10]

Louisa, writing to Joseph from Maine, seconded this, saying, "From what I hear it seems as if the race riots have brought well-meaning white people & colored people together. I understand there is a notice in the paper about white church ministers and workers inviting colored lawyers, doctors etc. to come to consult with them in regard to conditions. If they go on doing this & do it in each city we may hope for better conditions I feel sure."[11] It was that sort of impetus that brought Zia Bagdadi and Robert Abbott together in Chicago to work for improved interracial relations.

———

In August, Zia and Louis were asked to meet with the Bahá'í Temple Unity to discuss the riots in Chicago and Washington. They laid some of the blame on "the greed and schemes of certain white landlords," who thought they'd benefit by driving out African Americans. Louis well-knew that component of prejudice and persecution: as we recall, his step-grandfather was murdered by the Klu Klux Klan because he had the audacity to own a horse as well as a mule.

From Chicago, Louis went to Green Acre to be with Louisa, but he was back down south in the autumn. Arriving in Helena, Arkansas (also called Elaine) shortly after the riot there, he found people "in a state of grim pessimism and despair." They were small town folks, suspicious of any newcomer, white or black, even under normal circumstances. Nevertheless, Louis managed to give six public talks. Roy Williams noted, "'. . . the Message of the Covenant is the safest thing for this part of the country and is the cause of both the surety of mind and the surety of limb.'"[12]

Louisa, in the meantime, kept trying "to solve this problem of where to live when Louis is not in the South & it seems likely to get more & more difficult to find a suitable home at a reasonable price & we do not expect to live in Washington again. It does not suit my health. Louis & I ought to have a little home somewhere we can be together . . ."[13]

When she was in Atlantic City, Pauline Hannen came to visit her now and then and also gave Bahá'í presentations. Louisa lived on her small "income from home," which had been reduced during the war but that was temporary. She took her landlady to a Bahá'í meeting with a black family, having first told the landlady of their color, but admitted that she hadn't told the woman "of Louis's race just yet."[14]

Louis kept moving on, as did Roy Williams, and it became possible to discern certain victories. In May of 1920, Roy wrote to a friend in Boston who was dedicated to children's education, "There has been for some months past a real live assembly of both races in Atlanta, Georgia, and there are some children who have been very active in giving out the Message to both their school teachers and other children and also in establishing a correspondence that is very beautiful between themselves and other Bahai children in the north . . ."

He continued, "I am speaking to school children in every town and their shining faces make me very happy and they are very happy too when I speak and tell stories of 'Abdu'l-Bahá and they never forget them . . . Sometimes the Greatest Name both in Persian and English is written on the black-boards and explained to them and I have known it to stay on black-boards for nearly the entire year . . . the children would not let it be erased . . ."[15]

Of course lack of funds caused straitened circumstances for the two men, and they continued to hide their needs from the people they taught. Roy told Agnes Parsons, "Almost the first thing these folks want to know is the means of support of this Cause and its teachers." He said the question was "nearly always urgently made, because the condition of the people is entirely material." On hearing that Roy and Louis wouldn't accept reimbursement, "they seem mystified," Roy observed, "and wait to see if these things be true and to see if the teacher moves about with that independence which he claims . . ."[16]

Sometimes, also, the milieu in which they taught was particularly challenging. As the year of the Red Summer drew to a close, Louis wrote to Joseph from Pine Bluff, Arkansas, that he was to address a gathering of Catholics and have dinner with the priest. Apparently, he found that prospect a bit daunting, and a remarkable prayer flowed from him, born of experience and devotion:

I hope and pray that 'Abdu'l-Bahá will set His angels to guard my mouth, so that His Wisdom may speak through this moving dust.[17]

Louis and Roy, never still except when exhaustion claimed them, had found their métier, but the racial warfare disturbed them as it did many of their brothers and sisters. After the riots in Washington and Chicago, an outstanding black Bahá'í couple from Boston, Sadie and Mabry Oglesby, expressed their views in a letter to Harlan Ober, who, with his wife, Grace, had brought them into the Faith.

The Oglesbys became Bahá'ís in 1914 and were immediately active, expressive defenders and promoters of their new Cause. Mabry ran a real estate company, and Sadie was a home-maker. They had one child, an adopted daughter, Bertha Parvine. At first, Mabry, an eloquent speaker who had been a power in his labor union for years, was the bolder one of the couple. He served as a Bahá'í administrator in Boston, was frequently elected as delegate to the yearly Bahá'í National Convention in Illinois, and was appointed to Bahá'í national committees. But after Sadie met Shoghi Effendi in Haifa in 1924 and he exhorted her to be a leader, she plunged more assertively into the fray. The Guardian was impressed with her "pure faith, tender devotion and ardent zeal."[18]

Back in 1919, after the Red Summer, the Oglesbys wrote: "'. . . We believe that the Bahá'ís have a great opportunity as well as a great responsibility to bring this great life-giving information to the world. To this end we suggest the following . . . 1st. United prayers over a continued period . . . 2nd. Conference initiated by Bahá'ís calling together leaders of races, churches groups . . . We believe that the general unrest at this time properly handled can be used to stimulate great Bahá'í activities everywhere . . . To sit, to talk, to listen—there is no virtue in that. To rise, to act, to help—that is a Bahá'í life. Deeds are the standard.'"[19]

Harlan Ober heartily concurred, but the Bahá'í Temple Unity was slow to come up with an action plan, though they did feature

Louis Gregory as their public speaker during their national conventions of 1920 and 1921. But, as it happened, Sadie, Mabry, Harlan, and other Bahá'ís who agreed with them were right on target with the thinking of 'Abdu'l-Bahá.

The Master wrote to the Temple Unity, setting in motion a program for Bahá'í-sponsored Race Amity Conferences in the United States. He chose as the leader for this work a most unlikely candidate who had no experience as an organizer or activist, and had even impressed some of the African-American Bahá'ís as being rather pro-segregation: the Washington socialite Agnes Parsons.

15

The First Race Amity Conference

with Agnes Parsons, Louise Boyle and family,
Joseph Hannen, Lucy Diggs Slowe

So many gods,
So many creeds,
So many paths that wind and wind
While just the art of being kind
is all this sad world needs . . .
—*Emma Wheeler Wilcox*

It wasn't only Bahá'ís familiar with Agnes Parsons' timidly moderate stance regarding race relations who were mystified by her assignment to spearhead the race amity program. She herself was mystified. She intellectually embraced the concept of oneness, but in practice, she couldn't really countenance what was called "social equality" in that day, though she tried. She was philanthropic and kind, always a help to Louis Gregory, Roy Williams, and others in their travels. She was beloved as a matriarch of the Washington Bahá'ís. They respected her stature as an outstanding hostess to the Master in Washington in 1912 and at her summer residence in Dublin, New Hampshire—yet they were mystified. The only one who didn't seem mystified was Louis Gregory.

He felt the Master had chosen wisely. Agnes (everyone called her Mrs. Parsons, but she wanted to be called by her first name) had wealth and social status combined with purity of heart: a rare combination, for didn't Christ say that it's harder for a rich man to get into heaven than it is for a camel to get through the eye of a needle? But how praiseworthy is the camel that can get through!

Agnes' social status was something she had in common with many she wanted to attract to the conference, and her purity of intent was an attraction for all. Her discernment calls to mind Robert Turner. As Phoebe Hearst's butler, he saw the wealthy Mrs. Hearst's affections get alienated from the Bahá'í Faith when Dr. Fareed and other nakazeen were terribly nice to her because of her money and used various schemes to try to defraud her of it. Robert, however, as we saw in an earlier chapter, remained firm in his beliefs, refusing "to let the world throw dust in his eyes."

Agnes didn't let her own wealth and influence throw dust in her eyes, either, yet she was able to use her wealth, as well as her purity and steadfastness of faith, to pull together diverse people of power in an event meant to be love-producing, unifying and elevating, not a political forum leading to squabbles, schisms, and ego-battles. Louis felt that he himself, as an African American of no particular worldly position in that time of strife, might appear opportunistic if he took the lead. But no one could question Agnes' motives: what did she have to gain by organizing a race amity conference?

During the misery over the Pythian Temple meetings, he'd come to know Agnes well. A few of his letters betray frustration with her extreme prudence and caution, but tolerance and empathy prevailed, and he always counseled his more impatient coworkers to give her time. After the first Race Amity Conference, which finally occurred in 1921, he and Agnes would do crucial work together.

But the main thing with Louis was that 'Abdu'l-Bahá had selected Mrs. Parsons to lead the way, and 'Abdu'l-Bahá wanted that amity conference. Therefore, he, Louis, was at Mrs. Parsons' service. But initially he limited his involvement. The main reason was his commitment to his travels in the Deep South. Also, he preferred active adventure over manipulating conferences and other administrative affairs. Not only that, he didn't want to disappoint 'Abdu'l-Bahá with a conference that failed; and he feared it might fail in the current climate, the aftermath of the Red Summer, which was lasting much longer than just one summer.

Agnes received her marching orders from the Master during her 1920 pilgrimage. She'd had a long association with Him, beginning with her first pilgrimage in 1910, which she embarked upon after Lua Getsinger told her about the Bahá'í Faith. She wanted to see if Lua's description of 'Abdu'l-Bahá was "real."[1] She was curious, hopeful, and quite dubious. When the Master kept her waiting in an anteroom before meeting her for the first time, her doubts increased. She was also annoyed. No one kept Agnes waiting.

She was the daughter of Brigadier General William Bedford Royall, who could just as well have been called *The Virginian*. Despite his Southern roots, he was a renowned Union Army officer and then became a famous Indian fighter. He was the first employer of "Buffalo Bill" Cody, who would, in his dotage, become a star of "Wild West" shows. The general wielded saber, rifle, and a Colt 45 in dirty fighting on the frontier in the European-American struggle to wrest land from the Native Americans—who had never thought of "owning" land in the first place. He got severely wounded in the process. But Agnes grew up sheltered in the wealthy world of her mother, Elizabeth Coxe Howell Royall. At least that's how it appeared to her friends. If she'd ever camped out at a frontier army post, brushing flies off her hardtack, nothing about her gave it away.

She was forty-nine when she made her first pilgrimage. She was married to Jeffrey Arthur Parsons, director of the rare prints division at the Library of Congress, and she was the mother of three children. The oldest, a son, was tragically disabled. The middle child, a daughter, had died at the age of one year. The youngest, another son, still very small, was at home. In short, Agnes Parsons, daughter of a doyenne of Southern society and a brigadier general, was a woman of years, long-suffering, and position. She had no time, after a long sea voyage made on a hope and a prayer, to wait for someone who might or might not be a holy man.

But when she was finally ushered into 'Abdu'l-Bahá's presence, she didn't think about any of that because she immediately collapsed at his feet. When she regained consciousness, He was helping her rise. She later said it seemed a beam of light passed from His eyes into hers, just before she fainted. Although she'd prayed for an omen to convince her that the Master was "real," apparently the beam of light wasn't enough, for the next day, at the Shrine of Bahá'u'lláh, she asked for another sign. A wind blew up and shook the shrubbery, and a small bird flew into Agnes' bodice and nestled there for a moment before taking wing again. Even after that, she requested a third sign. The next day, when she asked 'Abdu'l-Bahá, "Are you Christ?" she thought she saw Him disappear into a column of fire that crackled like a burning tree trunk. She never received a yes or no to her question, but then, she never asked again.

As we can see, Agnes didn't do things halfway. During that first pilgrimage she resolved to build a house for 'Abdu'l-Bahá to stay in when He came to the United States—she had no doubt that He'd arrive. She told the Bahá'ís He'd promised to stay in her house, so they weren't surprised when He received them in Washington, ensconced in the reception hall of the Georgian style mansion she'd built him. Juliet Thompson said it was "all white, its ceilings and paneled white walls carved delicately with white garlands; a platform set in front of the fireplace was always banked high with crimson roses, while at the many windows hung curtains of transparent, luminous green silk."[2] On His second and third visit to Washington, the Master didn't stay at Agnes' house, choosing simpler quarters, but He still made use of her reception area, treating her with the utmost gratitude and courtesy while firmly refusing her offers of financial assistance. He told her to give the money to charity.

When He paid His fabled visit to her country home in Dublin, New Hampshire, He didn't stay at her family home there because it was on the mountain; He stayed in an inn, at a lower altitude, where it was warmer at night.

One of His counsels to Agnes was to give talks on the theme of "oneness." When she said she couldn't give talks, he told her to memorize Bahá'í writings on oneness and quote them from the platform. She evolved a graceful, elegant technique. In April, 1919, at the National Convention where the Master's Tablets of the Divine Plan were all received, the speaker, after reading the Tablet for the Southern States, said 'Abdu'l-Bahá had told him "prominent believers of the south like . . . Mr. Hannen, Mrs. Parsons, Mr. Gregory" and others must consult on effective promulgation of unity.[3]

Then, during her second pilgrimage in the spring of 1920, as Agnes sat at supper with the Master and about twenty other people in His house in Haifa, He told her, "I want you to arrange a convention in Washington for amity between the colored and the white." She reported, "I thought I would like to go through the floor, because I did not feel I could do it." The Master went on, "You must have people to help you."[4] And that was the extent of His directions. During the rest of the pilgrimage, Agnes gained confidence that she *could* accomplish the Master's wishes, even without further discussion of them, but she had absolutely no idea of *how* to go about it.

When she returned to Washington, she initially found her social circle uninterested. However, plenty of advice was available from people who did sympathize. (Such is the way of advice.) Since some of it was good advice, she took it. The counsel that impressed her most came from Moses E. Clapp, a former U.S. Senator from Minnesota. He was a white man known for his activism on behalf of the NAACP and Native Americans, and he also cofounded the law school at Trinity College in Connecticut. Louise Boyle, a white Washington Bahá'í who was also very supportive of interracial causes, invited him to tea and had Agnes come over, too.

Louise was a second-generation Bahá'í, which was fairly uncommon in those early days. She was a liberal and progressive thinker, having studied with Maria Montessori, the great Italian pioneer of early-childhood education. Louise's mother, Charlotte Dixon, had become a Bahá'í in Chicago and was regarded as the spiritual mother of the whole Bahá'í community of Washington, DC. She established the Bahá'í group there after moving home to nearby Maryland. Her father and siblings also became Bahá'ís. Her brother, James Brittingham, was the first Bahá'í in New York City, and his wife, Isabella Brittingham, was the great teacher called by the Master "our Bahá'í-maker" and named a Disciple of 'Abdu'l-Bahá.[5]

With Louise, Mrs. Parsons and Senator Clapp talked for about two hours. He suggested getting a group of women together to help organize the Race Amity Conference and adopting a "conventional" approach: avoiding argument and being positive. Mrs. Parsons' expressed it, "Do not make a protest about anything. Lift the whole matter up to the spiritual realm and work for the creation of sentiment."[6]

Sentiment is generally defined as refined or tender emotion: feelings welling from the heart. 'Abdu'l-Bahá explained that racism is rooted in the heart and can only be annihilated by a transformation of the heart. We have seen this occur in Pauline Hannen. We've seen it occur in the heart of Mírzá Abu'l-Faḍl when he finally accepted the oneness of God and all religion, and, thus, the oneness of the human race: no castes, no outcasts because of color, nationality, or any other spurious reason. Louis Gregory had to allow his heart to be transformed, and he had to constantly nurture and renew that transformation so that he could consistently practice patience, not only with his fellow believers but with the Jim Crow world. Then he had to push himself to reach the extra step—the giant step—to forgiveness. But he did allow himself a certain kind of impatience.

As Gayle Morrison notes in *To Move the World*, ". . . he was tired of empty rhetoric." He wrote to Agnes Parsons, "Nothing short of a change of hearts will do. Unless the speakers are able to make the power of love felt, the occasion will lose its chief value.' He felt that interracial conferences that focused on economics and politics could not in the end effect the unity and integration required for true change. He said, "There are many, many souls throughout the South today who are working and longing for a better day. But without the Light of Abha (Bahá'u'lláh) their efforts seem infantile and helpless. Even some members of the state inter-racial committee, earnest, thoughtful hard-working men, have voiced to me despair.

If the Washington inter-racial congress is along these conventional lines I fear it will like the others, be fruitless. But if it be aflame with the fire of the divine Love, the hearts will be powerfully influenced and the effect will be great in all the years to come."[7]

After the 1919–20 season of race warfare, many people were indeed bitter, disappointed with themselves and with each other. New organizations responded to the tragedies but avoided the root problem: segregation, the fact that black and white people didn't mix, didn't know each other, and didn't meet on equal terms to form loving bonds with each other. The Commission on Interracial Cooperation, for example, created in Atlanta in 1919, aided black schools, fought certain injustices in court, and opposed white supremacist organizations, but didn't directly counter segregation. And many black people were attracted to the flamboyant, separatist, back-to-Africa movement led by Marcus Garvey instead of to integrated movements.

The Race Amity conference would present the Bahá'í point of view that human oneness, the foundation of world peace and integration, goes beyond black and white to embrace all ethnicities, nations, and religions, and that it can't exist without gender equality. So Louis Gregory, in his address to the conference, would stress "the elevation of the station of women, who must no longer be confined to a limited life but be everywhere recognized as the equal and helpmeet of man."[8] Moving as he did in a circle that included the indomitable women of his own family, including his wife, Louisa, his friends Coralie Cook and Pauline Hannen, and many more, he was deeply cognizant of women's worth.

He also knew that 'Abdu'l-Bahá's message of race amity was holistic, emphasizing the need for *all* people equally to cast out *all* forms of prejudice. 'Abdu'l-Bahá said when he spoke with a group of socialists in Chicago, "It is prejudice that destroys the world. Every enmity, war, misunderstanding and suffering that has ever occurred in this world has been from either religious, patriotic, racial or political prejudice . . ."[9] Only by freeing themselves of prejudice can humans shake off the disease of war and settle into an ever-evolving peace.

Religious prejudice may be the most lethal prejudice of all. In one of his last speeches in New York, 'Abdu'l-Bahá said, ". . . In all religious teachings of the past the human world has been presented as divided into two parts: one known as the People of the Book of God, or the pure tree, and the other the people of infidelity and error, the evil tree . . . one part of humanity the recipients of divine mercy, and the other the object of the wrath of their Creator. Bahá'u'lláh removed this by proclaiming the oneness of humanity . . . He has submerged all mankind in the sea of divine generosity. Some are asleep, they need to be awakened. Some are ailing, they need to be healed. Some are immature as children; they need to be trained. But all are recipients of the bounty and bestowal of God."[10]

Sadly, Joseph Hannen, one of the greatest champions of oneness, a true race amity supporter and a devoted worker for harmonious international East-West relations, was not present to help with arrangements for the Race Amity Conference or grace it with his gentle presence. He died a little over a year before it took place.

On January 27, 1920, Joseph was struck by a vehicle (Roy Williams said it was a postal truck) and run over as he left the Washington post office, where he went every day because he was communications-central for the Orient-Occident Committee, Bahá'ís in far-flung localities, and Bahá'í travelers, especially those such as Louis and Roy who were working in the South.

In his voluminous correspondence, in which he took care of incredible amounts of detail, Joseph never struck a cold or distant note. In December of 1919, he told Roy, "You will . . . be interested in knowing that, last night, at our . . . Unity Feast, we had the unexpected and very great pleasure of meeting your Mother and your

Grandmother. It was our first meeting with the former. . . . Both of these ladies were made to feel very much at home, and decidedly lionized by the quite distinguished audience present, because they were the parent and grandparent of Roy Williams! You would have been glad, I am sure, and happy because of the tribute to your worth and their charm of manner. Juliet Thompson, of New York City, was there, with a social leader from Washington, Mrs. Noel, one of her patrons; also M. and Mme. Dreyfus-Barney . . ."[11]

Roy was in Cleveland, Ohio, working in a steel mill, and Louis was in Dallas, Texas, when an ambulance took the stricken Joseph to a hospital. The hospital sent him home. Someone forwarded to all the proper recipients the last packets of letters Joseph had picked up at the post office. Sixty years later, Roy wept when he recalled receiving his correspondence—the envelopes were spattered with Joseph's blood.

Roy had hoped to see Joseph soon in Washington and to have a reunion with other friends there and with his family. But at the end of January, the Bahá'ís were gathered at Joseph's bedside, praying ceaselessly for him. He was able to converse with people; he "seemed quite unconcerned over his condition." But his strength was ebbing, and on the morning of February 1, he died.

They laid Joseph to rest in a coffin in his house, and "both colored and white" gathered, bringing "flowers until not only was the bier hidden from view by these floral offerings, but the chimney piece and various articles of furniture in the room were likewise smothered with blossoms, while the entire house was filled with fragrance . . ."[12]

An interracial group of pallbearers carried Joseph's remains from the house. He was buried near Pauline's mother, Amalie Knobloch, in Prospect Hill Cemetery.

Louis regarded Joseph as his spiritual father while, to Joseph, Louis was both son and senior; he once said he felt Louis was like a great, patriarchal forest tree sprung from his (Joseph's) spiritual root. Only a month before he was killed, Joseph wrote to Louis,

"'Let me say that you can never ask anything of me that I shall not gladly grant. For you have done much for me if I may have been privileged to be of some little importance in your life. Often, when I wonder what I have done in the Bahai (sic) work that is worth while, my thoughts go to you and your splendid work, and I feel that it is quite worth living for, to have helped to guide such a noble soul to the Kingdom.'"[13] This is one of the few letters that Louis preserved, over long years, until the end of his life.

Louis was traveling when Joseph died and while Agnes Parsons was on her fateful pilgrimage. He wrote sympathetically to Pauline and to Joseph's mother from Monroe, Louisiana, of "thinking, thinking, thinking, as so often I do about him (Joseph) . . . His labor was ceaseless, his service to the friends of God and all humanity universal in its nature and his forgetfulness of self characteristic of the martyrs . . ."[14]

'Abdu'l-Bahá, deeply grieved, wrote that Joseph was a "pure and spotless soul," always serving, always unselfish, "an illumined soul, merciful, kingly, lordly," and said to Pauline, "This calamity is overwhelming and painful . . . A thousand times alas, that like unto a star, that glorious personage disappeared from the horizon of the immensity of space. He has arisen from a horizon that knows no setting and has . . . hastened to the Center of Light . . ." He assured her that she would find Joseph "in the divine realm." The separation was only temporary; the two would "enjoy eternal companionship . . ."[15]

Pauline was brokenhearted, yet she maintained her spirit. A delicately floral-spiced spirit like hers doesn't break—it just wafts on.

———

Neither Pauline nor anyone else wanted mourning for Joseph to delay the Race Amity Convention. Agnes Parsons seemed hesitant, so, on Louis' behalf, Louisa Gregory "collected together some ideas expressed in" his "daily communications to her and submitted the facts" to Agnes "as reasons for holding the inter-racial congress as soon as possible."

Louis also wrote to Agnes himself, saying that 'Abdu'l-Bahá's comments "about the general condition makes me feel that even our efforts cannot avert the calamity, but that the Bahá'ís would regret it if disaster struck before they had their conference. He felt the conference would be effective only if "its spiritual vibration, God willing, should go throughout America," and that Bahá'ís in America and the world over should say special prayers simultaneously with the gathering.

Louis had encountered "racial conferences being held throughout the South," but he believed that "despite them . . . both sides are to some extent secretly organizing and perhaps arming for a conflict that seems irrepressible. If the Washington congress is only like the others, it, too, will have no results."

He offered to come and help if the committee required it although to him the pressing needs of his Southern teaching came first. On a cheerier note (he always included something bright) he mentioned a new African-American Bahá'í in Chattanooga, Tennessee, known as "the oracle of the fourth ward" for putting up "a daily bulletin at his (grocery) store . . . with a wholesome motto. It is widely read, often reprinted by the daily press . . . Now his bulletin often contains the Bahá'í teachings . . ."[15]

Finally, a committee formed by Agnes set the conference date for May 19–21, 1921, in Washington. Once it was in motion, they found themselves with eager helpers. Some of Agnes' aristocratic lady friends budged from their apathy to lend their patronage; Howard University assisted, supplying its stunning choir and other resources; a senator and two congressmen signed on as speakers. In a brilliant public relations campaign by Martha Root, schools, churches, and other venues throughout the city received nineteen thousand programs / invitations, and there was plenty of press coverage. But of course, there was no predicting the outcome. How many people would attend? And would the speakers really promote harmony and develop an atmosphere of fellowship?

To everyone's joy, two thousand people showed up on the night of May 19 in the First Congregational Church. And when the Bahá'í chairman, having set the tone with his opening remarks, introduced a senator who was to speak, the senator said to him, "I was going to make a political speech, but would it be better for me to try to follow what you have said in a harmonious way?"[16] Of course, the chairman encouraged that. And they were off!

Each subsequent session drew up to 1,500 people, and programs included songs by the Howard University singers and recitations of work by black poets. Audiences included the entire student body of the M Street Junior High, which was Washington, DC's first middle school for African-American children and "the first (school) of its kind in the United States."[17] The students were led by the school's founder, the African-American educator Lucy Diggs Slowe, a former student of Coralie and George Cook's, who, among her many other achievements, was the first Dean of Women at Howard University.

Coralie would write of Lucy Slowe that she'd evinced "the Divine Law of the Oneness of Mankind" and did not leave anyone behind as she struggled to reach her goals, "sharing as she gained, lifting up as she climbed; blazing trails for any ambitious girl to follow."[18]

Alain Locke, a Bahá'í since 1918, was a session chairman; he was the famous African-American philosopher and writer—the first black Rhodes Scholar in history—who would soon become the guiding light of the Harlem Renaissance. And Louis was one of the speakers, as we have seen.

To sum up, the first Race Amity Convention was prestigious, heart-touching, and harmonious: in short, a success. An African-American member of the audience, M. F. Harris, wrote a letter to Agnes Parsons in which he said, "I attended every session, day and night . . . Many times throughout the meetings did with much effort restrain my tears. My heart leaped and throbbed and many times almost burst within my breast. I am a colored man . . . My race as a whole, I believe, is quite ready to welcome the glad day when all will be brothers . . . The trouble is nearly unilateral. God give us the day."[19]

'Abdu'l-Bahá was pleased with it and with His protégé, Agnes Parsons. He wrote, "'Praised be to God that the Race Convention was carried through in utmost perfection.'" He told Agnes, "'Really thou art a Bahá'í . . . Thank thou God that thou art the first person who established a Race Convention . . .'"[20]

Louis Gregory was encouraged by the gathering, attributing to its influence the increase in race unity efforts by churches and other groups that he noticed during subsequent travels.

Another Race Amity Convention quickly followed. It was organized by a small group of Bahá'ís (two women, to be exact), in Springfield, Massachusetts, who asked Roy Williams to help them. After that, a progression of Race Amity events, patterned after the first, went on for some years. The U.S. Bahá'ís as a whole began tuning into and becoming leaders in what today's National Race Amity Center at Wheelock College in Boston has dubbed "America's other tradition."[21]

Needless to say, there were serious setbacks and agonizing stops and starts. The course of true love, as Shakespeare said, never does run smooth. On the whole, it was a long and painful process for Agnes Parsons, to whom everyone looked for support and wisdom, knowing the "implicit confidence" placed in her by 'Abdu'l-Bahá. Despite this confidence and His unstinting praise, it was several years until she could actually say "'all consciousness of racial differences had left her heart and mind when she attended the Amity Conference at Rochester, NY . . .'" in around 1926.[22]

As for Louis, because of his unquestionable capabilities he inevitably became heavily involved in Bahá'í administration, management, and coordination, and this included serving on the National Race Amity Committee during almost all the years of its existence, speaking at conventions and helping to organize them, and instituting race amity events at Green Acre Bahá'í School. For the rest of his life, in fact, in many ways, no matter what Bahá'í administrators and communities did or failed to do, Louis Gregory *was* race amity.

16

Pure Gold

There is a future for the man of peace . . .
—*Psalms 37:37*

The organizers of the second Race Amity Convention—Olive Krez, Grace Decker, and Roy Williams—had been besieged by doubts during their planning. Roy was especially dubious; he'd been given much of the responsibility for the conference and felt "entirely inadequate," he said, "to deal with this matter personally." So they cabled 'Abdu'l-Bahá, asking if they should go ahead, and He cabled back on November 7, 1921, "Approved; God confirms." At which Roy said, ". . . it is evident it is the Will of God . . . We should quickly rally and make this a great success and a victory."[1]

A little more than two weeks later, on November 28, 1921, the Master died. There had been no lingering illness and no warning. The Bahá'ís were completely unprepared, and completely grief-stricken. However, upheld by His cable, Olive, Grace, and Roy opened the doors to their amity conference on December 5 in the Central High School Auditorium in Springfield, Mass.

The mayor had helped the Bahá'ís secure the high school free of charge and was among the speakers, who included influential local clergymen. Despite such civic support, one of the Bahá'í speakers panicked right before the event, afraid they'd have a flop, an empty house, but Roy Williams said, "Here is the cablegram from 'Abdu'l-Bahá . . . Let us go to the auditorium and see what God confirms."[2] They found an interracial audience of nearly one thousand people, and the next night the audience was even larger. The conference was indeed a success and a victory.

However, it was almost two years before the Bahá'ís had another amity convention. The Master's death definitely disrupted their functioning on all levels, personal and communal. Each had felt a personal connection with Him, whether they'd met Him face-to-face or not. Now most of them felt lost, devastated, brokenhearted, and, worse, unsure of their new leadership. Even the new leader himself, the Master's grandson, Shoghi Effendi, designated in His Will and Testament as the Guardian, was sick with shock and grief. Distress was so profound that a large, bold headline on the front page of the *Star of the West* advised mourners not to injure themselves or commit suicide. The fact that the Guardian was a round-faced youth in his early twenties—a student in England at Oxford University, called back to Haifa by his grandfather's death—didn't help reassure people.

In this maelstrom, Louis Gregory's psychic balance was a real blessing. He was in the midst of a year-long, coast-to-coast teaching trip when he received the news of the Master's passing. Already known for bringing the presence of the Master with him wherever he went, he simply continued to do so, for he didn't feel abandoned because 'Abdu'l-Bahá was no longer on earth, and he was comforted by his abiding trust in the Master's love and by the appointment of the Guardian. He was also unshakably convinced of the urgency of the teaching mandate laid down for the Bahá'ís in the Master's Tablets of the Divine Plan, and of the mission given him personally by the Master. Steadfastly following his chosen path, he saw constant growth and progress among the Bahá'ís, so he brought good news with him from town to town and optimistically reported the victories he observed to the national Bahá'í secretariat and his many other correspondents, cheering saddened hearts in all places.

"Please convey my dearest love, the Master's Love, to your household and to all the dear friends," he wrote to Edith Chapman, and it was a sentiment he often repeated, for he felt deeply assured that "No one was ever disappointed who in sincerity of heart appealed to Him; and His power is not lessened because of His ascent from this mortal plane."[3]

Louis certainly lived his grandmother Mary Bacot's philosophy that it's better to be lighthearted than brokenhearted, and we know that he did it with an indomitable will, to solace his own soul as well as for the benefit of others. His natural good humor helped him along. He always found something to amuse him, something to learn, someone to admire. In Butte, Montana, where there was "a very small Bahá'í group," he was happy to see that the husband of one them was "the very image of Abraham Lincoln," and he spent time with this friend, descending deep into the earth to see the mine where he worked and learn the risky process of mining.[4]

'Abdu'l-Bahá had written of Louis to a Bahá'í woman in Texas, "That pure soul has a heart like unto transparent water. He is like unto pure gold. That is why he is acceptable in any market and is current in every country."[5]

Indeed he had golden successes on his coast-to-coast trip. At the National Bahá'í Convention in 1922, the first one after the death of the Master, Miriam Haney hailed his journey as "a very remarkable spiritual work . . . It is the first time that any teacher so marvelously illumined as Mr. Gregory has been able to reach thousands and thousands of people, colored and white . . ."[6]

Since she was addressing the convention, Miriam called him "Mr. Gregory," but Louis preferred that his friends call him by his first name because, he said, it made him feel young. At that time he was in his forties, which is youngish nowadays, but in the 1920s, one could be considered over-the-hill at forty. He lived to be much older, and the maintenance of youthful feeling and appearance was always important to him. He and Louisa gardened when they could and were early adherents of so-called health foods; he regularly did eye exercises so he could avoid wearing glasses, especially while giving talks, and he also did daily calisthenics.

But probably his most sustaining activity was race amity work, and that meant he constantly overcame rage, hate, and hostility with love. The rage, hate, and hostility was in his challengers; he had long since relinquished the easy sinking of self in the intoxicating, addictive energy of anger for the self-elevation of keeping a prayerful heart concerned with the greater good. Nevertheless, grief and pain weighed him down, sometimes to the point of agony, whenever he encountered enmity.

He mourned not only for the oppressed but for the oppressors. In his *Racial Amity* manuscript, he referred several times to the psychosis of oppression. He felt, "Racial amity is a bounty (that releases oppressor and oppressed) from a psychosis that generally goes with a denial of rights which should be the common heritage of the free, thus sowing the seeds of conflict present or future." He saw that each oppressed group "develops a psychosis similar to that of the others and each may think that his sore spot is unique." The terms he used in that era, the 1940s, for the oppressed groups were Jews, Indians, Orientals, Mountain Whites, and Negroes. He said, "The knowledge of each others' trials may strengthen their combined efforts to overcome." He was sure that, inevitably, oppression would cease, for humanity's reality and future was as one people. He wrote:

> Earth and air, fire and water, the stars in their courses, the high tide of destiny and the Will of divine Providence are all arrayed against the forces of oppression.[7]

"We Shall Overcome" became the mantra of the Civil Rights Movement in the 1960s, but long before that, Louis wrote, "The work of overcoming is full of hope, and adds immeasurably to the joy of life. The efforts are highly inspirational to the youth in life's green spring; and to the aged, they disclose the fountain of perpetual youth, another name for divine happiness."[8]

Charles Wragg, a white Bahá'í from Australia who toured the South with Louis in 1933, observed Louis' response to the "abrasive reactions" they sometimes received—not only from whites, but sometimes from African Americans as well. ". . . On such occasions . . . his facial expressions were most illuminative, changing quickly from one of great anguish to a completely passive inward-look, as though searching his innermost being and beyond for a solution to a change in the relationship. This was his invariable reaction to difficulties and problems. I never saw him show anger, impatience or resentment, always it seemed to be an expression of earnest self-searching and seeking for guidance from beyond self-identity. I imagine that this was a reason why 'Abdu'l-Bahá said of him: 'He is pure gold.'"[9]

———•———

For her part, Louisa also didn't repine, and though she was ten years older than Louis with multiple aches and pains, she was surprisingly sprightly. The Master had told her more than once that He always remembered her, never forgot her, and she firmly believed that His spirit would always sustain her. As noted before, she also believed He'd saved her life, so her life was His and she must use it to serve Him. In 1922, the year following the first Race Amity Conference, she began her epic years of journeying and teaching in Europe. She had traveled and lived in various regions of the United States and decided she could be of more use, spend less money, and feel more at home, in Europe, especially since Jim Crow, endemic racism, and the fact that interracial marriage was either not recognized or illegal in twenty-five states (mostly in the South), made traveling with Louis problematic, to say the least.

His travels without her were dangerous enough. Her long letters to Louis from various parts of the Balkans attest to her constant concern about him as well as to her joy in her own adventures. Her concern grew especially after he acquired an automobile and drove it through the Deep South. She worried that he'd be subject to violence from racists unhappy with a black man tooling freely along at the driver's wheel of a car, especially if he had white passengers (unless of course he was wearing a chauffeur's cap, which, needless to say, Louis was not doing). However, he found his car a lot more convenient and comfortable than Jim Crow railroad and bus seats, and public transport schedules.

She also questioned his driving ability—but circumspectly. She was very careful, not wanting to offend him. Her references to it in letters are masterpieces of tact. In later years, legends abounded at Green Acre, especially among the younger generation, of his driving prowess and determination; a tree near the dining hall was inevitably pointed out as bearing scars from a certain effort of his to reverse gears.

One trip Louisa did make with Louis was to Haiti in 1937, in response to the Guardian's call for the establishment of Bahá'í groups in all the American republics. No car was involved. And Louisa's fluency in French was especially helpful in Haiti. Both found that because of their status as distinguished foreigners, they had easy access to the great and the good (so to speak). They were politely received, but their message was largely ignored until it was, eventually, opposed.

Among the poor, people were more open to the message. And in visiting shanty neighborhoods, Louis and Louisa said they'd "never before" seen "such extremes of poverty and distress." This from a man who spent his early years in a shanty tenement on Blackbird Lane in Charleston. Louis went on, "Louise says that in the Balkans it is not unusual to see people literally in rags. But such I have never seen anywhere in the U.S. altho' at various times I have passed through all of them save the Dakotas."

Neither of the Gregorys spoke Creole, a definite drawback when working with the less educated Haitians. They befriended "a youth who can neither read nor write, but who can make himself understood in four languages" and began a study class with a "group of humble but very sincere souls."[10]

They had a three-month visa. They soon realized that three months wasn't nearly enough time to do all that was needed. They also found that the genteel and gracious government officials they met were watching "their every movement," because "a high ecclesiastical authority had warned the country that strangers would come to them, ostensibly to teach religion, but secretly to spread radical propaganda, with a view to sedition and revolution . . ." When they decided to hold a public meeting, they couldn't get police permission. Nevertheless, Louis felt that "obstacles to the spread of truth almost invariably increase its vogue in future." He and Louisa left Haiti when their visa expired, planning to return in autumn's cooler weather, but instead they were drawn back to the southern United States and the Balkans because of the crying needs there. Happily, Ruth and Ellsworth Blackwell, also an interracial couple, successfully took up the Bahá'í work in Haiti in 1939.[11]

Louis and Louisa necessarily returned to their pattern of working separately. They missed each other and worried about each other's health, as indicated by the advice to keep warm, eat well, and such, that they exchanged in their abundant letters back and forth, but they also described their adventures in places as disparate as Tuskegee, Alabama, and Belgrade, Yugoslavia. They pitied each other's loneliness; however, as Louis said, "Tho' I miss her (Louisa) greatly, the defense against loneliness is keeping busy."[12]

Louisa was the first Bahá'í pioneer* in Bulgaria and in the part of the Balkans then known as Yugoslavia. Martha Root pointed out in a letter to her that she was also the first Bahá'í teacher to arrive in Hungary and Austria since the Master visited those countries in 1913. The struggling souls nurtured by her, who comprised the

---

* A Bahá'í pioneer is one who voluntarily leaves home to settle in a city or other area where there are no Bahá'ís, or where the Bahá'í community needs special help, for the sole purpose of serving and teaching the Faith. The pioneer is self-sustaining unless there are no employment opportunities at her post, in which case the pioneer may receive a stipend from family or her home Bahá'í community.

first Bahá'í groups in those countries, were lost in the devastation of World War II and the Stalinist repression that followed, but they were the spiritual foundation of today's Bahá'í community in that highly sensitive region.

A slice of the Gregorys' life from that time:

1928: Louis, who is busy with NSA duties and a series of Race Amity conventions, as well as his tireless teaching travels, writes proudly from New York City in a letter to Pauline Hannen that Louisa "sailed for Europe last week. She will join Martha Root at Prague and afterwards go to the Balkans to teach. So this family is all in action . . ."[13]

A letter from Louisa written in Sofia, Bulgaria, in May, 1928, gives a sense of the atmosphere. She's started a study class with an enthusiastic Jewish doctor at the apartment of a lady who's been a helpful translator for both her and Martha Root. "We began the class last Sunday evening in an attic room with a ceiling so low I could almost touch it. I have thought of the Apostles of Christ who gathered in an upper room and am encouraged to hope that such a humble beginning may later have great results, otherwise the world would despise such a centre of Bahá'í activity . . ."[14] (Since Louisa's so tiny, one realizes it must be a very low ceiling!)

People coming to Louisa's meetings include an Esperantist who first heard of Bahá'í from a Japanese Bahá'í Esperantist; Theosophists; a professor of Romance Languages; and an editor of a newspaper named after Tolstoy. She can't find a lot of very responsive people because everyone is "distracted" by recent earthquakes. Sofia, built on rocky ground, she says, is relatively safe, but most of the town of Plovdiv is shattered. "Of course," she reports, "the shocks were rather alarming here when the whole room rocked like a boat. Even at Sofia to this day, the Professor told us last evening, many people sleep in their clothes for fear an earthquake shock should come in the night . . ." The big quake struck at 9:30 pm on April 28 and "half the population passed (the night) in the streets or in their gardens. I went to bed at 11:20 pm and slept all night on the 6th floor (the highest) of this hotel . . . and knew nothing of another slight shock at one a.m. . . ."[15] Although Louisa often suffers from insomnia and jangled nerves, clearly she also possesses the famous British sangfroid.

1929: Louisa has been basing herself in Sofia, at Shoghi Effendi's request, when she is not in the United States with Louis helping him recover from the demands of his long road trips, his administrative duties, and his teaching / organizing stints at Green Acre Bahá'í School. It's been "a dreadful winter" in Sofia, "so much intensely cold weather . . . so much illness . . . epidemics of scarlatina and flu, etc. . . ." But she gave a talk that was well-advertised on the front page of *Mir* (Peace) newspaper along with an article on recent events in Persia and Turkey that the editor wrote from information Louisa gave him using news Shoghi Effendi sent her. Despite the cold, she had an audience that included "a nice Bulgarian priest," she said, and (using one of Louis' words) "a disputatious professor . . ."[16]

Now she's going to Haifa on her second pilgrimage, and she'll meet Shoghi Effendi. She'll go "overland by the Orient express as far as Tripoli except for 10 minutes crossing the Bosphorus into Asia and from Tripoli by autobus to Beirut and Haifa—2 ½ hrs. to Beirut and three hours later Beirut to Haifa in three hours. The connection with Tripoli and Haifa is twice a week and the Fabre Line boat only goes once a month . . ."[17]

Thus we have an idea of travel complications in 1929. But, as of this writing, we can't describe her second pilgrimage or give her impressions of the Guardian because no relevant papers have come to light. Louis, who might have been more inclined to write an article about the experience, asked the Guardian for his consent to accompany Louisa, but the Guardian said he'd have to postpone it because he was too much needed in the United States.

By June, Louis is writing from Green Acre to Edith Chapman, "And now with my dear wife I am united once more after nearly a year of separation and we are happy in our little nook in the heart of the woods . . . we are getting some rest. The good wife seems greatly improved by her services abroad and especially by her visit to Akka and Haifa . . ."[18]

He adds that he hopes to go to Haifa one day with Professor Henderson, with whom he recently worked in Nashville. Louis reinvigorated the professor's faith, and a group of Henderson Business College students became Bahá'ís and wrote to Shoghi Effendi.

1930: Louis writes to Edith in June from a cottage he and Louisa have rented in Portsmouth, New Hampshire, that he'd gotten off the road "toward the end of May so very tired out that I fear something would have snapped had I continued a week more. Have been doing little work save routine . . . and with sleep, regularity of habits and a wise selection of foods seem to be nearly back to normalcy . . . It is really very pleasant to be at home once more and Louise, my wife, is doing all in her power to make me comfortable. She is truly one of the jewels of Bahá'u'lláh . . ."[19]

Louisa has learned to cook, at least enough to help Louis (whose digestion and nerves are aging along with the rest of him) recover from catch-as-catch-can meals taken at off-schedule hours; from long jaunts and jostles in loud, unsanitary, mainly unsprung moving vehicles (in which he often had to ride in the back, of course); and from the inevitable tension of tricky racial situations and speaking to large, varied audiences.

Louisa and Louis shared a certain quality with many of the people they befriended: their means were extremely constricted, and they had to practice great frugality. But that had long since become second nature to both of them. However, as previously said, also weighing on them was the difficulty of finding places where they could live together without the pressures of extreme racism. Louisa usually was the one to search out residences and make sure her landlords knew and accepted the fact that her husband was African-American.

Eventually they found refuge in Portsmouth, New Hampshire, where there was a colony of black intelligentsia. In 1933, Louis wrote, "I was greatly blessed . . . by the presence of my angel wife, Louise, who had a four months 'furlough' from her teaching campaign in Bulgaria. That Balkan region is . . . still as seething caldron of unrest . . . We were supremely happy together in our quaint old home near the sea. It is our hope that our enforced separation along the line of service to the Divine Case will mercifully bring to us eternal reunion in the worlds of God."[20]

Portsmouth is near Green Acre Bahá'í School. A cabin at Green Acre became their haven as they aged, although the school couldn't always be wholly a haven because Louis in particular was often hard at work there as a teacher or committee member.

During their travels and at Green Acre, Louis and Louisa had the privilege (and sometimes the test!) of working alongside stellar fellow Bahá'ís including Grace and Harlan Ober, Horace Holley, Dorothy Baker, Martha Root, Marion Jack, May Maxwell, Anna Kunz, Doris and Willard McKay, Matthew Bullock, Elsie Austin, Sadie and Mabry Oglesby, Ellsworth and Ruth Blackwell. Louis also served as an administrator and planner with many such strong personalities. A proof of their greatness is that despite inevitable conflicts, and the anger and hurt feelings that went with them, the shining strong ones of the Bahá'í community worked together in ever-evolving unity, with humor, grace, and love.

The Gregorys also wrote frequently to Shoghi Effendi, reporting their news, and in turn they received constant, warm guidance, as well as praise and gratitude in his replies. Active pioneering teachers such as Louis and Louisa kept the Guardian going, for he really was, because of internecine disloyalty and the persecution dogging the Middle Eastern Bahá'ís, a man of constant sorrows.

As the years wound on, Louis had the joy of seeing new African-American Bahá'ís rise to prominence in the community—but he was aware that not enough African Americans joined the community. This concerned Shoghi Effendi, too. Through his correspondent, Sadie Oglesby, he sent a message to African-American Bahá'ís:

> "... It is incumbent upon the Negro believers to rise above this great test which the attitude of some of their White brethren may present. They must ... accept the Cause of Bahá'u'lláh for the sake of the Cause, love it, and cling to it, teach it, and fight for it as their own Cause, forgetful of the shortcomings of others. Any other attitude is unworthy of their faith ...
>
> "The whole race question in America is a national one and of great importance ... The Negro friends must not waste their precious opportunity to serve the Faith, in these momentous days, by dwelling on the admitted shortcomings of the white friends. They must arise to serve and teach, confident of the future in which we know these barriers will have once and for all been overcome.
>
> "... The more Negroes who become Bahá'ís, the greater the leaven will be within their own race working for harmony and friendship between these two bodies of American citizens: the white and the colored."[21]

That essentially sums up the work and belief of Louis Gregory and the vision and counsels given him by 'Abdu'l-Bahá. He was true to his mandate to his final breath. During his last years, as his physical strength declined, he enjoyed greeting visitors at his cabin, from the greatest to the humblest, and serving cookies he and Louisa had made. Both he and Louisa particularly enjoyed visits from youth. He immersed himself in the study of biblical prophecies and how they were being fulfilled, and he shared his discoveries with guests from his seat at his huge desk in his study. His own Bible, currently archived at Green Acre, is annotated with his graceful, precise handwriting. He always remained eagerly capable of original insights, discerning intellectual and spiritual quest, and deep discussion.

He passed away at Green Acre on July 30, 1951, and Louisa died on May 20, 1956. Long ago, 'Abdu'l-Bahá had written to Louisa, "O thou revered wife of his honor, Gregory. Do thou consider what a bounty God hath bestowed upon thee in giving thee a husband like Mr. Gregory who is the essence of the love of God and is a symbol of guidance . . ."[22]

Louisa was always cognizant of the truth of the Master's estimation of Louis. All who knew her also knew her great love and respect for Louis, and her consistent concern and care for him. Yet she had no false submission to domestic duty; just as her search for faith had been independent, so was her service to her faith once she found it.

But she was lonely after Louis died; fortunately, she had good ties with his family, the Noisettes, and went to live among them. In the several years that she survived her husband, she took consolation in the message Shoghi Effendi telegrammed when Louis died: "'Profoundly deplore grievous loss of dearly beloved, noble-minded, golden-hearted Louis Gregory, pride and example to the Negro adherents of the Faith. Keenly feel loss of one so loved, admired and trusted by 'Abdu'l-Bahá. Deserves rank of first Hand of the Cause of his race. Rising Bahá'í generation in African continent will glory in his memory and emulate his example . . .'"[23]

Now husband and wife rest side-by-side. Their graves in Mount Pleasant Cemetery in Eliot, Maine, near Green Acre, are kept in a state of fresh, flowering beauty. Bahá'ís and friends of all ages, hues and nationalities, each with a story, a song, a language of his or her own, often pay them special visits, gathering around them in one shining circle.

17

Heritage: Doris and Willard McKay

with Howard and Mabel Ives, Dorothy Baker, Grace
and Harlan Ober, Louis Gregory, May Maxwell,
Martha Root, George Henderson, and others

. . . And you shall flames within the deep explore;
Or scoop the stream phosphoric as you stand,
And the cold flames shall flash along your hand;
When, lost in wonder, you shall walk and gaze
On weeds that sparkle, and on waves that blaze.
—George Crabbe

Crossing the Color Line

The slender young woman in the photo tilts the wide parasol
jauntily over her shoulder, and its white-striped radius makes a
sunflower background for her rather wry, heart-shaped face under
her cloche hat. It's 1923, and she's twenty-nine-year-old Doris Hen-
rietta Hill, teacher and artist, fiancée of Willard Judd McKay, who
is a geologist, agronomist, and hard-toiling farmer. She'll soon take
up residence at Emerald Hill, his family fruit farm in Geneva, New
York. Her teaching career will go on hold, for married women aren't
hired to teach in public schools, or, indeed, for many jobs at all.

She doesn't mind. Art—the charm of color, texture, and form—
is everything to her. She and Willard share "an almost pagan excitement" about nature and wildflowers. And the farm is a treasure.
Around July, the view from Emerald Hill is "a row of black tartan
cherry trees" still retaining "some stray fruit . . ." the crops of

string beans and corn "checkering the fields; the acres of apples and pears, fenced in by arbor vitae or spruce hedges . . . acquiring size and color." In springtime, the orchards are a mass of blossoms, and huge lilac bushes are in flower. There are fifty or sixty acres of orchards, and the slope of the hill runs for three miles to blue Seneca Lake.[1]

There's nothing Doris and Willard like better than sharing Emerald Hill with friends. An Emerald Hill guestbook—a slim school exercise book of the type Doris always uses for diaries and such—tells of one of their "announcement parties" and is illustrated by Doris' affectionate pen and ink caricatures. Willard's sister, Marguerite, writes, "Nothing was too good for this party—Doris and I . . . scrubbed, papered and painted two rooms and a ceiling that all might be fresh . . . We also planted violets, trillia (sic) and bloodroots in our wild garden and flower seeds in our tame garden . . . "

The party is such a success that others follow, so that eventually a guest comments, "Announcement party number three! I hope there are more!" It seems the only reason Doris and Willard forgo further announcement festivities is that they actually get married. But they don't stop celebrating; the champagne keeps flowing.

Doris' 1924 diary records card parties—mah jong, hearts, bridge—and skiing parties; ice cream and cake parties; playing anagrams; baking cakes; making fudge; cooking hamburgers for seventeen guests, and concert-going. She and Willard also spend long winter evenings among their piles of books and periodicals discussing theosophy, psychoanalysis, and the like, getting so "wound-up" they can't sleep.

Yet, there's more to their union than joie de vivre. A friend of Willard's hitchhikes 240 miles to "investigate the bride" and writes in the guestbook, "Here dwells Love, permanent, unchanging, miraculous. Thus it will ever be and I'm glad to have glimpsed it."

As their honeymoon year draws to a close, a new philosophy beguiles them. In November, 1924, Doris jots in her journal,

"Tonight we went to Doc Heist to study Bahaism—with the Collisons included. We spent a pleasant evening but did not get so very far with the Bahá'ís." A week later: "Went to the Collisons for Ba Ha . . ."[2]

Albert Heist, an osteopath with a reputation as a healer, and his wife, Lucy, are Christians, but he's curious about other religions and philosophies. When he reads in the paper that Howard Colby Ives will be giving a public talk on the Bahá'í Faith, he invites Howard to his office to discuss it. Howard visits the office, accompanied by his wife, Mabel. Doc Heist afterwards invites friends to his home to read an introductory book, *Bahá'u'lláh and the New Era*.

Rex (Reginald) and Mary Collison are atheists. Rex directs the agronomy department at Cornell University and works on the New York Experimental Farm, next to Emerald Hill. The Heists and Collisons are older than the McKays, and the newlyweds feel flattered to be included in the group, though Doris acts blasé, telling Willard, "I'm going to find out all about this Bahá'í thing and when I'm through I'm going to throw it away like a sucked orange."

Everyone seems to feel that way, for discussion rambles. However, they stumble across a phrase that stays with Doris: "Service is prayer." It inspires Doris to comment, as she and Willard stroll up Emerald Hill on an Indian Summer day, "Everything seems so heavenly the way it is, but in our lives we have no service and we have no prayer . . . So, if service is prayer . . . perhaps we should invite your mother and sisters to move out here with us." This is the answer to an unspoken desire of Willard's.

Soon Willard's mother, "dignified and erudite . . . in her wheelchair . . ." moves in, along with two of his sisters, Marguerite and Christine. The farmhouse now boasts a baby grand piano so Willard can play his beloved classics, and a book room with a "wide planked floor . . . painted orange with dark blue borders"—Doris' love of color and her penchant for painting everything making itself known.

Around the same time, the McKays go to a baked bean supper at the Collisons' to meet the Ives'. Howard is spare, a bit stooped, deep-eyed, with bushy white hair and brows accenting his lined, melancholic face. Mabel is blue-eyed with dark curly hair and a merry expression. Doris feels they are obviously *personages*, yet everyone is at ease with them. Sitting in a semicircle before the fireplace, Doris, Willard, and five friends listen to Mabel present the Bahá'í principles "in a strong, confident voice," and arrive at what Doris will describe as "the concept of oneness—a concept to be loved as a reality, for itself." Doris feels that with a "flash of illumination" she and the others accept "the integration of our ideas and of our world."

Then Howard tells them about Bahá'u'lláh, elevating oneness to a divine level. (Howard's eloquent response to the Master is immortally preserved in his memoir of search and discovery, *Portals to Freedom*, first published in 1937.) Bombarded with questions, Howard prays silently "with open palms and head thrown back." When he rises and gives the answers, his questioners' defenses melt. Doris later reports, "I believed. We all believed." She feels as if "a painting, obscured by dust," has been "restored to the artist's original colors." She has a final question for Howard: "How does one pray?" Without a word, Howard hands Doris his own, well-worn prayer book.

In her bedroom at the farm, Doris marvels that she's now convinced of "an Essence . . . a knowing and responsive ENTITY" dwelling in "the world of spirit." She's sure that Howard "addressed this Being" so he could give inspired answers to the group's questions. So it follows "that we too could pray, establishing a kinship with this Power, with Bahá'u'lláh as an intermediary."

However, she's "miserable . . ." She hears "Howard's voice . . . 'Mankind is one! All prejudices must be abandoned!'" Doris has "a couple of prejudices—one for race, and one for nationality" that are "like a cinder" in her "spiritual eye." She knows she must pray to be cleansed of her prejudices "simply because it's the way to get *in*."

As a teenager in Rochester, New York, Doris lived on Caledonia Avenue, where whites occupied the east side and people of color the west; the two camps didn't acknowledge one another's existence. "Any exchange of looks would have been considered an affront." This was the so-called Color Line, alive and flourishing as it did in many parts of the north—and upstate New York is far, far from the Deep South. "The prejudices on each side were leaden," Doris later recalled, "like the walls of a casket."

Willard, on the other hand, has always been "lead resistant, a neutrino of the spirit . . . a born crusader against that social barrier." As a student at Cornell University, he roomed with the only African American in the dormitory. While teaching at the University of Texas, where segregation was law, he proudly told people about his former roommate and championed equality. He got fired. That's why he was back on the farm.

Thus we see Willard sleeping the sleep of the just while Doris lights a candle, opens Howard's prayer book, and, in what is perhaps the first prayer of her adult life, begs God to eliminate her prejudices. Then she manages to sleep. In the morning she wakes up feeling "free, unsullied," her consciousness cleansed "pure as clear air."[3] Not only that, but she's discovered prayer, which will be, from then on, her lodestone. And her natural love of people has expanded so that she's eager to share home, food, and spirit with everyone, no matter their color, class, or culture. She's thirty years old, and she stands at the threshold of a new life.

"Fear Not!"

Doris was born on September 29, 1894, in Lindley, NY, to Henry Franklin Hill and Adaline Burr Hill. While pregnant, her mother had a vision of an angel saying, "Fear not!" It was good advice. At four months, Doris lay motionless in her cradle, apparently dead of pneumonia. Townspeople gathered in church, praying for "Brother

Hill's baby." Meanwhile, a neighbor named Mrs. Riffle slipped a teaspoonful of whiskey into Doris' mouth, and the baby "came back to life." As a teen-ager, Doris questioned whether it was the prayers or the whiskey that saved her.

At four, Doris told her mother she was going to go live with a rowdy neighboring family—Mrs. Riffle's?—so she could "kick and yell" as much as she pleased. Of course she had to stay home, where she was meant to be a model of moral virtue. Her father kept the town general store and was a superintendent of the Methodist Episcopal Church. He was an unusual storekeeper. He knew Greek and Hebrew and had two chief passions: his library, which was a gem of antiquity at the heart of his house, and the night sky—astronomy. Doris' mother led the church choir. There were prayer meetings, church services, Sunday School. Yet, as an only and cherished child, Doris enjoyed tremendous freedom in a string of five playrooms on the top floor of her house and in the halcyon outdoors. She often played in solitary splendor because her mother was picky about her companions.

She noticed the word "poor" when she was five years old, and her mother used it to describe the washerwoman. Doris realized that she herself was rich with her "black and white checked dress with its red buttons and red silk collar," the fires glowing in her hearths, and all her playthings. Her parents insisted that they were not rich, but Doris knew the truth: compared to the washerwoman and many others that she saw in her little town, she *was* rich, and she was grateful for it.

Then, suddenly, she became poor. When she was ten, her father's store failed, and the family moved to Rochester. She later said her mother had been a dressmaker; perhaps Adaline took up that trade after the store went out of business. At any rate, the family managed to stay afloat. Doris was fifteen when her mother informed her that her "moral apprenticeship" was over, and she didn't think Doris "would go to the bad."

A talisman for Doris at that time was a book of Persian poems. It had been a gift to her father, and, since Doris was "in love with it," he gave it to her. Doris recalled, "The book went with me through High School, Teachers College, and Art School . . . I grew . . . with my perceptions widened and colored by . . . Omar Khayyam, Hafiz, and Jal'u'din Rumi. I drew illustrations in the margins. I wore the cover off the book." (She would later draw and paint illustrations on the pages of other books, including her beloved copy of *Prayers and Meditations of Bahá'u'lláh*.) The Persian poetry book accompanied her everywhere throughout her life.[4]

Unfortunately, we have no information on formative influences in Willard's childhood and youth. He was born in Geneva, NY, in 1890, and no doubt grew up at Emerald Hill, accustomed to chores, surrounded by his siblings—at least one brother and three sisters that we know of—all of them under the watchful eye of parents who must have been hardworking and orderly. His mother was well-read, and it would appear that his father also respected a good education. Willard won a scholarship to Cornell University. After graduation, in 1912, he went to teach geology at the University of Texas. We know what happened there. When he returned to Geneva, he studied agriculture at Cornell and then began managing Emerald Hill.[5]

Blossoming

Now Willard and Doris are Bahá'ís, and they bloom in the attention showered on them by Howard and Mabel Ives; Grace Ober and her husband, Harlan; Louis Gregory; and others who, having met 'Abdu'l-Bahá, shed on all they meet what Doris calls "stardust." It isn't common for a group to enroll all at once as Bahá'ís, and the Geneva group gets larger when Willard's mother joins along with Marguerite and Christine. This is a nice bump for the small U.S. Bahá'í population, and Bahá'ís constantly visit the farm to teach the new wonder children.

"It seems as if you must be interested in all we do and think here although why I can't imagine," Doris writes to Mabel Ives. "It seems as if I ought to send you letters from home as I do the rest of the family." Indeed, the Ives become an extra set of parents to the McKays, and Doris and Willard embrace new activities and insights with no time to miss their former champagne and card-party lifestyle. Doris rejoices in "the experience . . . of reading *The Book of Ighan*** (sic) . . . I am being miserly, trying not to read too fast because, after all, one can only read it once for the first time."[6]

Slowly, Doris gains sensitivity to "the 'real' people inside others" and loses her fear of "what the others would think," her need for self-protection "through self-concealment." But she's acutely fearful en route in the Ives' car to gather with the Bahá'ís of Buffalo, NY, and it's not just because of Howard's driving, though that is indeed exciting. She feels like the proverbial country mouse as she enters Grace and Harlan Obers' well-appointed home on an affluent city street. At least she has her new hat, bought to fortify her self-image, "a large blue scoop lined with lavender-shirred silk." She later recalled, "This hat and I went to this meeting and listened to everything."

Two connecting rooms are lined with Bahá'ís; Doris and the Geneva group file past them "close together in defensive formation" to find seats. After scriptural readings, guests are invited to speak. "A slim young woman with smiling gray eyes, her pallor and luminosity set off by a wine colored velvet dress . . . tells a simple story to remind" her listeners that "all are children of one God." Her radiance and eloquence stun Doris. Asked to make a few remarks herself, she can merely rise, utter, "I am speechless!" and sit back down. Later, the young woman walks down the two rows of people with her hands stretched out to Doris, clasps both of Doris' hands, looks (past the hat) into her eyes and says, "You are the one."

---

* The Kitáb-i-Íqán, or The Book of Certitude, by Bahá'u'lláh.

Thus begins Doris' enduring friendship with Dorothy Beecher Baker. The young Dorothy just happened to accompany her grandmother to the Obers' house that night. Although Doris is struck by Dorothy's magnetism and inner grandeur, she also senses that Dorothy is somewhat childlike, fragile, and vulnerable.

She soon learns more about Dorothy from Dorothy's grandmother, Ellen Beecher—known to the Bahá'ís as Mother Beecher. In 1912, Ellen took thirteen-year-old Dorothy to see 'Abdu'l-Bahá, and He later told her that Dorothy was His daughter and she must train her for Him. That's Ellen's lifelong challenge: Dorothy resists. Dorothy just wanted to live an ordinary life, first as popular prep school girl, then as a bubbly schoolteacher, and now as a middle-class wife and mother, playing golf and going to PTA meetings. Yet her brilliance, gifts, calling, and destiny demand extraordinary deeds. Ellen, now in her late eighties, has been patient, and must school herself hard to remain patient. She's white-haired, tiny, just about always wrapped in a white shawl, and she brings a small cane chair with her wherever she goes. And she never stops going. Town to town, teaching tour upon teaching tour. Sometimes she makes a long visit, as when she spends two winters instructing the Bahá'ís of Geneva.[7]

On March 21, 1929, the first Naw-Rúz (New Year) celebration for the Geneva Bahá'ís, Doris feels her self-consciousness fade further when Grace Ober comes to the farm to prepare a feast. Grace, a tall, angular, emotive woman with a singularly animated face, creates the Master's Pilaf, a dish to feed a multitude, taught to her by the cook who accompanied 'Abdu'l-Bahá during His North American travels. On a huge brass tray she's brought with her, she mounds cinnamon-fragrant, baked, buttered rice; shredded chicken, chopped nuts, olives, and other goodies; and she adorns all of it with carrots and dates. Grace is an artist, and she loves to use her design skills on her pilafs. As she serves, she quotes 'Abdu'l-Bahá: "Food prepared with love is healing for the body, the mind and the spirit."

Doris soon learns that the Master's Pilaf—with variations, for it is a moveable feast—is a regular feature of Bahá'í hospitality. 'Abdu'l-Bahá Himself prepared and served it at times. May Maxwell and Louis Gregory are also pilaf experts, and it becomes part of Doris' cooking repertoire.

Doris continues to lose her self-consciousness as she observes how her Bahá'í teachers have no fear of simply being themselves, and when Louis Gregory comes to visit, Doris is happy to rejoice in her new freedom from prejudice and get to know him, her first African-American friend. Of course, she's afraid of doing or saying something offensive. She's awed by his height, and even more by his radiance and his aura of genuine inner oneness, his wholeness and balance. Like his fellow veteran Bahá'ís, he takes a nurturing interest in the new Bahá'ís of Geneva, so, finding Doris sitting before the fire in the dining room, he sits down with her and asks how they're all doing.

"I want to talk to you about this, Louis," Doris says. "There's one of us who doesn't seem to be quite as on fire as the rest of us. She's not quite as loving and she doesn't want to work as hard as the rest of us. What would you do in a case like that?"

Louis jumps up from his chair, snaps his fingers and leaves the room.

Doris would later explain, "I was backbiting. I was so virtuous about it. Just wanted a little advice. Louis' advice was 'shut up,' although of course he was too elegant to put it that way." She added that his action, if observed by someone deaf to the conversation, would have simply looked as if he'd forgotten something. But the lesson had the power to make her blush even when she was in her eighties.

Later in the day, she encounters Louis again when, not seeing him as she crosses a dimly lit room, she almost steps on him as he lies prostrate in prayer on a Turkish carpet. He rises "with agility and grace," smiles, and says, "There's a little of the oriental in me, I think." He doesn't, then or ever, refer to their "first little talk."

"Louis was so good and so witty," Doris later reminisced. "He had a certain spice. I don't think people realize the depth of humor in the man."[8]

———

Doris and Willard's receptivity, enthusiasm, and articulateness immediately put them in the forefront of national as well as local Bahá'í activity. They work with the National Teaching Committee, do public relations writing for the Bahá'ís, and help create study outlines for Bahá'í books—Willard is particularly interested in the harmony of science and religion. The 1929 National Bahá'í Convention in Wilmette, IL, is especially memorable for them. Willard is charmed by the simplicity and purity of Louis Bourgeois, architect of the to-be-built Mother Temple of the West, which at this point is merely Foundation Hall, an edifice that looks, Doris thinks, like a "cheese box." But Doris worries over Dorothy Baker.

Doris is a bit older than Dorothy, and now she steps into the role of "the listening ear, the counseling friend." Watching Dorothy stand by a doorway of Foundation Hall during an intense convention session, she sees Dorothy seem to sway, and she gets up and goes to her. Dorothy asks if Doris will take a walk with her. Dorothy sobs heartbrokenly as they walk, beating herself up with self-reproaches for struggling against her destiny as a public persona. When she does give talks on the Bahá'í Faith, she feels her "spirit explode into particles of light" and words come to her "that sometimes make people weep." Yet she buries herself in civic, secular activities, afraid of the toll her potential immersion in her religion might take on her family—and on herself. But resistance isn't benefiting her: it's making her ill.

Doris listens and silently prays. Returning to the vicinity of the Hall, they settle in a little oasis "in the structural wilderness of columns and beams . . ." There's a small round table covered by a gold and black cloth, a vase of pink roses, a bench softened by a Persian carpet. A young African-American couple is praying in the nook, and Dorothy and Doris sit and listen, "Dorothy wrapped . . . in the spirit of worship."

At last Doris looks at Dorothy and sees an "inner light" shining in her face—she'll never again see Dorothy's face without that light. Later, Dorothy writes to her, "And now may I tell you something? . . . you have given me unbounded strength! What you did I do not exactly know. The few minutes at the shrine will never be forgotten. How my throat ached, and when I looked up I saw you looking at me so serenely and oh, so sweetly . . . But what those moments at the shrine taught me cannot be put into words. I think my heart was laid at the Master's feet there . . ."[9]

Soon Doris' quietude of listening, loving, and praying must embrace a new dimension. Mabel Ives arrives in Geneva and gives Doris and Willard a new task. Mabel was appointed to organize a Race Amity Conference in Rochester on March 7, 1929, but she doesn't have time—the MacKays will have to do it.

Pioneering Oneness

With the 1921 Race Amity Conference in Washington, DC, held at 'Abdu'l-Bahá's behest, the Bahá'ís presented diversity as a blessing and oneness as a principle and way of life, the basis of world peace, and they received overwhelmingly positive responses. Three subsequent conventions were also well-attended and much-appreciated. Then plans for and actualizations of further amity meetings lagged until 1927, when the Bahá'ís launched a new series of Race Amity Conferences.

So it is that, soon after the start of 1929, Doris and Willard take the interurban trolley into Rochester to meet their helpers, Elizabeth Brooks and Constance Rodman, so they can organize the gathering. They only have a week to do it! All four are white and inexperienced at conference-giving. Elizabeth—tall, broad-faced, middle-aged, with a ready smile—will be so affected by the work that she'll soon devote her life "to the friends over the (color) line," renting a house in the African-American part of Rochester, supporting herself "by taking in roomers."

The four traverse the city in cold, slushy weather, visiting churches, offices, and homes to speak with "guardedly polite" African Americans (Doris' description) who judge them "with keen intuitive senses that necessity" has developed. Evenings, they pray in Constance's parlor. Doris and Willard sleep there "behind a pale blue curtain." A few days later, Doris has a severe cold and, more, she admits, a case of "cold feet." She is to chair the conference. She's never chaired anything in her life.

On the evening of March 8, she, Willard, and Louis Gregory take five African-American friends out to dinner in downtown Rochester. All are tense at first—an integrated meal anywhere, but especially in public, is taboo in 1929, and they well know the Klu Klux Klan is active in their area. But soon human conviviality takes over. After the meal they happily walk together, despite the stares of fellow pedestrians, to the Women's City Club, where the conference opens with music by the African Zion Church choir.

Doris introduces the speakers: Louis Gregory and a young white minister. From the podium during their addresses, she watches resistance and skepticism dissolve in the diverse faces of the audience of some four hundred people. She's deeply moved as the program closes with the "Negro National Anthem"—that poignant plea to "God of our weary years, God of our silent tears . . ." She's never heard it before.

She soon reports to a friend, "What a fool I have been these last two weeks to worry over the part I had to play. You must have been praying for me in my hour of need, for I felt a sublime happiness, love, assurance and power. I cannot describe the ecstasy I felt all through."[10]

Just about a month later, the Blossom Picnic, May 11–12, 1929, at Emerald Hill is another public challenge to segregation. Shortly before the picnic, Doris is in New York City for a Bahá'í National

Teaching Committee Meeting. Having an afternoon to herself, she takes a "Reconciliation Fellowship Tour" of Harlem.

With other white tourists, Doris visits a church, a library, the offices of the NAACP and the Urban League, and hears Harlem-ites explain the injustices they face. Like the rest of her group, she's mute. But at the Urban League she finally finds her voice, "What is being done to further friendship and unity between the races?" She's seen a lot of despondence on the Harlem streets, so she fears her question will be met with scorn. But she mentions the Bahá'í Faith and the Rochester Race Amity Conference, and is invited to lunch the next day with James Hubert, secretary of the league.

At lunch, sitting across from her host, whose face seems, she says, "both sharply keen and meditative," she explains that Bahá'ís build unity through fellowship.

"I wish it were true," James Hubert says, "but it can't be done."

"But it has been done. You can see it with your own eyes."

"I won't believe it 'til I see it done."

"Then come to our Blossom Picnic this weekend."

That Saturday, the Secretary of the Urban League gets off the train in Geneva, over two hundred miles from Harlem. Willard picks him up at the station and they drive in contemplative silence, finally rolling into the farm past an integrated crowd of youths playing ball. Other mixed groups stroll through the orchards where cherry blossoms are at their peak and the pink buds of apple blossoms are just unfurling. In the dining room, containers of food brought by guests proliferate while helpers fill the kitchen, where Doris is cook-ing twenty-five lbs. of rice. Guests include not just African Ameri-cans and whites but people of various ethnicities and nationalities from Cornell University's Cosmopolitan Club, of which Willard is a member.

About a decade later, in a letter from Hyderabad, India, Martha Root will tell Doris and Willard, "It is thrilling to meet Mr. Amir Ali who was your guest from Cornell at the Spring festival in Geneva in 1929. He is now private secretary to the Prime Minister." Amir Ali appends to the letter, "With the most delightful reminiscences of your beautiful farm at Geneva . . ."

That night, eighty folks feast together and enjoy the songs of the Zion Church Choir and stories of the Master, feeling His love and presence via Louis Gregory, the Obers, and the Ives, along with another great transmitter of His spirit, May Maxwell, visiting from Montreal. The intimacy and beauty of the gathering are complemented by the farm's lack of electricity, necessitating illumination by "two blue candles set in . . . (Doris') tall brass wedding candlesticks" and other means, while the scents of lilacs and fruit blossoms waft through open windows. Over the course of two days, 150 people picnic at the farm. Dorothy Baker addresses a large outdoor meeting with, Doris feels, "a power and sweetness" that thrills all hearts. James Hubert's reaction to the whole weekend: "I had to see it to believe it."

After the picnic, the Klu Klux Klan threatens to burn down the farm. Also following the picnic, Elizabeth Brooks arranges Bahá'í meetings in Rochester. Doris and Willard come into the city to address the meetings, and they stay overnight in African-American homes. Doris says prayers of thanks that, to her, the "Caledonia Avenue" of her girlhood is now "a phantom barrier." Soon, two African-American families in Rochester become Bahá'ís, and they are the bedrock of that community. But the first African-American, post-Blossom Picnic, post-Race Amity Convention new Bahá'í is Bert Jackson of Geneva.[11]

———◆———

Early autumn, 1930, brings another benchmark for the McKays: they're sent on a Bahá'í teaching tour through New York, Philadelphia, Washington, Baltimore, Boston, Portsmouth, and Montreal. The harvest is in, so they can leave the farm and farm animals in charge of others. Doris buys two blue outfits in velvet and silk. But when it comes to dressing-up, she admires Willard more than herself. She finds him aristocratic-looking in suit and tie.

The McKays consider themselves "the most unlikely people in the world to be making a tour of big cities," but they're upheld by "the certainty" that their friends are praying for them and their "recognition that 'of ourselves we can do nothing'" for "God doeth whatsoever He willeth." And things do pop right along as they speak successfully, and meet and mingle, in all kinds of venues.

In Manhattan, they manage a pilaf feast, cooked by May Maxwell and Doris, "bustling around in aprons," for a large, integrated group; the guest of honor is the star of the Broadway hit *The Green Pastures*, a show with a wholly African-American cast.

In Portsmouth, New Hampshire, they visit Louis and Louisa Gregory. They arrive by bus to see Louis awaiting them "with a look of boyish eagerness." They accompany him to a little house where Louisa, "with a red scarf wound around her head" is cooking dinner. "Yes we certainly are in residence," Louis announces with an air of triumph. In their eighteen years of marriage, he and Louisa have rarely been able to dwell in the same house. They are fatigued from their constant individual travels and the long periods of separation they endure, so this small home is a delight.

At a small gathering that evening, Doris is surprised to hear Louis, "the humblest, most self-effacing person you can ever imagine," say that his great stumbling block when he became a Bahá'í was his pride. "He prayed on his knees before Bahá'u'lláh for the elimination of his pride."

In Montreal, Willard and Doris are ensconced in the home of May and Sutherland Maxwell, a place permeated with the spirit of 'Abdu'l-Bahá, Who stayed there during His visit to the city in 1912, and with Sutherland's elegant interior design. They're charmed with the Maxwell's nineteen-year-old daughter, Mary.*

---

* In 1937, when she was twenty-six, Mary Maxwell married Shoghi Effendi, the Guardian of the Bahá'í Faith. She became known as Amatu'l-Bahá Rúḥíyyih Khánum, and was named a Hand of the Cause of God.

She has a youth group that she calls the Fratority Club because most of the people in it wouldn't be welcome in McGill University's fraternities or sororities. They include Japanese and Turkish students, and Eddie Elliot, an electrician who is the first black Canadian to become a Bahá'í. (He will become a leader of the Montreal Bahá'ís as well as of the city's African-Canadian community, and will officially represent Canada at the Bahá'í world's historic intercontinental conference in Kampala, Uganda, 1953.)

For a Fratority gathering during Christmas week, Doris wishes she had something more ornate than her simple blue silk dress. As she starts downstairs, Mary offers her "a glamorous Spanish shawl: blue roses embroidered on a square of white silk, with a fringe of shaded blue at least 18 inches wide." Mary drapes Doris in the shawl, which sets her off perfectly, and makes a gift of it to her.

Despite the joy at the Maxwell's, Doris has to work to keep up a cheerful front. She feels she can hardly raise her head. The problem is her response to 'Abdu'l-Bahá's great disciple, May, who is so beautiful, so elegant and angelic. Doris feels unworthy, cast down, sullen. Her disappointment in herself at these feelings only intensifies them. She's sick with what she calls her "self-thing." At last she throws herself across the bed in the guestroom and gives way to sobs, only to be discovered by May, who insists on knowing the reason for such grief.

Doris tells all, adding that she feels, "as if part of myself has been burning away." May doesn't waste time taking this personally. She tells Doris that now she can "begin to understand Shoghi Effendi's anguish when called to the station of Guardian" and says, "To the extent that we elect to carry that cross ourselves, will he be relieved of his burden."

That's the stardust Doris sees in May and others like her who transmit the presence of 'Abdu'l-Bahá; they also transmit His kind, forgiving love, His fatherly indulgence and His call to rise up, rise higher. May elevates Doris' ego-war to service and sacrifice. She communicates to Doris "a tenderness not of this world."

Years afterwards, at a much older age than May ever lived to attain, Doris said, "The memory of May is a perfume that can't be put into a bottle. May wanted us to understand that unity was a hidden mystery, the key to the treasure house, to be worn next to our hearts. She had a pearl-like luster, and her concept of unity was *profound*. 'Abdu'l-Bahá called her 'the Center of the Love of God in the western world.'"

On their return to the farm, Willard and Doris ski up Emerald Hill on a glistening winter night and watch the stars. Willard knows all the constellations, as had Doris' father. Like the white light of the stars, May's "spiritual intonations" echo through their memories "with the clarity of a silver trumpet."[12]

Soon afterwards, Doris attends the Urban League convention in Buffalo at James Hubert's invitation. She has ten minutes at the end of the last session to speak to the African-American delegates from forty-three states about the Bahá'í Faith. Her listeners greet her talk as a benediction. James Hubert and Sam Allen (another Urban League secretary) drive her back to Emerald Hill, and they stop to eat at a crowded roadside restaurant.

Diners turn from their meals to stare at Doris entering with her escort of two burly African-American men. Seated at a side table, the trio orders the "choicest food on the menu" and are "treated with a dazed deference." On their way out, James and Sam stop to buy cigars and notice, by the desk, "KKK," in two-foot high capital letters, representing the Klu Klux Klan.

Nothing daunted, Mary Collison spearheads a presentation by James and Sam at the Geneva Women's Club, with songs by Harry T. Burleigh, renowned African-American baritone, folklorist and composer. The all-white audience, possibly containing some members of the KKK, reacts favorably, if with some bewilderment, for the "'enemy' . . . stirred their love and their respect."

The Urban League then invites Bahá'ís to come and be entertained in Harlem households. Doris stays with Sam Allen and his wife, Lois, who confides, "I can't help it. If there is a knock on the door and a white man stands there, my heart sinks. Whoever it is, if he is white, I feel the same." Yet Doris will visit the Allens several times, always finding their apartment "an island in the sky, a place of safety and understanding love."[13]

At One with the Dispossessed

So life blesses Doris and Willard, but as their spiritual fortunes rise, their material ones plummet. The Great Depression is choking the United States and the world. At the beginning of 1932, the McKays lose their home forever. Fruit prices have dropped disastrously and Willard's brother, while working in town, must take over the farm. (Eventually, he'll have to sell it.) Doris' "bubble-dome" of security bursts. Here's a new kind of oneness: she and Willard are, she realizes, "suddenly at one" with "the dispossessed . . ."

In March, 1931, the McKays drive away from the farm into a landscape of icy winds, grayness, and fog that's "like the minds of bewildered people . . ." In the rattletrap Studebaker they've bought for $25.00 from Howard Ives, they head for Pittsburgh, Pa., comforted by a foot-warmer of their "own invention, a lighted farm lantern under a blanket." Grace and Harlan Ober now live in Pittsburgh, and Doris and Willard will live with them; Willard is to have a job with Harlan. Driving through the grimy "coal mining valleys of the Alleghenies" they see "the miners . . . plodding home from their shifts, tunnel lights still burning in their caps" to "rows of small square houses planted down in the shadow of steep hills." Gray and brown clouds billow from the blast furnaces around Pittsburgh, the Steel City, and at times burst into orange flame. The McKays are far from their honeymoon nest among the cherry blossoms and lilacs.

But in Pittsburgh they enjoy a diverse Bahá'í community ranging "from the brilliant minds of the academic world to near illiteracy, from those with economic security to poverty, from black to white . . ." Sadly, much of the economic security proves short-lived. When the McKays first arrive, the Obers seem in a relatively good situation, but that quickly changes. With Grace, Harlan, and their three children, Doris and Willard move into a ramshackle house, Tilbury Tenement. The McKays occupy a meagerly furnished attic that's blessedly shaded by large trees and has more than one window so there's cross ventilation. Harlan's business is failing—there's no job for Willard, so he works as a fundraiser for a breadline. Grace and Harlan are out all day, struggling for subsistence. Doris can't find a job and undertakes the housekeeping.

While Willard dials the phone and talks on behalf of the food program run by an old Roman Catholic church in the Strip, which is a squatters' town on unwanted land between a cliff and the Ohio River, Doris labors like Cinderella. Fresh soot falls daily from the Pittsburgh mills and coats all surfaces, and the Obers' "upright perfection" includes cleanliness. Doris, never a fussy or enthusiastic housekeeper, used to "send out" the laundry from the farm, but now must wash everyone's clothes, scouring shirt collars with a stiff brush and yellow Sunshine Soap, ironing, then folding every item according to Grace's standards. She dusts with an oiled cloth, cleans upholstery, vacuums, follows Grace's system of rubbing grime from the wallpaper with "pink dough," attacks carpets with scrubbing brush and hot suds. She also does the cooking.

She and Willard have one dollar between them. Willard's life insurance is gone. They've sold almost all their heirloom furniture. Even Doris' diamond ring is "in and out of pawn." Though she's been a farm wife, she's been a relatively pampered one. She sometimes breaks down despite her efforts at self-control and Willard's solace. One morning Grace sees the traces of her tears and asks why she's been crying. "It's the feeling of being trapped . . . Of no future, no solution. It's being covered with soot and sticky heat, and not knowing what will happen, and being so terribly tired. And it's hiding ourselves from one another."

"I know, Doris," Grace answers, enveloping Doris in a bear hug, "because I feel exactly the same way." Despite her own worries, Grace manages to pour cheer into Doris' cup, as do other friends.

One evening, Louis Gregory, in town for a visit and for Bahá'í activities—these go on apace no matter what—calls the wan Doris aside and says, "Experience has shown that it's not always easy for Bahá'ís to live together." He slips a $5.00 bill quickly into her hand and darts to the other side of the room, so she has no chance to refuse it. It would be rude to run after him and insist. Yet she knows "he doesn't have any more $5.00 bills than anybody else." She will later observe, "$5.00 was like a fortune in those days. You could live on it for a week." She can only be grateful, warmed by his love—and she makes sure, ever after, to give similar gifts as often as possible. She probably later met others who had been sustained by five dollars from Louis slipped into a palm or tucked into an envelope with a letter—Edith Chapman and Roy Williams are two who come to mind, and there were more.

Soon Mabel and Howard Ives come to live in Tilbury Tenement. The Ober family with the McKays and the Ives sustain themselves with nightly prayer sessions. Lack of work and shortage of food are just two of the trials they face. The Obers' teenage daughter is convalescing from polio and also having pangs of teenage rebellion, with which Doris too readily sympathizes. The melancholic Howard Ives is suffering a breakdown. Harlan is nearly broken by his inability to keep up his business, which necessitates firing his employees. Prayers and service are the bootstraps by which they all pull themselves up.

Grace never stops being hospitable. At one point she invites an entire NAACP convention to tea at Tilbury Tenement. Twice the expected number arrives. Thirty sandwiches, prepared for thirty guests, are each cut in half, and all goes forward merrily.

On another occasion, having received a special plea for contributions to building the Bahá'í Temple, Tilbury Tenement earns $14.00 with an "economy dinner" of baked potatos and rabbit gravy. The rabbits are courtesy of Howard, who tried to breed them to make money. Unfortunately, they died. Doris becomes quite proficient at cooking rabbit a la king, stuffed rabbit, spiced rabbit . . . What with the bunny suppers and the failure of his rabbit project, Howard's depression only increases.

Undaunted, in October, 1931, the Pittsburgh Bahá'ís host a Race Amity conference. Willard is the organizer, and Doris chairs the meeting at Louis Gregory's request. About 175 show up, and all dine later at the "colored Y," where Louis tells Doris he wishes she could chair all his meetings. Meanwhile, Doris writes in her diary of the "usual turmoil and stress" in Tilbury Tenement. "It is ever on, and on, and ON with the alternative of NOWHERE."[14]

But Willard is going somewhere. On December 1, he boards a bus and is off on an odyssey: three weeks in the South with Louis Gregory. Doris will later describe the tour as "a truly historic step and one of the highlights of Willard's life . . . The two tall men, one dark, one very fair, both radiant" eat together and share lodgings, bus seats, and podiums despite segregation laws.[15]

In 1961, they would have been called Freedom Riders. Miraculously, they're personally spared the violence that dogged the Freedom Riders, though violence, as we will see, was rife along their path.

On the Road with Louis Gregory

"I shall always think of it as The Trip," Willard says, reporting the tour. "Louis thinks this is the first time a colored man and a white man have traveled together on terms of equality through the Southern states, riding together in a public conveyance." Willard and Louis, deputized by Bahá'ís, always take the cheapest possible buses. Willard sits with Louis, which means he rides in the back of those buses because of Jim Crow law.

Louis has been a Johnny Appleseed of oneness for years, and now Willard meets many of his sprouts and saplings (so to speak). People who listened to Louis "with a grain of salt" (Willard will later explain) now see brotherhood in action. In Atlanta, he and Louis speak at Morris Brown College, the Atlanta School of Social Work, the Spellman Preparatory High School, Morehouse University, and the Home Training School. They also meet privately with individuals and groups, including the city interracial committee.

A Bahá'í named Mae C. Hawes, tells them an indelible story. She's just back from New York City, having gotten her master's degree in library science at Columbia University. She relates that, toward the end of the year, in her sociology class, "the 'Negro problem' came up" during discussion. A young man from St. Louis said, 'In Missouri we like our Negroes black and our whites white. But the yellow Negroes . . . we can't stand . . .'" A girl from Ohio contributed, "We think the light-colored Negroes have it a little easier because the whites think they must be better than the dark ones because they have more white blood."

Mae related that she, a fair-skinned blonde, listened in shock, realizing that these friends of hers thought she was white. She said, "I thought you all knew that I am a Negro." Silence. She added, "Let's talk this thing through . . ." She calmly advanced scientific evidence for the oneness of the human race.

Finally the Missouri student commented that he'd been trying to understand where he'd gotten his point of view. "And now I know," he said. He remembered that as a child walking with his father he'd doffed his hat to an African-American woman. His father scolded, "Don't ever do that again." But a few days later he politely greeted another African-American woman. His father took him home and beat him within an inch of serious injury, saying, "I'll teach you to show respect to a nigger."

Our reporter, Willard, caps this with Louis' observation, "There's great good in the theory advanced in Plato's 'Republic' that children should be taken from their parents before they have a chance to learn their vices."

Onward the two roll to Tuskegee Institute in Alabama. Seated in the back of the bus, Willard finds he has more leg room, but the motion is "more perceptible." However, when the bus begins to empty the porter seats the two further front.

At last they pass through Tuskegee, "a small white village" and get off the bus at the Institute, "which is a separate world . . . It has its own stores, post office, and even its own student bank, which accepts accounts and honors checks as small as one cent." At Tuskegee, they're quartered in The Oaks, the old home of the school's founder, Booker T. Washington. After a first meal in a dining hall for white guests where they're seated in a room apart from "three white gentlemen from Georgia" so they won't cause offense, they take the rest of their meals with the faculty.

They address various classes and students are amused at Willard's difficulty understanding their accents. "Their best Alabaman," he finds, is "a language which is musical and delightful to hear, but . . . (it's) composed entirely of vowels without any consonants . . ." He edges over "as close as possible to the questioner and after asking him about four times" can "begin to separate some of the words . . ."

"Why don't white folks like Negroes?" the students ask. "What can we do to overcome the prejudice against us?" "Do you think the Amos 'n Andy broadcast is harmful?" "In your personal opinion is prejudice against Negroes . . . due to jealousy or to the inferiority of the Negro?" "Why do white and colored children play together but tend to separate as they grow older?" Soon warmth and spontaneity characterize the exchanges. Later, Louis and Willard address a Sunday evening assembly of the entire student body and faculty. Someone describes their joint teaching method: Willard gives the basic Bahá'í tenets and Louis "furnishes the *rousement*."

On their last morning at Tuskegee, Willard and Louis meet with George Washington Carver, the world famous agriculturalist and chemist—most well-known as the inventor of peanut butter—who has his laboratory and fields at the institute. He's an old friend of another veteran Bahá'í, Roy Wilhelm. "Boys, you can thank Dr. Carver for the quality of your beloved peanut butter," Willard will tell the Obers' two sons when he returns home. "He has experimented with over forty varieties of peanut . . ."

Willard finds the aging scientist to be "unpretentious and quite poor," a member of "'Abdu'l-Bahá's 'superior race' who are the 'lovers of mankind.' He remains at Tuskegee from choice. He's turned down remunerative positions offered by commercial companies because he's needed at the institute to create revenue through his agricultural researches."

In Huntsville, Louis and Willard arrive at Alabama A&M University to be met by a student who tells Willard, "President Drake says that we have no separate accommodations, but that if you will room with Mr. Gregory we shall be very glad to entertain you." Later, in the washroom, Willard meets an African-American student who tells him "all the boys" think "it's wonderful that you'll sleep in a Negro's bed. They never heard of such a thing . . . my father will hardly believe it when I tell him. This will be the most interesting news I've ever brought home from school."

But faculty and students at A&M are generally "under a cloud of sadness and discouragement." Shortly before Louis and Willard's arrival, their football coach was murdered by a truckload of white men for no reason except that the men were "in a bad mood, presumably over the progress" of a trial in Binghamton. Louis and Willard give several talks to large audiences at the university, and among the people who express the most appreciation is a man who tried to save the coach from his murderers and suffered a vicious beating himself.

At Fisk University in Nashville, Louis and Willard stay in Dunn House with bachelor faculty members. The student body is African-American, but the faculty is integrated. "Many of the Fisk students," Willard observes, "come from wealthy homes . . . (and) are sophisticated, discriminating, critical and intensely dissatisfied. The faculty likewise, but tempered by maturity and tolerance . . ."

Willard especially marvels at their tolerance because of another recent tragedy. Their Dean of Women had been killed in a hit and run collision, and she needn't have died. She and the female students she was driving were all "thrown out of their car upon the State road . . . They lay there while traffic rolled by, and no one stopped to help them because they were colored. After a while, some colored people driving by picked them up and telephoned to a nearby hospital . . . This hospital refused to even administer first aid to colored people. It was necessary to drive 50 miles to a Negro hospital . . . As a result this able and brilliant woman (the Dean) *died* for lack of proper care."

After proffering what comfort they can in their talks at Fisk and at a nearby agricultural college, Willard and Louis meet the noted archivist and researcher Arthur Shomburg in the Fisk Library, where he curates the Negro Collection.* He responds to their visit enthusiastically, telling them that he met 'Abdu'l-Bahá in 1912.

Traveling northward, Louis and Willard make some stops in Ohio. Finally, after addressing thousands of students and scores of others, Willard heads home to Pittsburgh while Louis goes on to West Virginia, following his tireless path of apostleship, his heart greatly solaced. Traveling with Willard has been one of the "crowning experiences of his life . . . a fulfillment of the dreams of equality that had been shattered in his Southern boyhood, a testament to the viability of the Bahá'í path to reconstruction, and a compensation for the manifold sacrifices, hardships, and lonely humiliations he had endured along the way . . ."[16]

As for Willard, when he speaks later of "The Trip" his eyes often fill with tears of love and hope for all the poignantly promising young men and women he met, for he knows their difficulties and

---

* The New York Public Library, at the time, housed the Shomburg Collection of Negro Literature and Art, and it still does, but now the archives is called The Arthur Shomburg Center for Research in Black Culture.

the wounds they carry because of apartheid. And he writes of Louis, "He is really a man who would be a great hero to his valet, if he had one. In his case the more intimate the association the greater the love and admiration . . ." Both men are thrilled by the Guardian's response to their journey when he states his "deepest appreciation of their remarkable and historic services, and says, "We all feel indebted to them for their heroic efforts."[17]

"All the capital we need!"

Willard had gone on the tour at the request of another peripatetic, much-treasured teacher, Martha Root. She had asked him to "represent her." Doris and Willard got to know Martha when Martha visited Pittsburgh in the early 1930s. Doris attended a Press Club luncheon with her and marveled at how the ostensibly unassuming Martha shone in the "witty, sophisticated, fashionable" company. (But Martha, who used to get four-inch bylines as a feature-writer for a Pittsburgh newspaper, knew this company very well.) At the Ebeneezer Baptist Church, Doris took a back pew as Martha, in the pulpit, addressed the African-American congregation. After a while, Doris felt she wanted to "go, if necessary, crawl, up the long aisle to her (Martha's) side, such . . . (is) the magnetic pull of her presence . . ." She observed that Martha's talks seemed "chiefly a means to convey a Universal Love and its Source . . . a communication of Spirit," a return to "some lost music . . ." She wrote of Martha's "perfect transparency" and said, "I have looked more than I have listened. There is a light burning in that fragile porcelain."

Perhaps after 'Abdu'l-Bahá Himself, and Táhirih Qurratu'l-Ayn, there has never been and never will be a Bahá'í teacher of the caliber and effectiveness of Martha Root. And she's another of Doris' kindred spirits; she becomes an intimate friend, cherishing Doris as much as Doris cherishes her.[18]

After a painful year of communal living in Tilbury Tenement, the household breaks up when the Obers, having "tarried dangerously close to the margin of destitution," go to stay in a little house they own in Eliot, Maine, and the Ives move away, too. It's a great release from tension for all of them. Doris observes that Willard begins "to beam like the sun." In later years, when they remember Tilbury, it's "no longer a prison but a patch of sacred ground" for all the victories over selfishness that were won there.

Willard and Doris decide to stay in Pittsburgh to continue the work the "graduates of Tilbury Tenement" started, establishing and nurturing the Bahá'í community. They rent a very humble apartment, and after they climb the stairs, let themselves in with their new key, unpack, and put away some groceries, Willard exclaims, "This place is Heaven on Earth!" They settle in quickly, welcoming a parade of guests. Doris writes in her journal, "Now that the Obers and the Ives are gone, the community says that they are depending on us . . . I must stop feeling little and unimportant . . . and I must strive for faith, initiative and responsibility . . ."

But the community isn't blind to their struggles. Willard has a job, but it's temporary and due to come to a halt soon. One evening a Bahá'í tells them, "I took it upon myself to write the Guardian about the work you are doing and about your affairs. The answer has come back. He said about you . . . 'They are well versed in the Teachings and have the Bahá'í spirit and that is all the capital a Bahá'í needs.'" Often, over the years, those words will comfort Doris and Willard. Often, they'll remind each other, when their pockets are empty: *we have all the capital we need.* And something always arrives—a job, a check, a $5.00 bill—to sustain them.

Doris becomes active in the Women's International League for Peace and Freedom (WIPL) and in the Lucy Stone League for Colored Women. Many Jewish women volunteer in the WIPL, and they inhabit "desperate mental realms" because they're "worried about relatives in Germany as news of Hitler's atrocities is spread." Willard volunteers as a helper to an African-American social worker.

But Doris writes in her diary, "It seems weeks since Willard has taken in any real cash. My ring is pawned again. We are adapting ourselves to two meals a day. We are becoming better and better hikers; it is the carfare that kills. But, my shoes . . . Willard is out early up at the stores. He is trying to rent parking spaces to people . . ." This was a sad effort because he found out that many of the pedestrians he approached were walking because they'd lost their cars.

When Doris is asked to write a study guide on the newly released tome, *The Dawn-Breakers*, it's a sorely needed respite: deciphering the "forest of unpronounceable names," learning how titles and places of birth are part of the Persian names, trying to say the names using the guide at the back of the 600-page book, and, mostly, getting lost in the passion-play, the heroic stories. Someone once said absorption is happiness, and Doris finds that's indeed true.

Friends and humor also offer respites. Then, after three and a half years in Pittsburgh, Willard finds a job selling hardware and farm machinery in a Sears Roebuck Store in Jamestown, Pa., and the McKays move there.[19]

— · —

Martha Root's cousin, Lucy Wilson, temporarily resident in Jamestown, becomes quite dear to the McKays, but despite this new friend, jobs, creative writing studies and a rented house with a huge yard, fruit trees and a grape arbor, Doris misses Pittsburgh, which she calls "the mainland." It's a boon when Bahá'ís come to visit.

Eve Nicklin, soon to resettle for life in Peru as its first Bahá'í pioneer, and the pianist and vocalist Emogene Hoagg, are two who give Doris the cheer and stimulus she needs. But she really blooms on the day in winter, 1936, when Lucy Wilson brings Martha Root to see her. Afterwards, she writes, "Something BIG happened. 'Abdu'l-Bahá had said that He saw His father's face in the faces of those who came to Him and that was the reason they came forth from His presence radiant. Martha did that to me today and I know that she and Lucy carried away a picture of my true self that few see . . ."

For her part, Martha feels so encouraged by the McKays that after some weeks in Jamestown she began signing her letters "Martha 'McKay' Root." Martha is only in the United States because she's ill. She's used to spreading her wings and spanning the world. She longs to go to India. One day, Martha gives way to bitter tears, sobbing in Doris' arms. Martha, Doris writes in her journal, "calls out all my tenderness . . ." When Martha is able to travel on, Doris sees her off at the train and then writes, "Martha is ours forever. She has renewed the call to action and I hope will always continue to call loudly from the heights . . ."

But Doris and Willard feel frustrated in Jamestown, where the establishment of a Bahá'í community goes very slowly until, after a visit by Dorothy Baker, a "Jamestown Fireside" group is born, a study circle of some thirty people. One woman becomes a Bahá'í after dreaming repeatedly that the group surrounded her, chanting, "Bahá'í, Bahee, Baho, Bahum!"[20] The chant becomes the Jamestown Bahá'í cheer.

Doris writes to a friend in 1939, "What great and wonderful days these are," as on April 21, Mabel Ives comes to meet a robust little crowd of new Bahá'ís, regarding them as her "grandchildren." In July of that year, Doris and Willard take some of the "grandchildren" to a picnic organized by Mabel just across the Canadian border, and Howard comes from Toronto to meet them. He's aged and enfeebled, at once wrung out and radiant from spending the past year writing *Portals to Freedom*. Yet he's familiar with Doris' letters to Mabel, knows each Jamestown Bahá'í by name.

With the picnic in Canada, Doris' urge to pioneer in that country begins. In August, Mabel has Doris take charge of the Bahá'í Booth in Toronto at the Canadian National Exposition and Doris "falls in love with Canada," with the "story-book quality" of Union Jack flags floating high overhead instead of the Stars and Stripes, and the differences of accents and culture.

But World War II is underway in Europe. The United States isn't yet at war, but Canada, being a British dominion, is. Doris records, "I am churned inwardly by the new phases of the war. I am haunted by a sense of the dipping motion of airplanes that I saw in a news-reel . . ." She continues her trips to Canada and writes to Willard, ". . . the Bahá'ís . . . pass me around and around like a box of candy and it is like a perpetual love feast. I am . . . praying for them and trying to lift them all into a self-sufficient band who will do their own teaching . . ."

By Christmas, 1940, at home in Jamestown, Doris is blue. "The holiday time makes so much more poignant the world conditions, the confused and willful humanity, even the Bahá'ís themselves." And now that she's gotten accustomed to journeying north to her beloved Canada, she's slated to travel south to Memphis, Tennessee, where the Bahá'í community is divided, crippled by racism and she is to heal the rift. She's unsure of her capacity to do so, and she's sad to be going so far from Willard for an unknown period of time.[21]

Mission to Memphis

At the beginning of 1941, Doris is en route to Memphis after stops in Cleveland and Lima, Ohio. In Cleveland, she gives an afternoon presentation and that evening shares a podium with Louis Gregory. Both events are for integrated audiences. The Cleveland Bahá'ís, particularly the African Americans, eagerly promise prayers for her mission in Memphis. In Lima, she enjoys an evening with Dorothy Baker's family, especially Dorothy's husband, Frank, who is in an "expansive and beaming mood."

She loves seeing Dorothy—now an important traveling teacher and administrator—as "a homebody" and Dorothy treasures Doris as much as ever; they stay up talking all night. The next day they confer about Memphis during a drive through the countryside that takes them to Ellen Beecher's burial site. Later, Horace Holley arrives for more consultation about Memphis. Very recently, Shoghi Effendi has cited "racial prejudice" as "the most vital and challenging issue confronting the Bahá'í community . . ."[22]

Aside from her task of integrating the Memphis Bahá'í community, Doris has another job, a very demanding one. Mabel and Howard Ives are in Memphis; Mabel must leave for Little Rock, Arkansas, and Doris is to stay in their house and look after Howard. She finds that his health is failing to such an extent that every time he recites a prayer with his habitual passion, it seems to her that he's about to die.[23]

Doris is attached to Howard as if he were her own father, and she hopes that if something happens "to snap his hold on life" her "chicken heart would turn into that of a lion." At the same time, she's "desperately homesick." She writes to a friend, "I had a letter from Willard today and its tenderness nearly capsized my frail craft. I said to Howard, 'Should I pray to have this homesickness taken away?' 'No,' he said. I guess he is right. I know I am winning through to a new sensitiveness . . ." Howard strengthens and inspires Doris despite his physical weakness.

She contacts the African-American Bahá'ís of Memphis through Louis Gregory's friend, Professor George Henderson. As we saw previously in these pages, Professor Henderson made a great success of his business college and his Bahá'í activities. But by the time Doris gets to Memphis, the Bahá'í community is splintered and the situation has become achingly sad.

In general, interracial relations in Memphis are very bad. At one point, Doris sends a newspaper clipping to Horace Holley about an integrationist who was jailed for fourteen days without a formal charge, then "shooed from jail and city" (as the headline read). The Bahá'ís are not only prejudiced, they're scared. When Doris suggests an interracial supper, a white Bahá'í responds, "Out of the question! . . . The 'breaking of bread' with the blacks will ruin us and the Cause."

Understandably, George Henderson is feeling alienated. He now heads what *The Pittsburgh Courier* newspaper refers to as "a $50,000 institution, with dormitory accommodations, and a publishing and printing plant which turns out books, papers and commercial job work." Material success hasn't diminished his spiritual ardor; he's been a keen Bahá'í for a quarter of a century. Yet he, his students, his fellow African-American Bahá'ís, and other friends aren't welcome in the homes of white Bahá'ís in Memphis. Doris calls him several times to arrange a meeting and is put off each time. When he finally agrees to an appointment and sends a car to take her to his school, the car is "a dilapidated and battered hulk of a taxi . . ."

The school is nothing like the car. Doris finds "thirty or so bright and neat girls . . . tapping away at typewriters to the strains of victrola rhythms . . ." Escorted to George Henderson's office by his secretary, Doris finds him "a dapper person, more than well dressed, with a flower in his lapel and a white silk kerchief tied in a bow under his chin." He introduces Doris to the student body, the faculty and the dean, then dons "a light overcoat, throwing it over his shoulders like a cape, and puts on a wide-brimmed hat" and marshals Doris, students, and teachers outside for about an hour of picture-taking.

Back in his office, he plays the piano and sings to Doris while they wait for lunch, served by some students. Doris sups with him, the dean, a teacher, and two young typists who want to attend Doris' Bahá'í classes. Since there's only one knife, the professor cuts up everybody's steak and butters all the toast, calling it "the family knife."

Afterwards, Doris will write to Dorothy, "Suddenly I realized as I sat at our little 'family' dinner party . . . that for colored and white Bahá'ís to break bread together in the deep South is not any mere *feast* but a sacrament. Pray that they may one and all see that, before my work here is over. It is a symbolic act. A rite before God. What a Feast we will have here sometime, God willing . . ."

During lunch, discussing the situation of African Americans in Memphis, Doris finds that she could spend all her time addressing

African-American schools and congregations, attending meetings of the Urban League, etc. She writes to Dorothy, "The field is wide and I know it would be open to me. Fascinating as that would be I do think it would be going off on a tangent to my mission here to follow all those alluring avenues. But you know where my heart is . . ."

Riding home from the business college, she realizes she's passed certain tests: the ride in the dilapidated taxi driven by an African-American cabby who is *not* in livery, having her photo taken in public with African Americans, and sharing a meal with them. She's enjoyed every moment, and her new friends can feel that. She then goes to address a meeting of white Bahá'ís and ends up speaking about metaphysics. "A nice old lady and her daughter" give her a ride home. As she leaves the car, the nice old lady instructs her, "The Negroes are a lower race. God created them to be servants. It says so in the Bible."[24]

Suffice to say, Doris has her work cut out for her. She sets up three main activities for herself: classes at the Business College, meetings with the white Bahá'ís, and weekly drawing lessons for the daughters of an African-American couple, the Watkins, who became Bahá'ís seventeen years ago after meeting Louis Gregory. At an all-white Nineteen-Day Feast in February, she manages to help the group reach the consensus that a Local Spiritual Assembly would be formed if there were just nine Bahá'ís of any ethnicity dwelling in Memphis—and, in fact, there are.

So, Doris decides to host the next Feast at Howard's home and invite the African-American Bahá'ís. She runs into virulent opposition from some whites; they even want to write to Shoghi Effendi for permission to "indefinitely postpone" forming the (integrated) Assembly. Doris has the sickening task of informing the African-American Bahá'ís that they are disinvited—there won't be an interracial Feast after all. Soon after this, Doris, teaching two African-American students, reads them a quotation from 'Abdu'l-Bahá encouraging Bahá'ís to "sweeten the souls" of people who "poison your life" and be "a salve" to the sores of those who "inflict a wound on you." Her eyes fill with tears as she looks at the two young women. "These things have already happened to you because of racial prejudice, isn't that so?" she asks them. They answer in the affirmative. And they tell her they're ready "to accept the Bahá'í consciousness and live by that rule"—despite the behavior of some of the white Bahá'ís.

Doris has written to the National Spiritual Assembly and now receives from its secretary, Horace Holley, a reemphasis of the Guardian's statement about "the most challenging issue." She also hears from a Bahá'í in Nashville that they have Feasts in African-American Bahá'ís' homes because the white Bahá'ís aren't "keeping house," and they intend to have an interracial Naw-Rúz party. Doris' Bahá'í friends in Jamestown send a chin-up telegram, which she takes to George Henderson at the college. A white Bahá'í of Memphis, Clara Keller, accompanies her. They share the telegram, and he shares a recent letter from Louis Gregory. A meeting of minds and spirits occurs, "made even more magical" Doris later writes, when George passionately recites that great rallying cry of the oppressed, Edward Markham's poem "The Man with the Hoe."

Doris then asks if the Business College can be the venue for the Memphis Naw-Rúz celebration. The reply is yes. One of Doris' students makes the afternoon even more joyful by enrolling as a Bahá'í. On the day of the Naw-Rúz party an integrated community of twelve adult members and two youths meets at Henderson Business College to "break bread together" in a quietly reverent manner; it isn't ebullient, but, as Doris puts it, the diverse Bahá'ís discover they're "not oil and water." They belong together and can enrich each other. The Memphis Bahá'ís will all be on the same team from now on—at least, those who want to play ball will be.[25]

Home to Prince Edward Island

Returning to Jamestown, Doris also returns to her aspiration to relocate in Canada as a Bahá'í pioneer. McKaydia is the name she and Willard have for the home of their "affectionate dreams." After exploring several localities in the Maritimes region and settling in Moncton, Nova Scotia, they finally find McKaydia—Prince Edward Island (known as P.E.I.). Doris calls the island "a dimpled darling" of a place. It is a gem, as anyone knows who has ever read *Anne of Green Gables,* the children's classic set on the island. Yet L. M. Montgomery, author of *Anne,* an ardently loving daughter of P.E.I. who knew it painfully well, also called it a tight little island, and Doris and Willard will learn what that means, over the years.

But the world inexorably hammers at the island's door. Canada is on Eastern War Time. War ships are in the Gulf of St. Lawrence, and in the old Charlottetown Hotel the idyllic gentility of the dining area is shattered by loud radio reports of battles lost and won, and there are tables full of men in uniform. About a year later, Doris will record in her diary the death-at-sea of a Bahá'í noncombatant electrician in the Royal Canadian Navy.

The island weather is, Doris finds, "as moody as the sea" and she's intrigued by "the strange wild charm of the place." In 1942, the McKays, with Irving Geary's sponsorship, receive their immigration papers for Canada. By that time, the United States is also at war. Doris feels "it is destiny calling me to Canada" and things have fallen into place so fast that, she says, "I tweak my whiskers in wonder." (This expression is not as odd as it seems if we consider that any place Doris lives also houses a full contingent of cats.)

Nevertheless, both Doris and Willard feel that in going to Canada their real sacrifice is giving up "invitations to continue race amity work in the south." Doris later said it was "work for which we were better qualified and (in which we) probably would have been much more successful. The need in Canada, however was urgent."

According to Willard, writing twenty-three years after the fact, one of his reasons for moving to Canada was, ". . . if I was ever to see anything more of Doris it would only be if she and I went pioneering together." After his death, Doris wrote to one of his longtime correspondents in Jamestown that he always missed the place, had an abiding love for Jamestown and its people. He was too much of a stoic to ever admit the depth of his sacrifice.[26]

He and Doris both hold to their course largely because of a letter from the Guardian in 1944 asking if they would be willing to stay on the island for the rest of their lives, if necessary. He feels that in order to build a Bahá'í community there, lifelong commitment may be demanded, for, in his own words he agrees with P.E.I.'s preeminent writer: it's a conservative, tradition-bound place.

The McKays cable him, saying yes. Other pioneers also move to P.E.I. Doris will later note, "We all functioned actively for . . . years with only one declaration of an Islander, Leila Morris in 1956."

The pioneers must also function with next-to-no incomes. Elsa Vento, a Finnish newspaper woman, gives up a good job in Toronto to work as a maid for four to five dollars a week. Willard's sister, Christine, also works as a maid. Another pioneer hands out ice cream cones; one baby-sits twins. Willard tries everything to get work. He's even turned down for a job transporting bricks and stone via wheelbarrow on a construction site. Doris has some art pupils who come to her house and she charges them 25 cents per lesson—35 cents if two of them come together. After awhile she has some forty-five students. She later recalls "seeing a group of children standing outside our window, watching us do our art and thinking, 'Oh, if I could only get art to all these children.' That wish was to come true later."[27]

The Gearys are able to buy a farm in Vernon Bridge, and Willard, once the reigning king of his family's extensive orchards, is now a subsistence truck farmer. Irving, who has no experience as a farmer, works with him. None of the hard-toiling pioneers are young; their average age is about fifty.

The pioneers try everything to find some islanders willing to join them. They give teas, seminars, creative writing and art classes, and they publish newspaper stories about everything they do. Teachers visit and give presentations. One teacher reports, "I went many times to teach in Charlottetown . . . Everybody went to Charlottetown, because Charlottetown was the hardest nut to crack . . . When I would go to Charlottetown they would say Dorothy Baker was here and she prayed all night long for Charlottetown. There were always stories of people praying all night, hour after hour saying the Greatest Name, five hundred times, a thousand. It was ceaseless . . . You really felt that anything was an invasion and it seemed . . . invincible . . . Charlottetown was surrounded by what appeared to be an impenetrable wall of good willed indifference. The Bahá'ís there had to live on their inner resources and strength to an unprecedented degree . . . It was the most mystical community in Canada . . . You always saw into the life of things and Doris McKay was one of those and they lived in a world of art, in imagination, teaching art . . . There was no other community quite like it . . ."[28]

At Vernon Bridge, Doris has plenty of time to muse on evanescence as well as on harsher facts of existence. Willard drives a horse and cart until they can afford a car. They grow vegetables and fruit, and they raise chickens. They get off the island sometimes to teach at Bahá'í summer schools and in Moncton—expenses paid.

In 1947 Willard makes a monthlong teaching tour of Canada from coast to coast and manages to pursue his beloved theme of interracial harmony with individuals and in public talks, such as one titled Race and Religious Unity. He befriends a Cree youth and a Chinese gentleman; meets the sister of one of Canada's great artists, the late Emily Carr, who gives him a tour of Emily's lovingly preserved studio; visits a mosque and is charmed to see a crescent moon in the sky when he comes out; enjoys a visit to the home of a West Indian Bahá'í couple, Ernest and Rita Marshall, and chats into the wee hours of the morning with their West Indian roomer; enjoys a long discussion with a young Jewish woman whose intellectual theories remind him of his own thoughts "25 years ago, just before I met the Bahá'í Faith."

Back in Vernon Bridge, he feels "It may be that our most valuable activity (on P.E.I.) is being conducted on the spiritual plane."[29] Townsfolk come to visit, neighbors are in and out, and friends come from other places, too—some of them are artists who just want to paint. Doris paints constantly, at one point adorning old wooden shingles with landscapes and floral designs and selling them to tourists.

Eventually, Willard develops a heart condition, becomes hard of hearing, and has trouble with his eyesight. But things begin to look up when new pioneers come to the island, replacing earlier pioneers who couldn't support themselves and had to leave. Then Doris nets a plum of a job—art supervisor for all the public schools on the Island. She's fifty-eight years old. It's a first for the schools, as, up until then, there'd been no art instruction. And it's a steady income for the McKays after long years of drought. Doris comments, "My being able to get that job was as if we'd sold 19 or 20 calves." She instructs teachers about how to give art classes and goes monthly into seventy-five schoolrooms herself to work with students. She writes a book, *Art in the Schools*, which goes through three printings. She makes a lifelong impression on many students.

One of her former pupils, Ann Doyle, remembers, "Doris was my first art teacher in grades one through six. I fell passionately in love with her. She was the most magical person I'd ever met—she could make things appear out of nothing. She was very tough. If we didn't behave, Mrs. McKay wouldn't come. We had a couple of devils in the class and one day they wouldn't calm down and she walked out of class. After that we all kept them in line."

For fifteen years, Doris works that job, living in Charlottetown part of the week. When she's at the farm, she stays there, because of Willard's health, so she rarely gets off the island. Whenever Willard can get near a piano, he sits down and plays his beloved Wagner, though his hands are very aged and gnarled from his farm work. One of the P.E.I. pioneers, Bob Donnelly, likes to play mystery-fragments of classical music records for Willard and challenge him to identify composer and composition. He always can, but sometimes he disparages the quality of a recording. He's also a chess buff, and Doris and he play rapid-fire matches over lunch, zipping the pieces around so fast that Bob can hardly see them. Doris, always unwilling to lose, sometimes knocks the whole board to the floor if she's cornered. However, despite his prowess at chess, Willard doesn't "get" checkers. The neighbors can always beat him.

Scrabble is another McKay game. Doris, sharp into her nineties, will continue playing Scrabble and chess, handily defeating one of her favorite opponents, Patrick O'Neill, a young islander who has become a Bahá'í.

The neighbors, with whom the McKays take tea, celebrate birthdays, etc., are bemused by Willard and Doris. They're impressed with Willard's horticultural knowledge, but not with his mechanical skills. He often needs their help. Once, after a wild storm, one of the McKay barns falls down and the neighbors rush right over, for that's the typical reaction: get right to work shoring up the building. However, they find Doris and Willard outside calmly sketching the fallen-down barn. This shouldn't surprise them, since they're well acquainted with Doris' predilection for painting everything, including the bricks of her fireplace. Her huge, gorgeous flower garden also proclaims her love of color and form.

When she does get off the island to "the other side," as the islanders call New Brunswick, she's likely to return with a new, magnificent art book she just couldn't resist buying, even if it meant spending her and Willard's last few dollars. Willard never criticizes her for it.[30] Kindliness and humility are his outstanding traits, greatly appreciated by his many visitors and correspondents; his inner and outer life are centered in the true spirit of charity, and in prayer.

On June 4, 1966, he quietly passes away. Doris bears up well during the funeral, the meals, the visiting, the memorial, though of course she sheds copious tears. She remembers how she wept as a new bride the first time he went away on a trip, and she felt embarrassed for acting so tragic, but Willard said, "What would be tragic would be if you *didn't* cry."

However, after things quiet down, after the adrenaline of calamity ebbs, Doris is out in her garden one day when she suddenly doubles over in pain, the pain of intense grief and loss tearing right down the center of her body, rending her very soul. In March, 1967, she writes to a friend in Jamestown, "I have been sitting here in the apricot light of dawn after saying . . . prayers and thinking of Jamestown days . . . I was asked to write a brief biographical . . . sketch of Willard's Bahá'í life for the *Canadian Bahá'í News*, and this I made a draft of Sunday, the tears rolling down my face . . . after all these months I never forget him at all . . . and have to strive very hard to fill the hole of longing for him." The pain doesn't really leave her for the rest of her life.

She makes a painting of Willard's farm hat and jacket as they hang in the farmhouse doorway. And she never takes the hat and jacket away. A friend later remembered, "They were always there, the first thing you saw going into the house." Doris lives in the house until she's too old to manage alone any longer and always feels, "The house was, and still is, a shrine for Willard. People who come feel his presence here. He was the real settler, still much beloved by the older Vernon neighbors. He never wanted to move, a saint in that place with his gardens, his fruits, his prayers, recitations and teachings."

Through all her travels apart from Willard, and during the years after his death, Doris keeps a studio photo of him with her, encased in a worn, much-fingered, green leather frame.[31] But she doesn't lose herself in memories, much as she loves them. On the contrary, she's blessed with rebirth. It's only after Willard dies that she regrets their childlessness, and just when that happens she's rewarded with more children than she can count. Young islanders become Bahá'ís and see in Doris the spiritual guide they've longed for, and they bring other youth to meet her, with many decked out in the splendid regalia of the 1960s. When islanders see people getting off the ferry wearing psychedelically painted sneakers or patchouli-scented dashikis, they say, "Must be going out to see Doris McKay."

Ann Doyle, back on the island from college "on the other side" is thrilled to be reacquainted with Doris and find that Doris remembers her name so many years after she was a child in one of Doris' art classes. Doris invites her to dinner at Vernon Bridge, so Pat O'Neill brings Ann to the farm.

"I forget what she was serving," Ann later recalled, "but it was strange. She was a very eccentric cook. They (Doris and Pat) started saying various things about Bahá'í. I was into Zen. After a while, it became uncomfortable. I think Doris sensed that. She could talk about anything—quantum physics, literature, art, she was interested in everything. She started talking to me about poetry and that was perfect . . .

"But after dinner we went into the little parlor to have tea and Doris suggested we each say a prayer. I had the same reaction as before. I thought, 'I'm leaving.' But good manners dictated otherwise. Doris read a prayer and I thought, 'That was quite beautiful.' Then they handed me the prayer book and I leafed through it and leafed through it looking for something I thought I'd be able to say without feeling like a complete hypocrite. Finally I saw one and thought, 'This looks harmless enough.' So I began to say the words. Before I got the first sentence out I was sure it was the most beautiful poetry I'd ever read. It was true. And if I denied it, I'd regret it forever. My life completely changed in that moment."

Paul Vreeland visits Doris as a new, young Bahá'í and notices her "cultivated intellect . . . (her) tremendous, cultivated receptivity to other people . . . (her) alchemical ability to sum up a person." He brings his mother, middle-aged at the time, to meet Doris so they can discuss Horace Holley, for Claire Vreeland is researching a book on him. Claire reads some of her manuscript to Doris and Doris exclaims, "You're a poet!" Claire, a journalist, has never thought of herself as a poet. But the spell is cast. She's a poet from then on.

Later, when Doris is confined to bed, Paul and Claire bring Paul's father to meet her. Paul's father has no interest in discussing prayers, physics, poetry, or the like, yet Doris finds common ground. Paul has been working with her on her memoir and his father knows about the rattletrap Studebaker she and Willard used to have. He's heard its whole story, including the sad tale of its demise. Doris turns to him and says, "What do you think was wrong with that car?" A twenty-minute discussion ensues, complete with car noises and theoretical diagnoses.

Louise Polland is in her twenties when Pat O'Neill brings her to meet Doris. Doris is in her seventies. Louise marvels at how comfortable she feels with Doris, loving the fact that she's nocturnal, and loving her artwork. Soon Louise is a frequent visitor ("although at somewhat odd hours"). Doris isn't concerned about that; she loves overnight guests, and, in fact, any friend who visits her expects to be pressed to stay the night.

Louise is a new Bahá'í from "a non-religious household." She doesn't know how to pray, and she asks Doris to help her, although she's afraid Doris will express disapproval or reproach. Doris, of course, is "kind and matter-of-fact" and tells Louise she just needs "purity of intent . . . detachment from the outcome (of the prayer) . . . and concentration."

Soon Louise is helping Doris pray. It seems the Canadian Bahá'ís have launched a massive prayer campaign with everyone "encouraged to say certain prayers in a certain sequence every day." Doris, according to Louise, always has "a copy of *Prayers and Meditations by Bahá'u'lláh* welded to her arm," but she finds it hard to pray "according to a schedule or plan." When Louise offers to say prayers in Doris' name, Doris accepts with delight.[32]

The youth come and go from the island, off to school, or to pioneer posts in far-flung corners of the world, and another joy to Doris is her constant correspondence with them. She reports their doings in letters to friends, mentioning this one in Zaire, another in Finland, someone else in Haiti; she's a very proud mother. She writes an essay, "Reflections of a Pioneer," for *Bahá'í Canada,* and tells how the new spirit among the Prince Edward Island Bahá'ís has affected her. "Young people and music and a magic hospitality. THEN ONE NIGHT IT HAPPENED. All those years of Bahá'í Administration and school teaching, and all the scar tissue of a barren and childless pioneering were swept way by a waterfall of universal love . . ."

Meeting the new Bahá'ís and seekers, she remembers the ones who taught her—May Maxwell, Grace Ober, Howard and Mabel Ives, Ellen Beecher, Louis Gregory, Martha Root, Dorothy Baker. She employs "their way of teaching—to reach out for the soul and to say inwardly the Greatest Name to establish the rhythm of the spirit."[33]

We are reminded here of what Louis Gregory wrote to Edith Chapman in 1938: "The new group at Tuskegee seem greatly worried because they cannot attract crowds at once. Wish you might go there to tell them of your patience and endurance during the years and final victory. 'Walk above the world by the Power of the Greatest Name!' If you are spiritually related to me you have to learn this lesson over and over."[34]

Doris and Willard were truly related to Louis Gregory and to his matchless brothers and sisters who carried the Master's touch with them. At the end of her long life of patience and endurance, Doris felt, "So much is said about Love in the Teachings, not only because it is kind! It is a great and vital Power, a worker of miracles because it is the key to the heart of the True One. It is, to quote from the short daily prayer, the reason why we were created. Bahá'í love is a heritage passed on to the young Bahá'ís, the first link in the love-chain that was made by 'Abdu'l-Bahá . . ."

Doris feels, at nearly eighty, that "life has just begun . . . I am welcomed back to love . . . If I had not stayed on Prince Edward Island I should never have known you (the young new Bahá'ís and pioneers); you are all iridescent motes in the atmosphere I breathe. I pray with you more than for you. With every one of you it is like rubbing two sticks together to make a fire . . ."

She'll live into her nineties, and when she must leave her house she's lovingly cared for in the home of Bob and Shirley Donnelly—Shirley is a skilled nurse. Her humor remains intact. During a hospitalization, she tells Louise Polland that being in intensive care is like "being in a Russian opera." When the entire National Spiritual Assembly of Canada comes to visit her, all nine of them appearing at her bedside, she looks at them with a little smile and murmurs, "Am I supposed to be impressed?"

With the devoted help of Paul Vreeland, she finishes her memoir (she calls it her "me-moir"), *Fires in Many Hearts*, which is chock-full of stories of her beloved teachers and tales from the deep well of her own heart. A determined group of Bahá'í islanders is able to get a preliminary edition published and in her hands before she passes away in 1992. To her, the book is the result of "love power."[35]

We can see all of her life, and Willard's life, in that light. The light of love. A shining circle, a ring of oneness uniting us with the noble souls we've met and journeyed with in this book, linking us to one another in Doris' "love chain," wedding humanity as a mystic bride to its great Lover, its Maker. Love power. So deceptively simple.

Notes

1 / Heritage: The Concept of Oneness

The epigraph is from McKay, *Fires in Many Hearts,* p. 14.

1. 'Abdu'l-Bahá, in *Bahá'í Prayers,* pp. 332–33.

2. Ruhe-Schoen, *A Love Which Does Not Wait,* frontispiece and p. 67.

3. Letter from Doris McKay to Mabel Garis dated August 5, 1980.

4. McKay, *Fires in Many Hearts,* p. 336.

5. Ibid., p. 14.

6. McKay, "Reflections of a Pioneer," p. 17.

7. McKay, *Fires in Many Hearts,* p. 336.

8. Ibid., p. 169.

9. 'Abdu'l-Bahá, quoted in Shoghi Effendi, *The World Order of Bahá'u'lláh,* p. 111.

2 / In Egypt

The epigraph is from Corrothers, from "Paul Laurence Dunbar," *Singers of the Dawn,* p. 5

1. Gregory, *A Heavenly Vista,* p. 15.

2. Ibid.

3. The Universal House of Justice, *The Century of Light,* p. 9.

4. Gregory, *A Heavenly Vista,* p. 9.

5. Ibid., p. 11.

6. Gregory, "Impressions of 'Abdu'l-Bahá While at Ramleh," *Star of the West,* Sept. 8, 1911, p. 5.

7. Gregory, *A Heavenly Vista,* p. 8.

8. 'Abdu'l-Bahá, *Tablets of the Divine Plan,* p. 51.

9. Gregory, *A Heavenly Vista,* p. 15.

10. Ibid.

11. Hayden, Robert, "Middle Passage," *Collected Poems,* p. 51.

12. Gregory, *Racial Amity,* unpaginated Foreword.

13. Paulson, Feny K., quoted in *239 Days*, p. 162.

14. 'Abdu'l-Bahá, quoted in Gregory, *A Heavenly Vista,* pp. 12–13.

15. Shoghi Effendi, quoted in "In Memoriam: Louisa Mathew Gregory," *The Bahá'í World, Vol. XIII,* p. 876.

3 / AN AMERICAN CHILDHOOD AND YOUNG MANHOOD

The epigraph is from Johnson, Georgia Douglas, from "Let Me Not Hate," *Singers of the Dawn*, p. 12.

1. Louis Gregory, quoted in Morrison, *To Move the World*, p. 12.

2. Gregory, *Racial Amity*, Ch. 15, p. 1.

3. Stevenson, quoted in "New Life," *Smithsonian*, p. 64.

4. Williams and Dixie, *This Far By Faith*, p. 3.

5. Robertson, *W. C. Handy*, p. 53.

6. Eleazer, *Singers in the Dawn*, p. 20.

7. Williams, taped personal recollections.

8. Gregory, *Racial Amity*, pp. 4–5.

9. Ibid., pp. 1–4.

10. Wilkerson, *The Warmth of Other Suns*, p. 11.

11. Hayden, "Runagate, Runagate," in *Collected Poems*, p. 59.

12. Willis, *Reflections in Black*, p. 35.

13. Gregory, "A Gift to Race Enlightenment," *World Order*, pp. 36–39.

14. DuBois, *The Souls of Black Folk*, p. 3.

15. Morrison, *To Move the World*, p. xiii.

16. Hughes, *The Big Sea*, pp. 11–12; Robertson, *W. C. Handy*, p. 4.

17. McKay, *Reflections in Black*, p. 35.

18. Dubois, "Address to the Nation," http://users.wfu.edu/zulick/341/niagara.html.

19. Ibid.

20. Johnson, "Lift Every Voice and Sing," http://www.poetryfoundation.org.

21. Gregory, "A Gift to Race Enlightenment," p. 37.

22. Morrison, *To Move the World*, p. 27; pp. 24–25.

23. Peterson, *Healing the Wounded Soul*, p. 120.

4 / Amity: Meeting the Other American Tradition

The epigraph is from Wright, *Haiku: this Other World,*
p. 181

1. Gregory, *Racial Amity*, ch. 18, pp. 1–3
2. Morrison, *To Move the World*, p. 26.
3. Williams, taped recollections, 1980.
4. Musta, "DC Bahá'í Tour 2012, Prospect Hill Cemetery #46," http://www.dcbahaitour.org, pp. 5–6.
5. Bahá'u'lláh, *The Hidden Words*, p. 20.
6. Stockman, *The Bahá'í Faith in America,* volume 2, pp. 224–25.
7. Ishtael-ebn-Kalenter (Ali Kuli Khan), "Translator's Preface," *The Bahá'í Proofs,* p. 5.

5 / Persian Prince of Amity: Mírzá Abu'l-Faḍl

The epigraph is from Leach, *Drawings, Verse & Belief,* p. 9
1. Taherzadeh, *The Revelation of Bahá'u'lláh*, Vol. 3, p. 434.
2. Ibid., Vol. 2, pp. 219–20.
3. Ibid., Vol. 3, p. 98.
4. Ibid., Vol. 3, pp. 97–105.
5. Ibid., Vol. 4, p. 259; Vol. 3, p. 433.
6. Mírzá Abu'l-Faḍl, *Bahá'í Proofs* (Translator's Preface), p. 14.
7. Taherzadeh, *The Revelation of Bahá'u'lláh,* Vol. 4, pp. 342–43.
8. Ibid., Vol. 3, pp. 436–37.
9. Gail, *Summon Up Remembrance*, p. 163.
10. Bahá'u'lláh, prayer revealed for Mírzá Abu'l-Faḍl, provisional translation found in the Washington, DC, Bahá'í Archives.
11. Gail, *Summon Up Remembrance*, p. 164.
12. Taherzadeh, *The Revelation of Bahá'u'lláh*, Vol. 4, p. 261.
13. Nakhjavani, *The Maxwells of Montreal*, p. 137.
14. Gail, *Dawn Over Mt. Hira,* p. 107.
15. Ibid.
16. Ibid., p. 112.
17. Khan, "1901–1903: Through the Vista of a Generation," *The Bahá'í Magazine*, Vol. 24, No. 2, May 1922, pp. 60–61.

18. Moomen, "Abu'l-Faḍl Gulpaygani, Mírzá," http://bahai-library. com/momen_encyclopedia_abul-Faḍl_gulpaygani.

19. Banani, introduction to *Miracles and Metaphors,* pp. xvii–xviii.

6 / Home

The epigraph is from Hayden, from "THE SNOW LAMP," *Collected Poems,* p. 186.

1. Hannen, "Mrs. Pauline A. Hannen (Heartpromptu Poem)," copy of undated handwritten manuscript.

2. Gregory, "Robert Turner," *World Order,* Vol. 12, Apr. 1946, pp. 28–29.

3. Ashraf, quoted in Moody, letter to Pauline Hannen, May 20, 1920.

4. 'Abdu'l-Bahá, letter to Joseph Hannen, provisional translation by Mirza Ahmad Esphahani, July 4, 1906.

5. Gregory, Louis, letter to Joseph Hannen, June 7, 1909.

6. Ibid.

7. Gregory, "Robert Turner," *World Order,* Apr. 1946, pp. 28–29.

8. Ibid.

9. 'Abdu'l-Bahá, in *Lights of Guidance,* #569.

10. Gregory, *A Heavenly Vista,* p. 9.

11. Ibid.

12. Morrison, *To Move the World,* p. 7.

7 / And to Work

The epigraph is from Hayden, "a voice in the wilderness," *Collected Poems,* p. 96.

1. Chapman, "A Witness to the Power of the Greatest Name," unfinished two-page manuscript sent to Victoria Bedikian, p. 1.

2. Gregory, "Some Recollections of the Early Days of the Faith in Washington, DC," pp. 3, 4, 33.

3. Hayden, "a voice in the wilderness," *Collected Poems,* p. 96.

4. *The Holy Scriptures,* p. 885.

5. Gregory, "Some Recollections of the Early Days of the Faith in Washington, DC," p. 5.

6. Gregory, letter to Joseph Hannen, June 7, 1909.

7. Gregory, "Some Recollections of the Early Days of the Faith in Washington, DC," p. 4.

8. Ibid.

9. Buck, *Alain Locke: Faith and Philosophy*, p. 40.

10. Ibid., p. 41.

11. Hannen, untitled paper on the first Bahá'í children's classes in Washington, unpaginated, Bahá'í Archives, Washington, DC.

12. Hannen, *A Family of Spiritual Dynamos*, p. 5.

13. Buck, *Alain Locke: Faith and Philosophy*, p. 38.

14. Locke, "Educator and Publicist," *Bahá'í Magazine,* Vol. 22, #8, Nov. 1931, p. 255.

15. Ibid.

16. NAACP: 100 YEARS OF HISTORY, http://www.naacp.org.

17. Cook, "Votes for Mothers," *The Crisis*, 1915, http://www.monticello.org.

18. Cook, letter to Pauline Hannen, Nov. 29, 1913.

19. Gregory, letter to Joseph Hannen, Nov. 12, 1910.

20. Hannen, "News from the Occident," *Star of the West,* Vol. 2, #3, Apr. 28, 1911, p. 9.

21. Hannen, quoted in *A Family of Spiritual Dynamos*, p. 6.

8 / Happiness

The epigraph is from Milosz, Czeslaw, from "A Gift," *The Ecco Anthology of International Poetry*, p. 158.

1. Gregory, Louis, fragment of letter to unidentified recipients (probably the Hannens), from *Konigen Louise,* undated, Bahá'í Archives of Washington, DC.

2. Gregory, *A Heavenly Vista,* p. 15.

3. Ibid, p. 19.

4. Gregory, *Racial Amity,* Chapter IV, p. 4.

5. Gregory, *A Heavenly Vista,* p. 15.

6. Ibid, pp. 15–21.

7. Morrison, *To Move the World*, p. 63; Gregory, Louisa, letter to Agnes Parsons, Jan. 18, 1921.

8. Mírzá Abu'l-Faḍl, *The Bahá'í Proofs*, pp. 112–13.

9. Ibid.

10. Bahíyyih Khánum, *Bahíyyih Khánum: The Greatest Holy Leaf*, p. 212.

11. Bahá'u'lláh, The Hidden Words, Persian no. 19.

12. Gregory, *A Heavenly Vista*, pp. 23–25.

13. Ibid.

14. Ibid.

15. Mírzá Abu'l-Faḍl, "Tributes and Eulogies" from "Translator's Preface," *The Bahá'í Proofs*, p. 21.

16. Fraser, "A Glimpse of Mírzá Abu'l-Fadl at Ramleh, Egypt," *Star of the West,* Vol. IV, No. 19, March 2, 1914.

17. Redman, *'Abdu'l-Bahá in Their Midst*, p. 330.

18. Gregory, *A Heavenly Vista,* pp. 15, 27–8.

18. Redman, *'Abdu'l-Bahá in Their Midst*, p. 14.

19. Morrison, *To Move the World*, pp. 47–48.

20. Ibid.

21. Kipling, "The Ballad of East and West," *A Victorian Anthology, 1837–1895,* http://www.bartleby.com.

22. "Here to Study That She May Teach in Her Own Country," *The Washington Times,* June 15, 1911.

23. Da Silveira, "Ashraf, Ghodsieh," *Encyclopedia Iranica,* http://iranicaonline.org.

24. Morrison, "A New Creation," *Journal of Bahá'í Studies,* Vol. 9, No. 4, p. 9.

9 / Planting the World-Tree in the U.S.A.

The epigraph is from Ruhe-Schoen, Janet, "World Tree," unpublished ms., personal papers of Janet Ruhe-Schoen, 2012.

1. Redman, *'Abdu'l-Bahá in Their Midst*, p. 57.

2. Universal House of Justice, *Century of Light*, p. 20.

3. Redman, *'Abdu'l-Bahá in Their Midst*, pp. 90, 95.

4. Cook, Coralie, letter to 'Abdu'l-Bahá, March 2, 1914.

5. 'Abdu'l-Bahá, *The Promulgation of Universal Peace*, p. 44.

6. Blake, William, "The Black Boy," www.poetryfoundation.org; Ives, *Portals to Freedom*, p. 63.

7. Ewing, *Toward Oneness*, pp. 46–47.

8. Sobhani, *Mahmud's Diary*, p. 387

9. Lovelace, "To Althea from Prison," in Untermeyer, *A Treasury of Great Poems*, p. 472.

10. Parsons and Hollinger, *Abdu'l-Bahá in America: Agnes Parsons' Diary*, p. 31.

11. Etter-Lewis and Thomas, *Lights of the Spirit*, p. 51.

12. Buck, *Alain Locke, Faith & Philosophy*, p. 46.

13. Hannen, untitled manuscript on first Bahá'í children's classes in Washington, DC, undated, Bahá'í Archives, Washington, DC.

14. Buck, *Alain Lock, Faith and Philosophy*, pp. 41–42.

15. Ibid.

16. Morrison, *To Move the World*, p. 206.

17. Hannen, Pauline, untitled manuscript on children's classes.

18. Ibid., and DC Bahá'í Tour 2012, DC Bahá'í Center #14, http://www.dcbahaitour.org.

19. Sobhani, *Mahmud's Diary*, p. 57

20. Morrison, *To Move the World*, p. 60.

21. Ibid., p. 58.

22. Ibid., pp. 58–59.

23. Ibid., p. 59.

24. Ibid., p. 61.

25. Perry, "Robert Abbot and the Chicago Defender: A Door to the Masses," *Michigan Chronicle,* Oct. 10, 1995, http://bahai.uga.edu/News/101095.html.

26. Miller, "Echoes of the NAACP's Fourth Annual Conference," *The Chicago Defender,* May 4, 1912.

27. Sobhani, *Mahmud's Diary,* p. 70.

10 / A Marriage of Equals

The epigraph is from "Black is the Color," http://www.metrolyrics. com.

1. Hill, Joy, "In Memoriam: Louisa Mathew Gregory," *Bahá'í World Vol. XIII*, pp. 876–88; Savio, "Mayflowers in the Ville Lumiere," p. 13.

2. 'Abdu'l-Bahá, undated Tablet to Miss Louise Mathew in Paris answering her letter of Dec. 30, 1908.

3. Undated Tablet to Miss Louise Mathew, probably in London, provisional translations, Bahá'í Archives, Washington, DC.

4. Gregory, Louise, letter to Pauline Hannen, Oct. 15, 1912.

5. Gregory, Louise, letter to Agnes Parsons, Dec. 21, 1914.

6. Ibid.

7. Ibid.

8. 'Abdu'l-Bahá, quoted in Thompson, *The Diary of Juliet Thompson*, p. 76.

9. Gregory, Louis, Letter to Louisa Mathew, July 28, 1912.

10. Gregory, Louis, Letter to Pauline Hannen, Sept. 19, 1912.

11. Gregory, Louis, Letter to Edith Chapman, Feb. 20, 1935.

12. Gregory, Louis, Letter to Pauline Hannen, Sept. 30, 1912.

13. Shoghi Effendi, *God Passes By*, p. 457.

11 / "The Difficult Part of Peace-Maker"

The epigraph is from Drummond de Andrade, Carlos, "Your Shoulders Hold Up the World, *The Ecco Anthology of International Poetry*, p. xxxvii.

1. Queen, Hallie, letter to 'Abdu'l-Bahá from Joseph Hannen, August 3, 1913.

2. Ibid.

3. Hannen, Joseph, letter to 'Abdu'l-Bahá, Jan. 18, 1914.

4. *The Afro American*, April 14, 1928. http://news.google.com/ newspapers.

5. "Forward to Facsimile Edition," pp. 12–17.

6. Ibid., p. 12.

7. Ibid., pp. 12–17.

8. 'Abdu'l-Bahá, in *Bahá'í Prayers,* pp. 115–16.

9. Hannen, Joseph, letter to 'Abdu'l-Bahá, March 5, 1914.

10. Ibid.

11. Cook, Coralie, letter to 'Abdu'l-Bahá, March 2, 1914.

12. Gregory, Louisa, letter to Agnes Parsons, March 17, 1914 NBA; Morrison, Gayle, *To Move the World,* p. 82.

13. Gregory, Louisa, letters to Pauline Hannen, Aug. 15, 16, 17, 1913, NBA.

14. Gregory, Louisa, letter to Agnes Parsons, March 17, 1914, NBA.

15. Morrison, *To Move the World,* p. 82.

16. Gregory, Louisa, letter to Albert Vail, May 19, 1914, NBA.

17. Cook, Coralie, letter to 'Abdu'l-Bahá, March 2, 1914.

18. Ibid.

19. 'Abdu'l-Bahá, quoted in Morrison, *To Move the World,* p. 76.

20. Gregory, Louisa, quoted in Morrison, *To Move the World,* pp. 77–78.

21. Gregory, Louisa, letter to Agnes Parsons, May 4, 1916, NBA.

22. Gregory, Louisa, letter to unidentified "Dear Sister in el Abha," June 20, 1916, NBA.

23. Gregory, Louis, letter to Joseph Hannen, July 19, 1919, NBA.

24. Williams, Roy, taped personal recollections, Greensboro, NC, 1980, NBA.

25. Ibid.

26. Hannen, Joseph, letter to Agnes Parsons, January 15, 1917.

27. Williams, Roy, taped recollections, 1980.

12 / INTO THE MAW

The epigraph is from Cervantes, Lorna Dee, "Poem for the Young White Man Who Asked Me How I, an Intelligent, Well-Read Person, Could Believe in the War Between Races," *Women Poets of the World,* pp. 398–99.

1. Gregory, Louis, "Other News Notes," *Star of the West* Vol. II, No. 16, Dec. 21, 1916, p. 519.

2. 'Abdu'l-Bahá, *Selections from the Writings of 'Abdu'l-Bahá,* p. 320.

3. "Other News Notes," *Star of the West,* Dec. 21, 1916, p. 519.

4. Williams, Roy, personal recollections, 1980.

5. Ibid.

6. McMullen, Mike, "The Atlanta Bahá'í Community and Race Unity: 1909–1950," *World Order,* 26.4, Summer, 1995.

7. Morrison, *To Move the World,* pp. 84, 86.

8. Ibid*.,* pp. 66–67.

9. Ibid., p. 94.

10. Williams, Roy, Letter to Joseph Hannen, Nov. 7, 1919.

11. Williams, Roy, Letter to Joseph Hannen, Nov. 24, 1919.

12. Williams, Roy, personal recollections, 1980.

13. Williams, Roy, letter to Joseph Hannen, June 21, 1919.

14. Williams, Roy, letter to Joseph Hannen, June 27, 1919.

15. Gregory, Louisa, letter to Joseph Hannen, Sept. 1, 1917.

16. Gregory, Louis, letter to Louise Gregory, Oct. 21, 1917.

17. Gregory, Louis, letter to Louise Gregory, Nov. 5, 1917.

18. Ibid.

19. Gregory, Louis, letter to Louise Gregory, Dec. 7, 1917.

20. Henderson, George, letter to Louis Gregory, October 17, 1917.

21. Hannen, Joseph, letter to Shoghi Rabbani, April 30, 1919.

22. 'Abdu'l-Bahá, Tablet to Louis Gregory, July 24, 1919, prov. transl. by Shoghi Rabbani, Bahá'í Archives, Washington, DC.

23. Morrison, Gayle, "A New Creation: The Power of the Covenant in the Life of Louis Gregory," *Journal of Bahá'í Studies,* Vol. 9, No. 4, Association for Bahá'í Studies, 1994, pp. 1–4. www.bahaistudies.ca/journal.

24. 'Abdu'l-Bahá, quoted in ibid.

25. Williams, Roy, letter to Joseph Hannen, October 16, 1919.

13 / Sir Happy

The epigraph is from Cather, Willa, from "Prairie Spring," *April Twilights*, Alfred A. Knopf, NY, p. 131.

1. "Memorial Service to Dr. Zia Mabsut Bagdádí, Held in the Bahá'í House of Worship, May 8, 1937, Mrs. Corinne True,

Mr. Albert Windust, Chairmen," "In Memoriam," *The Bahá'í World, Vol. VII, 1936–1938,* p. 539.

2. Bagdadi, Dr. Zia M., *Treasures of the East,* pp. 94–95.

3. Ibid., p. 149.

4. Gregory, Louis, letter to Edith Chapman, Feb. 20, 1935.

5. Redman, *'Abdu'l-Bahá in Their Midst,* p. 132.

6. Ibid., p. 228.

7. "Zeenat Khanum," *Star of the West,* vol. 5, issue 4, May 17, 1914, p. 58.

8. Bush-Banks, Olivia, *The Collected Works of Olivia Ward Bush-Banks,* pp. 66–67, http://books.google.com.

9. "Memorial Service to Dr. Zia Mabsut Bagdadi," *Bahá'í World Vol. VII,* p. 538.

10. Perry, Mark, "Pioneering Race Unity," *World Order,* Vol. 20, No. 2, p. 49.

14 / Red Summer, Rough Ground

The epigraph is from DuBois, W. E. B., "A Litany of Atlanta," *Singers of the Dawn,* p. 8.

1. Wikipedia, *Red Summer of 1919,* accessed March, 2013.

2. Morrison, *A New Creation,* p. 2.

3. Wikipedia, *Red Summer of 1919,* accessed March, 2013.

4. Ibid.

5. Gregory, Louisa, letter to Joseph Hannen, July 23, 1919.

6. Gregory, Louis, Letter to Joseph Hannen, August 4, 1919, NBA.

7. Ibid.

8. Ibid.

9. Ibid., September 21, 1919.

10. Ibid., September 30, 1919.

11. Gregory, Louisa, letter to Joseph Hannen, July 31, 1919.

12. Williams, quoted in Morrison, *To Move the World,* pp. 130–31.

13. Gregory, Louisa, letter to Joseph Hannen, undated, 1919.

14. Ibid.

15. Williams, Roy, letter to Miss Ella M. Robarts, May 27, 1920.

16. Williams, Roy, Letter to Agnes Parsons, Sept. 19, 1919.

17. Ibid., November 3, 1919.

18. Shoghi Effendi, letter to Mabry Oglesby, May 23, 1927.

19. Mabry and Sadie Oglesby, quoted in Etter-Lewis and Thomas, *Lights of the Spirit*, pp. 76–77.

15 / THE FIRST RACE AMITY CONFERENCE

The epigraph is from Wilcox, Ella Wheeler, from "The World's Need," http://www.veganpoet.com.

1. McKay, Doris, *Fires in Many Hearts*, p. 47.

2. Whitehead, O. Z., *Some Bahá'ís to Remember*, pp. 79–80.

3. Ibid., p. 87.

4. Morrison, *To Move the World*, p. 136.

5. http://bahaicalendarthismonthinhistory.blogspot.com/...february 1852.

6. Morrison, *To Move the World*, p. 137.

7. Ibid., pp. 137–38.

8. Ibid.

8. Sobhani, *Mahmúd's Diary*, p. 364.

9. 'Abdu'l-Bahá, *The Promulgation of Universal Peace*, p. 454.

10. Hannen, Joseph, Letter to Roy Williams, Dec. 13, 1919.

11. Remey, Charles Mason, "Obituary, Joseph H. Hannen," *Star of the West*, Vol. 10, No. 19, Mar. 2, 1920, pp. 345–46.

12. Joseph Hannen, quoted in Morrison, *To Move the World*, p. 316.

13. Gregory, Louis, Letter to Pauline Hannen, Feb. 18, 1920.

14. "Set up this esteemed soul in Thy Glorious Kingdom," *Star of the West*, Vol. 11, June 5, 1920, p. 90.

15. Gregory, Louis, Letter to Mrs. A.S. Parsons, Dec. 16, 1920. WBA

16. Morrison, *To Move the World*, p. 140.

17. Miller and Pruitt-Hogan, *Faithful to the Task at Hand*, p. 58.

18. Ibid, p. 34.

19. Harris, M.F., quoted in Buck, "The Bahá'í Race Amity Movement and the Black Intelligensia in Jim Crow America," *Bahá'í Studies Review*, Vol. 17.

20. 'Abdu'l-Bahá, quoted in Morrison, *To Move the World,* pp. 142–43.

21. http://ncra.wheelock.edu

22. Parsons, quoted in Whitehead, *Some Bahá'ís to Remember,* pp. 95–96.

16 / PURE GOLD

The epigraph is from from "Psalms," *The Holy Scriptures,* Jewish Publication Society of America, Philadelphia, 1958, p. 802.

1. Morrison, *To Move the World,* p. 146; Williams, Roy, letter to Agnes Parsons, Nov. 7, 1921.

2. Morrison, *To Move the World,* p. 146.

3. Gregory, Louis, letter to Edith Chapman, June 21, 1929; Gregory, Louis, letter to Edith Chapman, Jan. 29, 1927.

4. Gregory, Louis, letter to George Miller, Nov. 3, 1948, Washington, DC, Bahá'í Archives.

5. Morrison, Gayle, "Gregory, Louis George," *Bahá'í Encyclopedia Project,* http://www.bahai-encyclopedia-project.org.

6. Morrison, *To Move the World,* p. 117.

7. Gregory, Louis, *Racial Amity,* unpublished mss, ca. 1947.

8. Gregory, Louis, a version of the Foreword to his Race Amity mss.

9. Morrison, *To Move the World,* p. 318.

10. Ibid, pp. 249–50.

11. Ibid.

12. Gregory, Louis, letter to Edith Chapman, Nov. 4, 1932.

13. Gregory, Louis, letter to Pauline Hannen, March 9, 1928, NBA.

14. Gregory, Louisa, letter to the Office of the Secretary of the NSA, May 6, 1928, NBA.

15. Ibid.

16. Ibid., Feb. 12, 1929.

17. Ibid.

18. Gregory, Louis, letter to Edith Chapman, June 21, 1929, NBA.

19. Ibid., June 17, 1930.

20. Ibid., Sept. 27, 1933.

21. Shoghi Effendi, quoted in Hornby, *Lights of the Spirit,* p. 38.

22. 'Abdu'l-Bahá, quoted in *Bahá'í World Vol. XIII,* p. 878.

23. Shoghi Effendi, quoted in Morrison, *To Move the World,* p. 310.

17 / Heritage: Doris and Willard McKay

The epigraph is from Crabbe, George, from "The Burough," in Parker, Elinor, Ed., *Echoes of the Sea,* Charles Scribner's Sons, NY, 1977, p. 85.

1. Emerald Hill Farm guestbook 123–25, photo, unpaginated; McKay, D., *Fires in Many Hearts,* pp. 11, 55, 62, 80; Vreeland, Paul, "Doris McKay," *The Bahá'í World 1992–1997,* p. 31; Andersons, audio interview with Doris McKay, 1978.

2. Emerald Hill guestbook, unpaginated; McKay, D., Diary 1924, unpaginated.

3. Ibid.; Ibid.; Donelly, R., June, 2011; McKay, *Fires in Many Hearts,* pp. 14–16, 68; Andersons, interview with D. McKay, 1978.

4. "Doris McKay," *The Bahá'í World 1992–1997,* p. 31; McKay, D., "My Other World," unpaginated; McKay, *Fires in Many Hearts,* p. 10; Boyles, Ann and Mould, Louise, conversations with the author, Charlottetown, June 2011; Andersons, interview with D. McKay, 1978.

5. McKay, D., "The Roots of the Cause in the West, Our Dawnbreakers: Willard McKay," *Canadian Bahá'í News,* Oct. 1967, p. 4.6. McKay, D., letter to Mabel Ives, July 20, 1925; Phillis, Valerie, conversation with the author, Charlottetown, June, 2011.

7. McKay, *Fires in Many Hearts,* pp. 21–22, 17–18; Ruhe-Schoen, *A Love Which Does Not Wait,* pp. 201–205.

8. Ibid., pp. 28–29; 31–32; O'Neill, Patrick, conversation with the author, Charlottetown, June, 2011.

9. McKay, *Fires in Many Hearts,* pp. 75–77.

10. McKay, *Fires in Many Hearts,* pp. 69–70; McKay, D., "From the Platform," The Bahá'í Magazine, May, 1929, pp. 61–64.

11. McKay, *Fires in Many Hearts,* pp. 66, 70, 79–82; Andersons, interview with D. McKay, 1978.

12. McKay, *Fires in Many Hearts,* pp. 97–102, 120; van den Hoonard, *The Origins of the Bahá'í Community of Canada, 1898–1948,* pp. 89–91; Andersons, interview with D. McKay, 1978.

13. McKay, *Fires in Many Hearts,* pp. 109–10; 118–19.

14. Ibid., pp. 141–161.

15. Ibid., pp. 171–172; McKay, D., "Willard McKay," *Canadian Bahá'í News*, Oct. 1967, p. 4.

16. Morrison, *To Move the World*, p. 218.

17. McKay, Willard., *Account of His Teaching Tour*, pp. 6–21; *Fires in Many Hearts*, pp. 181–184; Scales, Jean, "Sarah Martin Pereira," *The Bahá'í World 1992–1997*, pp. 208, 221–29.

18. McKay, D., letters to Mabel Garis, Aug. 5, 1980, pp. 1–8, and Sept. 17, 1980, p. 1.

19. McKay, *Fires in Many Hearts*, pp. 197–250.

20. Ibid., pp. 252–69; Andersons, interview with D. McKay, 1978; McKay, D., Letters to Mabel Garris, Aug. 5 and Sept. 17, 1980.

21. McKay, *Fires in Many Hearts*, pp. 251–91.

22. Ibid., p. 292; Andersons, interview with D. McKay, 1978.

23. Rutstein, Nathan, *Corinne True*, pp. 32–33, 45, 71, 104; McKay, Doris, letter to Mabel Ives, July 4, 1941.

24. Gregory, Louis, "Faith and the Man," *The Bahá'í World 1938–1940*, pp. 901–902; McKay, *Fires in Many Hearts*, pp. 294–96, 302; McKay, D., Letter to Dorothy Baker, Jan. 17, 1941.

25. McKay, *Fires in Many Hearts*, pp. 302–8, 314.

26. Ibid., pp. 313–24; McKay, D., "The Lure of the Island," undated handwritten notebook diary, ca. 1945-46, Courtesy LSA of Charlottetown; McKay, D., Letter to Greg and Evelyn Wooster, Charlottetown, March, 1967.

27. McKay, *Fires in Many Hearts*, pp. 325–27; McKay, D., Letter to the Woosters, Charlottetown, March, 1967; Anderson, audio interview with Doris McKay, 1978.

28. McKay, *Fires in Many Hearts*, p. 324; Anderson, audio interview with Doris McKay, 1978; van den Hoonaard, *Origins of the Bahá'í Community of Canada*, pp. 195–96.

29. McKay, *Fires in Many Hearts*, pp. 325–27; McKay, W., "Report of a trip undertaken by Willard McKay at the request of the Canadian Teaching Committee, Jan. 8 to Feb. 15, 1947," Courtesy of L.S.A. of Charlottetown; van den Hoonaard, *Origins of the Bahá'í Community of Canada*, p. 229.

30. Boyles, Ann, Conversation with the author, June, 2011; Group discussion by Bahá'ís of Charlottetown, P.E.I., with the author, June, 2011; Andersons, audio interview with Doris McKay, 1978; Polland, Louise, email to the author, July, 2011; Mould, Louise, email to the author, September, 2011.

31. McKay, D., "Willard McKay," *Canadian Bahá'í News,* Oct. 1967, p. 4; McKay, D., Letter to Greg & Evelyn Wooster, Charlottetown, March, 1967; McKay, *Fires in Many Hearts,* p. 335.

32. Boyles, Ann, conversation with the author, June, 2011; Phillis, Valerie and Chris, Conversation with the author, June, 2011; Group discussion by Bahá'ís of Charlottetown with the author, June, 2011; Vreeland, Claire, emails to the author, May and June, 2011; Polland, Louise, email to the author, July, 2011.

33. McKay, D., "Reflections of a Pioneer," *Bahá'í Canada,* Vol. 9, No. 11, January, 1988, p. 17.

34. Gregory, Louis, Letter to Edith Chapman, August 30, 1938.

35. McKay, D., "Reflections of a Pioneer," *Bahá'í Canada,* Vol. 9, No. 11, January, 1988, p. 17; Bahá'ís of Charlottetown in conversation with the author, June, 2011; McKay, *Fires in Many Hearts,* p. 338.

Bibliography

Works of Bahá'u'lláh

The Hidden Words. Translated by Shoghi Effendi. Wilmette, IL: Bahá'í
Publishing, 2002.
The Seven Valleys and the Four Valleys. Translated by Ali-Kuli Khan and
Marzieh Gail. New ed. Wilmette, IL: Bahá'í Publishing Trust, 1991.

Works of 'Abdu'l-Bahá

Tablets of the Divine Plan. Wilmette, IL: Bahá'í Publishing Trust, 1993.
Tablets to Louisa Gregory. Translations of Tablets of 'Abdu'l-Bahá. U.S.
National Bahá'í Archives, Wilmette, IL.

Works of Shoghi Effendi

God Passes By. Wilmette, IL: Bahá'í Publishing Trust, 1974.

Works of the Universal House of Justice

Century of Light. Haifa: Bahá'í World Center, 2001.

Other Works

"'Abdu'l-Bahá's Legacy to Egypt Recalled." *Bahá'í World News Service*. Apr.
20, 2011. http://news.Bahai.org/story/818.
Banani, Amin. "Introduction." *Miracles and Metaphors* by Mírzá Abu'l-
Faḍl. Los Angeles: Kalimat Press, 1981.
Bankier, Joanna and Deirdre Lashgari, Eds. *Women Poets of the World*.
NY: MacMillian Publishing, Inc., 1983.
Balyuzi, H. M. *'Abdu'l-Bahá*. Oxford: George Ronald, 1971.
———. *Eminent Bahá'ís of the Time of Bahá'u'lláh*. George Ronald,
Oxford, 1985.

Barney, Elsa Clifford. Handwritten copy of talk given on the 17th of October in Chicago, 1901. U.S. National Bahá'í Archives.

Buck, Christopher. *Alain Locke: Faith & Philosophy.* Los Angeles: Kalimát Press, L.A.: 2005.

Da Silviera, Mahnaz A. "Ashraf, Ghodsieh." *Encyclopedia Iranica.* http://iranicaonline.org.

Dayton, Donald W. "The Holiness Churches: A Significant Ethical Tradition." *The Christian Century.* Feb. 26, 1975. http://religion-online.org.

"DC Bahá'í Tour 2012." http://www.dcbahaitour.org.

Dove, Rita, ed. *The Penguin Anthology of 20th Century American Poetry.* New York: Penguin Books, 2011.

Drake, St. Clair and Horace R Cayton. *Black Metropolis: A Study of Negro Life in a Northern City, Vol. I.* New York: Harper & Row, 1962.

Du Bois, W. E. B. *The Souls of Black Folk: A Celebration of Black American Artists.* New York: Harry N. Abrams, 2004.

———. "Address to the Nation, 16 August 1908." http://users.wfu.edu/zulick/341/niagara.htm

Edith Chapman Papers. Louis Gregory Correspondence, U.S. National Bahá'í Archives, Wilmette, IL.

Eleazer, Robert B., comp. *Singers of the Dawn.* Atlanta: Commission of Interracial Cooperation, Southern Regional Council, Inc., 1943.

Etter-Lewis, Gwendolyn and Richard Thomas. *Lights of the Spirit.* Wilmette, IL: Bahá'í Publishing, 2006.

Ewing, Tod, ed. *Toward Oneness.* Riviera Beach, FL: Palabra Publications, 1998.

Fraser, Isabel. "A Glimpse of Mírzá Abu'l-Faḍl at Ramleh, Egypt." *Star of the West* 4, no. 19 (March 2, 1914).

Gail, Marzieh. *Dawn Over Mount Hira.* Oxford: George Ronald, 1976.

———. *Summon Up Remembrance.* Oxford: George Ronald, 1987.

Gregory, Louis. *A Heavenly Vista: The Pilgrimage of Louis G. Gregory.* Washington, DC: R.L. Pendleton, n.d.

———. "Impressions of 'Abdu'l-Bahá While at Ramleh." *Star of the West* 2, no. 10 (Sept. 8, 1911).

————. Letter to Mabel Turner Taylor, May 3, 1951. From personal collection of Christopher Ruhe.

————. *Racial Amity*. Wilmette, IL: Louis Gregory Papers, U.S. National Bahá'í Archives. Unpublished ms.

————. "Robert Turner." *World Order* 12 (April, 1946).

————. "Some Recollections of the Early Days of the Bahá'í Faith in Washington, DC," Tuskegee, AL: 1937. Bahá'í Archives, Washington, DC. Unpublished manuscript.

Guillaume, Bernice F., ed. *The Collected Works of Olivia Ward Bush-Banks*. New York: The Schomburg Library of 19th Century Black Women Writers, 1991. http://books.google.com.

Hannen/Knobloch Collection. Bahá'í Archives. Washington, DC.

Hannen-Knobloch Family Papers. U.S. National Bahá'í Archives. Wilmette, IL.

Hayden, Robert. *Collected Poems*. New York: Liveright, 1996.

"Here to Study that She May Teach in her own Country." *The Washington Times*. June 15, 1911.

Hill, Joy Earl. "In Memoriam: Louisa Mathew Gregory." *Bahá'í World, Vol. XIII 1954–1963*. Haifa: Bahá'í World Center, 1970.

Hogenson, Kathryn Jewett. *Lighting the Western Sky*. Oxford: George Ronald, 2010.

The Holy Scriptures. Philadelphia: The Jewish Publication Society of America, 1958.

Hughes, Langston. *The Big Sea*. New York: Hill and Wang, 2001.

Ishtael-ebn-Kalenter (Ali Kuli Khan). "Translator's Preface." *The Bahá'í Proofs* by Mírzá Abu'l-Faḍl. New York: Bahá'í Publishing Committee, 1929.

Ives, Howard Colby. *Portals to Freedom*. Oxford: George Ronald, 1974.

Kaminsky, Ilya and Susan Harris, eds. *The Ecco Anthology of International Poetry*. NY: HarperCollins Publishing, 2010.

Khan, Dr. Ali Kuli. "1901–1903: Through the Vista of a Generation." *The Bahá'í Magazine* 24, no. 2 (May, 1922).

Locke, Alain. "Educator and Publicist." *The Bahá'í Magazine* 22, no. 8 (Nov. 1931).

Louis Gregory Documents. Bahá'í Archives, Washington, DC.

Louise Gregory Documents. Bahá'í Archives, Washington, DC.

McKay, Doris. *Fires in Many Hearts*. Manotock, ON: Nine Pines Publishing, 1993.

———. Taped interviews with Doris McKay by Joan and Fred Anderson, ca. 1990 and by Robert Donnelly, n.d., P.E.I., provided by Louise Mould, Robert Donnelly, and the Local Spiritual Assembly of Charlottetown, 2010, 2013.

———. "Reflections of a Pioneer." *Bahá'í Canada* 9, no. 11 (January, 1988).

McMullen, Mike. "The Atlanta Bahá'í Community and Race Unity: 1909–1950." *World Order* 26:4 (summer, 1995).

Miller, Carroll L. L. and Anne S. Pruitt-Hogan. *Faithful to the Task at Hand: the Life of Lucy Diggs Slowe*. Albany: State U. of NY Press, 2012.

Miller, Mildred. "Echoes of the NAACP's Fourth Annual Conference." *The Chicago Defender*. May 4, 1912. http://centenary.bahai.us/news/echoes.

Mírzá Abu'l-Faḍl Documents. Bahá'í Archives, Washington, DC.

Moe, Judy Hannen. *Hannens and Knoblochs: A Family of Spiritual Dynamos*. 2012. Unpublished manuscript.

Momen, Moojan. "Abu'l-Fadl Gulpaygani, Mirza." http://bahai-library. com/momen_encyclopedia_abul-fadl_gulpaygani.

Morrison, Gayle. "A New Creation: The Power of the Covenant in the Life of Louis Gregory." *Journal of Bahá'í Studies* 9, no. 4. Association for Bahá'í Studies, 1994. http://www.bahai-studies.ca/journal.

———. "Gregory, Louis George." *Bahá'í Encyclopedia Project*. http://www.bahai-encyclopedia-project.org (accessed 19 June 2012).

———. To Move the World: Louis G. Gregory and the Advancement of Racial Unity in America. Wilmette, IL: Bahá'í Publishing Trust, 1982.

Nakhjavani, Violet. *The Maxwells of Montreal, Vol. 1*. Oxford: George Ronald, 2011.

Parsons, Agnes S. and Richard Hollings. *'Abdu'l-Bahá in America: Agnes Parsons' Diary*. Los Angeles: Kalimat Press, 1996.

Perry, Mark. "Pioneering Race Unity: the Chicago Bahá'ís, 1919–1939." *World Order* 20, no. 2 (winter, 1985–86).

———. "Robert Abbot and the Chicago Defender: A Door to the Masses." *Michigan Chronicle,* Oct. 10, 1990. http://bahai.uga.edu.

Peterson, Phyllis K. *Healing the Wounded Soul.* Wilmette: Bahá'í Publishing Trust, 2005.

Redman, Earl. *'Abdu'l-Bahá in Their Midst*. Oxford: George Ronald, 2011.

The Research Department of the Bahá'í World Centre. *Bahíyyih Khánum: The Greatest Holy Leaf.* Haifa: Bahá'í World Centre, 1982.

Robertson, David. *W. C. Handy: The Life and Times of the Man Who Made the Blues.* New York: Alfred A. Knopf, 2000.

Sammons, Mark, and Valerie Cunningham. *Black Portsmouth.* Lebanon, NH: University Press of New England, 2004.

Savio, Julio. "Mayflowers in the Ville Lumiere." *Lights of Irfan*, Book 12. http://irfancolloquia.org.

Stevenson, Bryan. "New Life." *Smithsonian,* Dec. 2012.

Sobhani, Mohi, transl. *Mahmúd's Diary.* Oxford: George Ronald, 1998.

Stockman, Robert H. *'Abdu'l-Bahá in America.* Wilmette, IL: Bahá'í Publishing Trust, 2012.

———. *The Bahá'í Faith in America, Vol. I.* Wilmette, IL: Bahá'í Publishing Trust, 1985.

———. *The Bahá'í Faith in America, Vol. 2.* Oxford: George Ronald, 1995.

Taherzadeh, Abib. *The Revelation of Bahá'u'lláh, Vol. 2.* Oxford: George Ronald, 1977.

———. *The Revelation of Bahá'u'lláh, Vol. 3.* Oxford: George Ronald, 1983.

———. *The Revelation of Bahá'u'lláh, Vol. 4.* Oxford: George Ronald, 1987.

Thompson, Juliet. *The Diary of Juliet Thompson.* Los Angeles: Kalimat Press, 1983.

Untermeyer, Louis. *A Treasury of Great Poems*. New York: Galahad Books, 1992.

van den Hoonaard, Will C. *The Origins of the Bahá'í Community of Canada*. Waterloo, ON: Wilfred Laurier U. Press, 1996.

White, Roger, comp. *A Compendium of Volumes of the Bahá'í World, I–XII*. Oxford: George Ronald, 1981.

Whitehead, O. Z. *Some Bahá'ís to Remember*. Oxford: George Ronald, 1983.

Wilkerson, Isabel. *The Warmth of Other Suns: The Epic Story of America's Great Migration*. NY: Random House, 2010.

Williams, Juan and Qunton Hosford Dixie. *This Far by Faith: Stories from the African American Religious Experience*. NY: Blackside, Inc., 2005.

Williams, Roy. Taped recollections from Greenville, NC, 1980. Wilmette, IL: U.S. National Bahá'í Archives.

Willis, Deborah. *Reflections in Black*. New York: W. W. Norton and Co., 2000.

Wright, Richard. *Haiku: the Other World*. New York: Anchor Books, 1998.

"Zeenat Khanum." *Star of the West* 5, issue 4 (May 17, 1914).

Bahá'í
PUBLISHING
AND THE BAHÁ'Í FAITH

Bahá'í Publishing produces books based on the teachings of the Bahá'í Faith. Founded over 160 years ago, the Bahá'í Faith has spread to some 235 nations and territories and is now accepted by more than five million people. The word "Bahá'í" means "follower of Bahá'u'lláh." Bahá'u'lláh, the founder of the Bahá'í Faith, asserted that He is the Messenger of God for all of humanity in this day. The cornerstone of His teachings is the establishment of the spiritual unity of humankind, which will be achieved by personal transformation and the application of clearly identified spiritual principles. Bahá'ís also believe that there is but one religion and that all the Messengers of God—among them Abraham, Zoroaster, Moses, Krishna, Buddha, Jesus, and Muḥammad—have progressively revealed its nature. Together, the world's great religions are expressions of a single, unfolding divine plan. Human beings, not God's Messengers, are the source of religious divisions, prejudices, and hatreds.

The Bahá'í Faith is not a sect or denomination of another religion, nor is it a cult or a social movement. Rather, it is a globally recognized independent world religion founded on new books of scripture revealed by Bahá'u'lláh.

Bahá'í Publishing is an imprint of the National Spiritual Assembly of the Bahá'ís of the United States.

For more information about the Bahá'í Faith,
or to contact Bahá'ís near you,
visit http://www.bahai.us/
or call
1-800-22-UNITE

OTHER BOOKS AVAILABLE FROM BAHÁ'Í PUBLISHING

THE DAWNING PLACE
The Building of a Temple, the Forging of a Global Religious Community
Bruce W. Whitmore
$45.00 US / $47.00 CAN
Hardcover
ISBN 978-1-61851-083-9

The incredible story of the Bahá'í House of Worship in Wilmette, Illinois, and of the small devoted community that built it and turned a dream into reality.

Added to the National Registry of Historic Places in 1978, the Bahá'í House of Worship in Wilmette, Illinois is a stunning building with an inspiring and storied history. Drawing upon decades of research, author Bruce Whitmore brings to life, in rich and vivid detail, not only the story of how the Temple came to be built, but the story of the birth of a religious community and the many trials and victories it would experience in its establishment. In 1903, a small group of Chicago Bahá'ís made a decision to build a place of worship that would be open to people of all faiths. The search for a location; the choice of a forested bluff overlooking Lake Michigan; the 1912 dedication of the Temple site by 'Abdu'l-Bahá, the son and appointed successor of the Faith's Prophet-Founder; the selection of a design in 1920 that attracted international attention; and the decades of planning and building that led to the 1953 dedication tell only part of the story. The members of the fledgling Bahá'í community of the time, who pooled what meager resources they had to set in motion an extraordinary nationwide enterprise, serve as inspiring examples of sacrifice and devotion. The endeavor proved not only to be a unifying and galvanizing force for the North American Bahá'ís, but a rallying point for the entire worldwide Bahá'í community, which was still in the earliest stages of its development when the plan was set in motion. Now in its second edition, *The Dawning Place* has been updated to cover the years that have elapsed since the Temple's dedication with stunning, never-before-published photographs of the building and its surrounding environs.

DISCOVERING THE SUN
Jacqueline Mehrabi
Illustrated by Susan Reed
$12.00 US / $14.00 CAN
Trade Paper
ISBN 978-1-61851-079-2

Follow the story of a fifteen-year-old girl as she takes charge of her own spiritual destiny and participates in her first religious fast at boarding school.

Discovering the Sun follows Fern, a fifteen-year-old girl who has grown up on the remote Orkney Islands of northern Scotland and who is preparing to leave home for the first time to attend boarding school. Faced with the prospect of being away from the familiarity of her loving family, she is apprehensive about what lies ahead. She is also preparing to take part in the nineteen-day Bahá'í Fast for the first time. Concerned that she will be an outsider because of her faith, Fern soon makes friends with a number of classmates and discovers that she is not the only one who comes from a slightly different background. She also comes to learn that the Fast cannot only be a source of nourishment for her and for others but that tests and blessings can come from some unexpected directions. This is the second book in a trilogy. The first title in the series, *Discovering the Moon* (978-1-61851-072-3), was published in Fall 2014, and the third book, *Discovering the Sea,* will be published in Fall 2015.

THE RIDDLE OF THE HOLLOW REED
Charlotte Harman
Illustrated by Taurus Burns
$10.00 US / $12.00 CAN
Hardcover
ISBN 978-0-87743-716-1

A beautifully illustrated hardcover picture book that teaches children to love and care for others.

The Riddle of the Hollow Reed is a children's story about a traveling dervish who arrives in a city and becomes the catalyst for its transformation. When he arrives, he begins to play his flute to the townspeople, telling them that God created them because He loves them. Although the rulers of the town, not wanting change, scheme against the dervish, the townspeople begin to believe in his message, and the forces of corruption in the town are defeated through the power of the dervish's love.

THE SECRET OF DIVINE CIVILIZATION
'Abdu'l-Bahá
$21.00 US / $23.00 CAN
Hardcover
ISBN 978-1-61851-082-2

An outstanding treatise on the social and spiritual progress of both nations and individuals.

The Secret of Divine Civilization is a thorough explanation of the view of the Bahá'í Faith on the true nature of civilization. It contains an appealing and universal message, inspiring world-mindedness and soliciting the highest human motives and attributes for the establishment of a spiritual society. Written by 'Abdu'l-Bahá in the late nineteenth century as a letter to the rulers and people of Persia, it is still profoundly relevant today as a guide to creating a peaceful and productive world. This new edition, ideal for gift-giving, is leather-bound with foil stamping and a ribbon page marker.